# Prisons: Present and Possible

# Prisons: Present and Possible

Edited by

**Marvin E. Wolfgang**
University of Pennsylvania

**Lexington Books**
D.C. Heath and Company
Lexington, Massachusetts
Toronto

**Library of Congress Cataloging in Publication Data**

Main entry under title:
  Prisons, present and possible.

  Includes bibliographical references and index.
    1. Prisons—Addresses, essays, lectures. 2. Prison administration—
Addresses, essays, lectures. 3. Imprisonment—Addresses, essays, lectures.
I. Wolfgang, Marvin E., 1924-
HV8665.P76                            365                            77-3860
ISBN 0-669-01674-8

Published simultaneously in Canada

Printed in the United States of America

International Standard Book Number:  0-669-01674-8

Library of Congress Catalog Card Number:  77-3860

# Contents

# List of Figures

# List of Tables

# Prisons: Present and Possible

# A Prologue to Prisons

*Marvin E. Wolfgang*

Prisons have always shared in the history of mankind, but mostly as places of detention for individuals awaiting trial, or for the convicted awaiting some form of corporal punishment, exile, banishment, or harsh public labor such as galley slavery. When prisons themselves became the instruments of punishment and deprivation of liberty was perceived as punishment for crime, then cries of injustice arose when denigration, degradation, and infliction of physical pain exceeded the limits of deprivation alone. There have always been some souls who, without losing sight of the suffering of victims, have wished to mute the harsh consequences of the closed custody of the convicted. The Buonuomini of fourteenth-century Florence, the Quakers of seventeenth- and early eighteenth-century Philadelphia, the Foxes and Frys, and the Howards and Maconochies are illustrative advocates of prison reform and of the noble notion of rehabilitation. The rationales of punishment—revenge, retribution, expiation, deterrence, reformation, and social protection—have not marched like a phalanx through history, and each has influenced the development of the others. The focal, pivotal point for each rationale has been the prison.

It is the prison that is the last resort (except for the death penalty), and it is here that the most troublesome aspect of democracy pricks our conscience. The prison remains with us as a necessary, noxious aberration of one of democracy's most cherished values—liberty. Because we cannot clearly and accurately attribute cause to each crime and its author, prisons represent society's failure. Whether we blame the criminal citizen, his family, educational, economic or other institutions, or the entire social system, the prison remains symbolic of pervasive, systemic failure. It offends our sense of equality and equity, it reflects our lack of successful socialization, it cripples our confidence in good genes or the good society. It is the opposite of love, friendship, and harmony. It is the very antithesis of freedom. The prison remains because we are imperfect specimens of our own visions of proper humanity. As an end product and as a temporary solution to our imperfections, the prison continues to pose perennial questions: Who should go to prison? for what crimes? for how long? under what living conditions?

These questions form the stage  for which our authors have written their plays. The reward in reading them will not be answers but should be the stimulation to think more reasonably and constructively about these issues.

This volume was generated by the interest of a private foundation, the Cornerhouse Fund. The members of the board of the Cornerhouse Fund were interested in the controversial issues surrounding the discussion of prisons and

1

prison reform in the United States. Approached by vice-president Marvin Bressler to consider a project that would produce a response to the board's interests, I agreed to function as coordinator of the effort.

There have been many studies about prisons, imprisonment, prison subcultures, management, and organization. The National Institute of Law Enforcement and Criminal Justice has a special section devoted to corrections and correctional research. Neither new research studies nor inmate literature, neither antedotes nor systematic evaluation was the focus of my search for ideas about an approach to the topic of imprisonment. Some capably written books have recently appeared on the subject. For example, Norman Johnston's *Human Cage* and Thorsten Sellin's *Slavery and the Penal System* deal with the history of prisons. William Nagel's *New Red Barn* surveys American jails and prisons and Norval Morris's influential *Future of Imprisonment* provides models for prisons. Tom Wicker's *Time to Die* and Jessica Mitford's *Kind and Usual Punishment*[1] are among the more popular, intelligently written accounts for the wider public audience interested in the closed and controlled custody designated as prisons. These are only a few of the many new publications about prisons that range from description to prescription.

It is the intent of this volume to provide something slightly different. I wanted to bring together a few persons who had experience with prisons and prison research, who were not currently committed to the establishment of corrections, and whose professional and fiduciary rewards were not dependent on the bureaucracy of prisons or government. I wanted scholars whose erudition was a basis for their role as Socratic gadfly, and who were capable of standing outside the system in order to criticize it and to suggest revisions of it. The small group of authors represented in this volume became the cadre of the conscience of informed opinion.

We met several times to discuss the directions each author might pursue. I encouraged no abiding theme that would link each chapter neatly to its neighbor. Only prisons and prescriptions from each author's wisdom were the foci of their tasks. New and unpublished commentaries were requested, but freedom of framework, of expression, of style, and of normative suggestions was to be the hallmark of this compendium.

In the task of coordinating and editing the writing of these authors of different experiences and styles of expression, I was aided by Selma Pastor, my able librarian at the Center for Studies in Criminology and Criminal Law at the University of Pennsylvania. Syntax, accuracy, attribution, quotations, and the like were checked as usual. But I decided, after reading the second drafts of these chapters, not to interfere in the substantive suggestions and recommendations made by these fertile minds. As editor I neither endorse nor reject the suggestions made here. In all of them there is merit and I am most pleased with the collection. These scholars have written seminal and informative chapters with uncommon lucidity, succinctness, and literary grace. They are neither liberal nor conservative in the traditional ideological sense. They are rational, humane, and democratically conscious of due process and of the importance of protecting society while seeking to preserve the dignity of persons captured, convicted, and controlled. As any student of human history knows, scholars with these attributes are not easily assembled for discussion of the limited life space we call prison.

I shall not summarize the main points of these chapters, for both a summary and a critique of them are provided in the delightfully written Epilogue which is itself a contribution and a unique feature of this collection. It provides in the same volume a penetratingly substantive criticism of the original works. I do, however, wish to draw attention to the fact that these chapters contain some of the most provocative, creative, and stimulating commentary on prisons to be found in the literature: ghost towns converted to prison colonies; incapacitation disentangled from deterrence and the closest custody outside of imprisonment; the most comprehensively compact discussion of the lauded Swedish system; and a rationality offered for the assignment of persons to imprisonment.

## Notes

1. Norman Johnston, *The Human Cage* (Philadelphia: Walker, 1973); Thorsten Sellin, *Slavery and the Penal System* (New York: Elsevier, 1976); William Nagel, *The New Red Barn* (Philadelphia: Walker, 1973); Norval Morris, *The Future of Imprisonment* (Chicago: University of Chicago Press, 1974); Tom Wicker, *A Time to Die* (New York: Quadrangle, 1975); Jessica Mitford, *Kind and Usual Punishment* (New York: Random House, 1973).

# 1

# Prison Management: The Past, the Present, and the Possible Future

*Thomas O. Murton*

*Abner was at the reins as the matched team of bay mares pulled the buggy along the narrow roads winding through a bustling eastern Pennsylvania hamlet. As they approached the town square, his companion, Elijah, mused about the progress made in the decade since the American Revolution and reflected upon the achievements of the new nation.*

*"We have come a long way, Abner, since the overthrow of the oppression of the Crown and the arbitrary control over our lives. Remember that only 10 or 15 years ago we were subject to the arbitrary whims of a remote king who made the laws which governed us, required us to work for the enrichment of his coffers, and denied us any voice in governing ourselves? Those were indeed dark days!"*

*Abner nodded in silent assent, concentrating his attention on maneuvering his team through the edge of the square where a large number of townspeople, and some from the country too, had gathered for an afternoon picnic. Not all of the lunches were eaten; some vegetables were thrown at the miscreants locked into the stocks. But this was only warm-up entertainment; the main event was to be a hanging, from the gallows situated prominently in the center of the square. For most, it was to be a festive occasion indeed.*

*Abner and Elijah had casually observed posters several days before announcing the public punishment of these criminals. But today they had forgotten that the square would be crowded; forgotten, because their thoughts were on the meeting of the church membership that afternoon to discuss their role as Quakers in continuing social reform under the new-found freedom in democracy.*

*Abner skillfully guided the team through the crowd and, as they extricated themselves from the masses, he turned to Elijah in a moment of inspiration. "There must be a better way to deal with those unfortunate sinners. Public disgrace causes more shame than conversion to Christianity. And for the poor soul who suffers hanging, there is no redemption."*

*"You speak the truth," Elijah assented. "What is needed is separation of the malefactors in a place . . . maybe a monastery . . . where they may think upon their evil deeds and repent. A time to become penitent is the key."*

*"Elijah, you have great vision! Perhaps we can make a contribution to our new country—to the world—before the 18th century passes. Let us hurry on to the awaiting congregation and discuss this new revelation."*

*So saying, Abner flicked the reins, bringing them down with a loud noise on the backs of the horses, goading them into a gallop for the last few yards to the waiting group. A discussion was already in progress. Members of the congregation were alternately chronicling the evils of the autocratic English form of*

5

*government or decrying paternalism and exploitation and the concomitant oppression which had stifled self-determination and "the inalienable rights of man." Others responded with praise for deliverance from the tyranny of monarchs.*

*Abner and Elijah sat in dutiful, if impatient, silence while the others spoke, and later stood in quiet respect as prayers of thanksgiving for the new-found freedom were offered. But at the first lull in the rejoicing, Elijah climbed onto the buggy, called for attention, and proclaimed his half-formed thoughts conceived during the ride with Abner.*

*"Friends, we must continue the struggle for justice in our new society. Brother Abner and I, this very day, have discovered a new idea for Christianizing the heathen; for saving the criminals from eternal damnation; for furthering the ideals of democracy. . . ."*

*And so was born the penitentiary.*

The penitentiary failed to achieve its purpose and the reformers, almost immediately, set about to improve it. Subsequent reformation efforts resulted in the industrial prison, the educationally oriented reformatory, and more recently the rehabilitative prison. All have at least one thing in common: they have failed to reduce criminality.

After nearly a century of prison reform efforts, congressional hearings were held in Washington by Senator Thomas J. Dodd in 1969. That year may have been the starting point for contemporary efforts to implement major reforms of the penal system.

A more dramatic event was the revolt at Attica nearly two years later. Since then there has been a proliferation of media coverage about prisons. Magazines, newspapers, and journals have carried articles about prisons regularly. "In-depth" studies have been reported on radio and television. Scores of books have been written on the subject by professors, penologists, prisoners, and the public. Old prison movies have been rerun on television; new films have been made.

Some of us have been actively involved in lecturing, attending conferences, and endeavoring to put together a national coalition of prison reform groups. Attica spawned over six hundred such groups, most of which have long since faded away.

What has been the cumulative result of all this effort? Not much more than the reformers achieved over the past century. The net result seems to be that the diversity of problem analyses and solutions have riled up the troubled waters of prison reform more than they have clarified or calmed them.

A prison reform coalition was never realized because of the spectrum of ideology about reform; lectures on the subject are no longer in vogue on campuses; conferences have returned to "business as usual" topics such as the effective use of mace and the need for indestructible commodes.

Several years ago while speaking on a radio talk show in Canada about prison reform, I was verbally attacked by a listener. "I am furious with you," she said. "I am an involved citizen and have been concerned for years with the plight of the blacks in America. I have also been upset about Vietnam, mercury poisoning in the swordfish, and poverty. And now, I'll be damned if I have to start worrying about prisoners, too!"

It is too simplistic to attribute the waning interest in prison reform to public apathy. In the past five years the public has been presented with overlapping problems unparalleled in our history. John Q. Citizen has been inundated with evidence that in addition to wars and a polluted environment, there are problems with injustice, Indians, recession, and inflation (with attendant higher costs of living and unemployment), rising crime, political corruption at the highest levels, and a seemingly endless upward spiral of controversy, conflicts, and difficulties.

It is said that the squeaking wheel gets the grease, and the squeakiest wheel is the one nearest the listener. Even if he is convinced of the long-range benefits to the citizen from humane incarceration of the offender, the average person is more concerned with the immediate problems of putting bread on the table, a roof over head, and a lock on the door. In this sense the citizen is no different from the inmate in terms of focusing on creature comforts before considering more esoteric improvements.

Reform died along with the forty-three men at Attica. The central modality of prison reform thus far has been cosmetic in nature as evidenced by funding from the W. Clement Stone Foundation for courses in "Guides to Better Living" for male prisoners and "Feminine Development" for female prisoners.

The dimension of change required does not reform the monster without dealing with its nature; it is a revolution in thought, objectives, and practices. Semantics is a trap. Rejecting the word *reform* and simply substituting something like *regeneration*, while being more precise in intent, may in fact only be masking the same phenomenon. In other words, "a rose by any other name still has thorns."[1] Although it means different things to different people, the term *reform* used in this discussion will be redefined to mean a significant change of the entire organism in a direction thus far not explored systematically.

Perhaps one reason that prison reform has failed is that the right questions have not been asked of the right people at the right time. Appointing a traditional penologist to a study commission whose purpose is to evaluate present practices in prison management is not likely to be productive.

Perhaps it is time to reject the notion that prisons do or can rehabilitate. As a society we seem embarrassed to admit that some offenders are sent to prison simply for punishment. Corporate criminals, draft dodgers, professional criminals, accidental offenders, and the Watergate crew are not sent to prison for rehabilitation; they are sent for punishment. Why not eliminate the hypocrisy of adherence to the treatment concept of rehabilitation? Some prisoners are dangerous; some may be psychologically ill. A more logical approach to prison management may be to provide different experiences for different kinds of inmates in the same or different institutions.

Why write another treatise on prison reform? Prisons exist, and despite the efforts of the abolitionists (with whom I essentially agree), they will continue to exist for some time. Some of us concentrate our efforts on assuring a more humane existence for—and survival of—the inmates until that great day arrives when the walls come down for all but the dangerous offender. There seems to be some justification in this scheme.

What is being set forth here is not a more-of-the-same variety of change, but an effort to provide a different view of the view. Reformation of the prison is not dependent on more money to build more buildings to accommodate more staff who are paid higher salaries to do more (of the same) to more inmates. We need to do different things, and among those things is treating prisoners like human beings—not a particularly new idea in the history of man. Reform is based on interpersonal relationships between staff and inmates and is more a function of personalities than of concrete and steel.

The prison can be viewed from the perspective of society, the criminal justice system, the inmates, the administration, the scholars, the victims, or the philosophers. The focus of this discussion will be on management practices because the locus of power to bring about the essential changes resides in the administration. Arguments that the prime responsibilities for change lie with the governor, the legislature, the judiciary, or the public are diversionary, invalid, and counterproductive.

This essay begins with a historical overview of prisons and contemporary reform efforts. The latter sections deal with alternative modalities of prison management and reflections on reform as a concept. The emphasis must be placed on the essence of reform and not on the appearance of reform. Captain Alexander Maconochie stated it well in 1839:

> The operation of a principle is uniform; everything around it either flows from, or is accommodated to it; its effects appear necessary and unavoidable; and their inconveniences under firm and skillful superintendence being remedied in detail by improved apparatus, a thorough revision long seems unnecessary. . . . But, in all cases I am persuaded, such palliatives will be found eventually to aggravate, rather than mitigate, a real evil. They disguise some of its rankness; they thus prolong its duration, and give deeper root to its injurious results; they give the ingenuity of administrators a wrong direction by leading them to endeavor to suppress the indications of error, rather than remove error itself.

> And they ultimately make entire change more difficult, because a certain amount of apparent good undoubtedly following each supposed improvement, people are led to believe themselves in the right way when they are really only going further astray, as in the case

immediately in question, in which, instead of seeking to improve the apparatus of physical coercion, the real problem is how we may, in whole or in part, advantageously dispense with it.[2]

## A Historical Overview of Prison Management

It must be acknowledged that the penitentiary system in America is severe. While society in the United States gives the example of the most extended liberty, the prisons of the same country offer the spectacle of the most complete despotism. The Citizens subject to the law are protected by it; they only cease to be free when they become wicked.[3]

### Treatment Models

The prison, America's contribution to efforts to stem criminality, came into existence in the early nineteenth century under rather curious circumstances —as the result of efforts to lessen the harshness of capital and corporal punishment. The prison was thus viewed as a reform of the system. But almost since its inception, there have been ongoing attempts to reform the "reform."[4]

The original model of prison management which was established in Pennsylvania in the 1820s was a theocratic one. It was assumed that there was an equation between sin and crime and that the cure for both was to be found in Christianity. Inmates were isolated to reflect on their evil deeds until they became converted. They were denied contact with other human beings, including the guards who silently pushed trays of food through special doors. Each prisoner was given a Bible (regardless of his ability to read), provided with some craft materials, and allowed out into a pen adjoining his cell to exercise and to commune with nature.

This severe sensory deprivation resulted in mental impairment to many of the inmates, and the Pennsylvania system was generally abandoned after the construction of the New York prison system a few years later.

The religious model was rejected for the work-ethic model which was implemented in New York prisons in the mid 1820s. The work-ethic model kept inmates under secure custody while they performed mandatory work tasks. The model assumed that criminality was a function of slothfulness; the cure, therefore, was to teach the inmate good work habits. The work offered was nonproductive and consisted of digging and filling holes and working on the rock pile.

In the 1870s the reformatory model came into existence. Its purpose was to train and educate youthful offenders. Rejecting the religious and work models, the reformers concluded that criminality was the result of a lack of education and vocational training. Efforts were made to segregate first offenders from the hardened criminals who were incarcerated at the state prisons. After a time, however, overcrowding and an emphasis on industrial production forced the reformatory into operations very similar to those of the prison.

The current rehabilitation model gained widespread acceptance following the end of World War I and increased in popularity after World War II. This model of treatment assumes that the inmate is psychologically sick and that he can be cured through a variety of treatment techniques imposed by a professional staff of healers.

### Management Models

The different methods for correction of criminal behavior have been connected with different forms of prison administration. Under the Pennsylvania system the warden governed as a moral leader, monitoring the austere existence of his charges in a fashion closely patterned after the monastery. The warden was assigned the role of father to his flock—but without direct personal contact—providing an environment in which conversion to the righteous life could take place.

In the New York system the warden was required to assume more managerial tasks, since prisoners in congregate were allowed into the dining hall and assigned to work. More concern for custody was necessary, and rudimentary organizational methods were needed to provide supervision of work performance. Although the warden was not viewed as a father figure, he was nonetheless charged with exercising his authority in the best interests of the inmates.

Under the reformatory model the warden's role remained much the same as in the industrial prison except that he was required to devote more time to providing educational and training opportunities. For the first time a realm of expertise emerged apart from the warden himself. Wardens, who were generally appointed to their positions for political reasons and not for their personal vocational skills or academic training, were not equipped to supervise new activities such as vocational training or teaching.

The division of prison responsibilities into custody and training segments reached its culmination in the rehabilitation model and in the professionalization of the treatment team. Under this model the role of the warden is to maintain custody, to protect society, to provide creature comforts, and to organize the prison to support the main treatment effort. The model assumes that undesirable behavior can be modified only through the inmates' interaction with the professionally trained treatment staff. The guard is viewed as a neutral actor in the drama, whereas in the first three models he had a more positive function.

The warden is not likely to view the treatment team with the same enthusiasm as the clinicians. His role is to supervise the dichotomization of treatment and custody and to achieve some harmony between the two groups. The role of the warden has become increasingly complex as the function of the prison has become more complex. The multiplicity of goals and objectives, increased services, rising prison populations, and radicalization of some inmates have all added to the warden's responsibilities and obligations.

Nonetheless, while his role has become more complicated, there are more similarities than differences in the warden's functions over time. His duties have always been paternalistic, autocratic, and dictatorial. Since the inmates are wards of the state, control over them beyond the mere obligation to protect society has been deemed appropriate. A totalitarian regime is a more efficient system in the short range and, when stablized, is more easily managed. However, efficient should not necessarily be equated with better. The current combined dictatorial-medical model of prison management-treatment can be viewed as a natural evolution, reflecting the often-conflicting perceptions of criminality and the fickle demands of the larger society. The following discussion sets forth some of these contradictions.

## Conflicting Philosophies of Imprisonment

Under the best conditions the prison warden has been a benevolent dictator; under the worst, a despot. But it can be argued that the prison managerial structure has been predetermined by the philosophy operative at the time of innovation in each era. Once set in motion, such a political organization has been difficult to modify. In particular a major peaceful change in the structure of a dictatorial agency often seems impossible.

The philosophy of *incapacitation* is the most easily implemented mandate for the warden. As a result of incarceration, the offender's capacity to commit crimes against the free society becomes nil—unless he escapes. But the larger dimension of incapacitation implies the inability of the prisoner to follow a course of action under any circumstances. While sending an offender to prison will protect the larger society, the prison society becomes vulnerable to attack by the offender. The oppression of the prison environment, the overcrowding, the congregation of offenders, and the innate hostility of the inmate body all exacerbate the potential for violence which can be discharged only against other inmates or staff.

The options available to the warden for total incapacitation are limited. He seeks (usually without success) the transfer of mentally impaired prisoners to a mental facility. Prisoners with physical illnesses can be isolated in a hospital. Inmates who commit offenses inside the prison can be isolated in individual cells until these too become overcrowded. But with reasonable facilities and fairly competent guards, incapacitation is one objective of the prison that can be achieved more easily than some others.

Some *punishment* is achieved instantly at the time of incarceration when the prisoner loses a considerable degree of freedom of choice and mobility. In theory the basic punishment nature of the prison is resident in this denial of freedom. Yet the prison imposes further punishment on the inmate. The inmate is subjected to what he may perceive as arbitrary rules, is allowed little control over his affairs, and has to live with inmate power, constant fear, and a struggle for survival. He may also be abused in one way or another by staff members.

These negative effects are not the result of a predetermined plan by the warden to increase the harshness of the prison experience; with rare exceptions, violence is not institutionalized nor sanctioned by prison authorities: it is the inevitable result of a philosophy based on authoritarianism. By design or default, the prison achieves the objective of punishment. Yet there is some evidence that increasing the severity of punishment has little effect on specific deterrence.

The prisoner can be *deterred* from committing crimes against the larger society while he is in prison, but such deterrence results from incapacitation, not attitudinal change. He may or may not be deterred from criminal behavior after his release; the recidivism rate indicates that prison does not deter most of those who have been incarcerated.

General deterrence of potential criminals is assumed to result from punishment; there is contradictory evidence about this assumption. Whatever general deterrence exists may be in the law and the enforcement of that law. The fact that burglar A goes to prison five years after committing an offense is probably not a deterrent to burglar B, who calculates the improbability of his being detected, apprehended, tried, convicted, and sentenced to prison. Burglar B, perceiving the odds in his favor, may still pursue criminal endeavors.

Societal requirements for *vengeance and retribution* are usually met by incarceration. In extremely heinous crimes, such as murder, brutal rapes, child abuse, and sexual perversions, the public may not be satisfied with simple commitment to prison. More severe penalties such as castration or execution may be demanded. However, some element of retribution is always served by sending the offender to prison. Early parole, on the other hand, may later upset the public's perception of equity and justice in the specific instance.

*Reformation, rehabilitation, and reintegration* (the three R's of contemporary prison reform) are stated objectives of the prison and are sometimes mandated by statutes. They are attempted through a variety of educational and training programs in addition to psychological treatments and experiences.

The increase in rates of crime, recommitment to prison, and institutional violence all attest to the failure of the prison to rehabilitate the criminal offender. It is erroneously assumed that the prison is the prime social institution bearing responsibility for creating and curing criminality.

It appears self-defeating that a prison warden should be commanded to carry out rehabilitation programs in the context of incapacitation, deterrence, punishment, and retribution. It would require the wisdom of Solomon, the patience of Job, and the supernatural power of Christ to achieve these objectives simultaneously. Since wisdom, patience, and divinity are not requisites for appointment as a warden, it is understandable that the multiple objectives society has imposed in layered fashion on the warden have not been achieved.

*Statement of the Problem*

Historically it has been assumed that the American prison model is the most effective one to provide an opportunity to modify human behavior positively in an institutional setting. It has been further assumed (incredibly) that a paternalistic-authoritarian-dictatorial setting is the most productive one for teaching responsibility in a democratic society.

There have been four major changes in treatment concepts in the prison with accompanying lesser changes in prison violence, in recidivism, or in criminality. Nevertheless, many clinicians remain passionately committed to the notion that given sufficient time and resources, the prison will gradually become a citadel of good works and will somehow fulfill its mission of reformation.

It would appear that the 175-year history of the American prison has allowed ample time to test the validity of this belief. Because changes thus far have not resulted in any real reform of inmates, it seems reasonable to conclude now that the problem lies, not in the lack of special (unidentified) treatment programs, but in defects in the organizational structure of the prison and the conceptualization of the problem.

So long as the traditional model of prison management is considered inviolate; so long as reformers are content to graft good ideas onto a sick organism; so long as inmates are treated as subjects under a ruling monarch, the day of real reform will remain in the future.

**Contemporary Reform Efforts**

American penology today falls far short of its theoretical potential. Even in contrast with the significant but rare forays into prison reform by men such as Alexander Maconochie, Thomas Osborne, and Howard Gill or with contemporary prison practices in foreign jurisdictions, the current state of the art of prison management in the United States is woefully deficient.

Regionalization, small institutions, and treatment in the community are all current fads on the correctional scene. Alaska has had regionalization of facilities since it was acquired by the United States in 1867. The largest institution in the state has a capacity of only 125 inmates. The principal juvenile and adult institutions are located within the corporate boundaries of local communities (exceptions are two honor camps located in more rural locations and the new Eagle River facility). These "progressive" aspects of the Alaska correctional system are a product of geography, climatic conditions, and congressional apathy before Alaskan statehood.

Until 1974 no prison had ever been built in Alaska. Long-term or dangerous offenders were transported outside Alaska for housing with the Federal Bureau of Prisons. Lack of attention to Alaska's institutional needs resulted in what is now considered a model of progressive thought. But, alas, while Alaska survived the climate, limited funds, congressional neglect, and presidential apathy for over a century, it was destined to succumb to the reform zealots.

After all it is very difficult to reform a prison if there is no prison to reform. Even though respected correctional study groups now uniformly urge a moratorium on prison construction and the closing of prisons in favor of small local treatment facilities, Alaska was forced to go through the complete evolutionary cycle.

Three persons converged on Alaska in the early 1970s and proved invincible. Professor LaMar Empey, of the University of Southern California, had been a consultant to Alaska for several years. His major impact was the conceptualization of the Alaskan prison, euphemistically known as the South Central Regional Correctional Institution. Empey argued successfully that Alaska could benefit from an enclosed facility where officials could intensively do more things to more inmates.

Austin MacCormick, executive director of the Osborne Association, was a consultant on prison reform to forty-eight states. He went to Alaska to reform the prison system but found no prisons. That "deficiency" was remedied, and he endorsed the new facility.

> The design is excellent, I'd say. There's a feeling here of a small community rather than a large institution. Alaska was lucky. You could have been stuck with upgrading an old penitentiary. Instead, you started from scratch.[5]

Some would argue that Alaska could have continued without a prison and thus would have been luckier still.

Edith Flynn, of the National Clearinghouse for Criminal Justice Planning and Architecture, was instrumental in lending support to the building program by arguing that Alaska would become a model for the other states to follow. Yet the prison, built at a cost of $5.2 million to house one hundred inmates initially, is located on 207 acres of moose range, thirteen miles from the nearest town, Anchorage. Because of the remoteness of the institution, educational and vocational services available in Anchorage are difficult to use. The inmates are idle because there is a lack of useful work and educational programs in the institution. Medical, dental, and other health facilities had to be built into the institution because of its isolation. A work-release center operating in Anchorage for several years was closed to lend weight to the contention that the Eagle River facility was needed to provide work-release opportunities. There was no need for the additional space for inmates in Alaska at the time of construction. Yet even with the new bed space and the lack of overcrowding, prisoners are still being sent outside to the Bureau of Prisons.

The new prison may offer employment to local hunters; it may give a boost to the construction industry; it may provide a laboratory to test notions of therapy; it may provide a model prison; but it will do nothing to provide new, needed services for the inmates and that, theoretically, is what rehabilitation is all about.

The facility was opened in June 1974; it was under grand jury investigation five months later.

> The problems at the center are due to poor and inefficient management, lack of foresight, and negligence in its operations. . . . A beautiful, shiny new facility with every physical comfort but lacking in direction and programs have [sic] little chance of rehabilitating anyone.[6]

While correctional authorities scurried to suspend, demote, or fire officers to appease the grand jury, the presiding judge pondered the fact that he had not yet received a satisfactory explanation for the release of an inmate on a work pass (although the court had ordered that he receive no such privilege) who had allegedly raped three women.

At the other extreme, the Arkansas prison system has evolved slowly—but not too far—from the slavery of the nineteenth-century traditions. Because the deficiencies of the Arkansas system are legion and have been widely reported, they will not be recited here. Suffice it to say that the Arkansas prisons were never known as models of therapeutic treatment. There was one brief moment in 1967-68 when the sordid history of that system over the previous century was temporarily interrupted. But Arkansas rejected its first chance at real reform and has insisted on progressing through all the evolutionary stages of development.

Although new facilities have been built, inmate guards replaced by paid officers, and many programs instituted, reform issues have been more obscured than clarified, and one is hard pressed to distinguish the present system from the pre-1967 era. The more blatant physical abuses have been replaced by other forms of brutality. The net result has been the condemnation of prison practices on three separate occasions and a ruling by a federal court in February 1970 that the entire Arkansas prison system violated the cruel and unusual prohibitions of the United States Constitution.[7] Efforts to reform the prison have included requests for Dale Carnegie courses for the inmates and a $281,660 grant from the Labor Department to train officers in "the proper use of firearms and the baton and the riot control stick." The men were tested on a firing range for accuracy with an assortment of weapons including a .38 caliber pistol, a .30-.30 caliber rifle, and shotguns.[8]

More recently, the Arkansas Department of Corrections has received a $39,000 grant from the Law Enforcement Assistance Administration (LEAA) to provide programs in transactional analysis for the inmates. It is unclear how either a Dale Carnegie course or transactional analysis will equip the inmates to survive the assault training of the guards.

Federal Judge J. Smith Henley ruled in August 1973 that sufficient progress had been made in the prisons to permit him to relinquish jurisdiction at that time. However, inmates appealed the decision to the Eighth U.S. Circuit Court of Appeals in St. Louis, arguing that the Arkansas correctional system was still unconstitutional.

The three-judge panel remanded the case to Judge Henley for immediate action "to eliminate the unlawful conditions which now exist in the Arkansas prison system."

> As the respondents urge, there is no such thing as a "perfect" prison system but this does not relieve respondents of their duty to make their system a constitutional one in which human dignity of each individual inmate is respected.
>
> We find major constitutional deficiencies particularly at Cummins in housing, lack of medical care, infliction of physical and mental brutality and torture upon individual prisoners, racial discrimination, abuses of solitary confinement, continuing use of trusty guards, abuse of mail regulations, arbitrary work classifications, arbitrary disciplinary procedures, inadequate distribution of food and clothing, and lack of rehabilitation programs.
>
> The continued infliction of physical abuse, as well as mental distress, degradation, and humiliation by correctional authorities demonstrates that mere words are no solution.
>
> Such unlawful conduct by correctional personnel is of major significance leading to this court's finding that the present correctional system in Arkansas is still unconstitutional.[9]

The Mississippi prison system is almost as notorious as the Arkansas system. Until recent times inmates were whipped with a leather strap called a Black Annie, forced to work in the fields as slaves, and not infrequently, murdered within the prison. Attorneys in Jackson filed an action in federal court to correct the blatant deficiencies of that system in 1970. After one year's litigation, then superintendent Tom Cook bowed to court pressure and agreed to increase the breakfast menu for inmates in the maximum-custody unit to "one eight-ounce glass of milk, two hot cakes four inches in diameter, two tablespoons of sorghum syrup and a cup of sauerkraut." The evening meal was even more appetizing. In addition to a beverage, the inmate received "a cup of beans, a cup of sauerkraut and one square of cornbread 3 and ½ inches in diameter and at least 1 and ½ inches thick."[10]

It was difficult to find a superintendent with the courage to tackle the Parchman facility—and one who would be acceptable to Governor Bill Waller. The post was vacant for a year while prison board officials traveled all over the country interviewing an estimated forty applicants for the position. By the summer of 1973 the post had been offered to and rejected by three penologists.

The nationwide search was concluded in November 1973 with the appointment of Jack K. Reed, an ex-marine, to head the prison reform movement. Reed had served eleven years as a parole supervisor in the California Department of Corrections but had reported no institutional experience.

Reed's first professional acts at the prison were the abolition of a work program for maximum-custody inmates, suspension of the inmate grievance committee, and elimination of conjugal visits for inmates in the maximum security unit. Advisory committeeman Doug Baker complained because Reed had not even visited many of the camps on the farm two months after his appointment.

Female offenders are housed on the same prison grounds but in separate facilities. Within the first few days of his appointment, Reed moved away from the current trend toward coed activities by ordering the fencing of the women's camp to isolate it further from the rest of the prison population.

Other innovations included proposals to dig a trench around the twenty-two-thousand acre farm to stop escapes by vehicle, to construct a fence around the entire farm, and to purchase uniforms for the civilian guard force. In addition Reed endorsed the new construction plans approved by the prison board.

Ignoring the proposed moratorium on prison construction, Mississippi has advocated long-range plans to build two regional medium-custody institutions in other parts of the state and has allocated about $5.5 million to upgrade the Parchman facilities. The present two dozen camps will be reduced in number to three new units housing 384 men in each of two units and 192 troublemakers in the third unit. Other plans include building a maximum-custody facility later. Each unit will be fenced, as will the twenty-two-thousand acre prison grounds, at a total cost of $200,000.

This is the future of Parchman. There is no question that the brutal system had to be changed; this was recognized by the federal court that ordered alternatives to bring the institution up to constitutional standards. Yet these reforms do not appear to be reforms but evolutionary steps in the traditional improvements of an archaic system. Is there an alternative?

Prison reformers in recent years have advocated breaking huge prisons into small units. Parchman was the only prison facility in the United States without a "prison." Although the Alaskan prison was operational at the time, it was not officially opened until the summer of 1974. At Parchman the largest congregation of inmates in any single component of the institution was fifty. This small size was not the product of progressive thinking but came about because the farm was broken into functional plots that could be managed by mules and the inmate "tenant farmers." Now the small camps are to be reorganized into more efficient but larger units, and a maximum-custody prison is to be built along with intermediate regional facilities.

Mississippi has led the nation in the implementation of conjugal visits. While verbally endorsing the practice, the new superintendent, Reed, suspended rudimentary due process provisions in existence at Parchman when he took over.

It has been suggested that prisons should not be isolated from the free-world community; yet the new facilities at Parchman will be fenced, and the entire prison, for the first time, will have a fence around it. Some may consider this fencing necessary to eliminate the entrance to the sprawling farm: an LEAA-funded massive brick and concrete entrance gate complete with guard house. It seems inappropriate, after all, to have a prison gate that is not connected to a fence or wall.

Parchman did not have a "prison"; it did not have a walled or fenced institution. It did have small units of inmates; it had the beginnings of a coed institution. It had it all—except a man with the vision to realize its potential. Parchman could have leaped the chasm of twentieth-century penology and become a forerunner in prison reform by retaining the good aspects of the prison and avoiding the intermediate steps in the customary evolutionary process.

Parchman had been unmolested by the reformers; and like Arkansas, Mississippi has rejected the risky possibility of real reform for the safer route of traditional reform. When the penologists are through, Parchman will pass inspection by the accreditation team from the American Correctional Association with their *Manual of Correctional Standards* in hand. It will even look like a prison.

Those who do not learn from history are condemned to live it, it is said. These contemporary examples of "new directions" in corrections seem hardly new at all. They certainly do not conform with successful innovations that have occurred in the past, with current innovative practices in other jurisdictions, or with future conceptualizations. But all is not bleak on the correctional scene. A candle has been lit in Vermont.

> The 165-year-old Vermont State Prison at Montpelier, will be closed by June 30 [1975] and its 85 inmates transferred to state and federal facilities. State Corrections Commissioner Kent Stoneman said at a news conference on Dec. 30 [1974] that the $1.6 million annual operating cost for the maximum security facility was a serious drain on his agency's budget. He said he expects a net savings of $615,000 by closing the prison.

> The prison employs 90 correctional officers and administrative personnel. Stoneman promised all career employees new jobs with the corrections department in other cities.[11]

Perhaps a word should be said about the contribution of scholars to reform efforts. A review of the prison literature of recent years does not reveal much about new directions for reform. A task force headed by William G. Nagel and sponsored by the Law Enforcement Assistance Administration studied over one hundred institutions throughout the United States in 1972 and 1973.[12] Nagel started with the famous saying of Austin MacCormick, "If only I had the right staff, I could run a good prison in an old red barn."

The study, however, did not focus on programs, but Nagel stated the objective thus: "When we first started this study we had in mind producing a very precise guidebook for correctional architects."[13] So from the beginning the focus was on concrete rather than programs. In spite of the current emphasis on locating new facilities within the community, the researchers found that:

[A]ll of the new correctional institutions which we visited were rurally located . . . removed from universities, unable to be reached by public transportation and seemingly designed to discourage citizen and community involvement. . . . Community correction, reintegration, and corrections' need for the auxiliary resources of the cities and universities all have been sacrificed to the pressures of pork barrel politics.[14]

The researchers concluded:

We did see some imaginative and innovative architecture which tried quite valiantly to make less obvious the fact of confinement. Ornamental grilles and hollow blocks sometimes are used instead of bars. Internal walls are well glazed. Winding paths replaced the long bleak corridors. Landscaped lawns and gardens cause some of the uninitiated to complain about "those country clubs for convicts." The grim stone wall is no longer built. The staff of these new facilities, many college trained, hustle at their innumerable important tasks—supervising, teaching, counseling, training, treating, disciplining.

These are all enlightened changes. Yet in our conversations with inmates and staff alike and in our observations, we heard and saw the old preoccupation—control. We also observed deep mutual suspicion, great cynicism, and pervasive hypocrisy as the kept and the keepers played old games with each other while using the new sophisticated language of today's behavioral sciences. I have not worked in a prison since 1960, but it was if everything had changed, yet nothing had changed. The institutions were new and shiny, yet in all their new finery they still seemed to harden everyone in them. Warm people enter the system wanting desperately to change it, but the problems they find are so enormous and the tasks so insurmountable that these warm people turn cold. In time they can no longer allow themselves to feel, to love, to care. To survive, they must become callous. The prison experience is corrosive for those who guard and those who are guarded. This reality is not essentially the product of good or bad architecture. It is the evitable product of a process that holds troubled people together in a closed and limited space, depriving them of their freedom, their families, and their humanity while expecting relatively few employees to guard, control, punish, and redeem them.[15]

The study certainly updates the knowledge about existing institutional design and, even if peripherally, reveals that there has been little change in staff-inmate interactions. That much is a contribution. Less helpful, perhaps, is the concluding section on what institutional design should be.

The author begins with a disclaimer, saying "It is foolhardy for me to try to describe the correctional institution of the future" and then proceeds to describe it.

[T]he nation's principal commitments . . . during the rest of this century should be to reducing crime by correcting the crime-producing conditions in our economic and social structures . . . to reduce the present fragmentation and accompanying ineffectiveness . . . [and provide] a total systems planning. . . .

[Local jurisdictions] must concentrate on reducing the [jail] populations . . . speedy justice . . . alternatives to confinement . . . improved probation and parole services . . . intensive treatment units . . . [and] small group residences. . . .

Until we invent an acceptable substitute for prisons in which to hold the relatively small numbers of intractable criminals among us, we will, in time, have to build better facilities. . . .[16]

Nagel concludes that the prisons of tomorrow will be of two general kinds. The first will be for low-risk, repeating offenders who should receive sentences of less than two years in community-based facilities. The second group, high-risk offenders, will be housed in small, local, secure facilities while they serve their lengthy sentences.

Nagel's study starts with the assumptions that the system needs to be improved rather than renovated, that programs are more important than facilities, and that there should be a moratorium on construction. In concluding that "more of the same" will solve prison problems, it emphasizes facilities over programs and urges new construction. The recommendations are neither new nor innovative. It seems that we have heard it all before—some of its as early as the correctional congress of 1870. There is little here that will spawn new ideas or new directions for those confused legislators, judges, and administrators who sincerely seek guidance.

In his most recent book Norval Morris defines as his task an "attempt to define the proper role of the prison in a democratic society." He describes his model as "jurisprudential" rather than operational. Morris correctly notes the danger that "diversionary techniques that will protect offenders from the greater rigors of imprisonment may lead to a substantial extension of social control by official state processes rather than to a reduction."[17]

Arguing an "optimistic view of the future of imprisonment," he contends that:

> [T]here is nothing at all wrong with the [individualized treatment] model; the fallacy lies in the reliance on its coercive application outside the proper constraints of a due respect for human rights [which will be achieved through] the substitution of graduated testing of fitness for freedom for parole predictions of suitability for release. . . . I think it is perfectly practicable to keep what is good within the individualized treatment model. . . .[18]

And thereby Morris falls victim to the trap that has ensnared so many of his predecessors in reform efforts: the tempting seduction of gradualism—that is, the erroneous assumption that the prison model is essentially a good one; all that is needed is to improve it.

Elsewhere in the book, Morris argues that we should "keep all that is of value in existing parole processes" and "everything that is good in our present plea bargaining processes." He suggests moving from "coerced cure to facilitated change" in the rehabilitation of inmates. "In order for this new modality to work, the prisoner must be freely allowed to reject [the treatment programs]." Yet the first four-to-six weeks in the reception and diagnostic center of the model prison would be mandatory, and participation would be "obligatory . . . in a small living and discussion group of eight inmates and two to four staff members." In addition each inmate "must fulfill his assigned stint in the daily work program." The inmate can be returned to the general population at any time for failure to "benefit" from the treatment program or adjust to the new environment. And, finally, "the [treatment] decisions will be imposed on [the inmate]."[19] While allowing any inmate the right to withdraw from the program without negative sanctions at any time, Morris imposes a fourteen-day cooling-off period during which the fellow members of his group endeavor to change his mind.

It could be argued that any plan that is obligatory, is imposed by the administration, requires participation in group therapy, demands work performance, and includes the sanction of return to the general population is indeed coercive. Morris indicates that he has some awareness of the danger in "shifting the source of coercion to stay [at the model prison] from the prison administration to the inmates' small living group."[20]

The general design is "that treatment of repetitively violent prisoners take place in a humane and secure setting"[21] in the milieu of a racially balanced staff which meets frequently under the leadership of a "neutral" warden such as one trained in law or business. One cannot quarrel with the advocacy of creating a humane prison. The ground gets a little shaky when Morris ventures into the quicksand of the medical-psychiatric-psychological model of treatment to the extent of urging twenty-four-man psychotherapy groups for those who do not benefit from one-to-one therapy.

Morris begins his book with a comment that "prisons have other purposes [than rehabilitation] —to punish, to deter, to banish—which assure their continued survival." Yet after making a valid argument for the necessity of evaluating this experimental program, he concludes that "the most important test of the new institution will be the recidivism rate of its group. . . ."[22] Not only does the proposed study not evaluate the purposes Morris initially enunciates, but it is based on the naive assumption that the future criminality of discharged prisoners should be attributed to the prison, as if there were no other variables in the offender's life that might cause him to commit another crime.

Morris tenaciously holds to his belief that the present system is not all that bad and can be made better. "If we can rehabilitate the rehabilitative ideal with these prisoners, a humane and effective prison system may not be beyond our grasp."[23]

The books by Nagel and Morris may not be representative of the dozens of prison books that have been written in the past five years, and caution must be exercised in generalizing. But these selections may well represent the better of the lot. Many of the other writings are even less insightful, less innovative, and less helpful to those who search for answers, or even to those who pursue the questions.

## An Alternative Mode of Prison Management

The present system of imprisonment has not worked. Prison problems, to a large extent, can be traced to the inequitable, arbitrary, unfair, and unjust system of management. To combat the traditional negativisim of the prison environment, a coalition of power between inmates and staff, based on honesty and trust, could form a strong power base for change. Before describing an alternative model of prison management, this section presents a discussion of the assumptions on which such a model rests.

### Criminological Assumptions

**Complexity of Criminality**. Criminality is a complex phenomenon manifest across cultures, ethnic groups, social statuses, age differences, occupational statuses, and geographic regions. Specific areas of a community are more crime-prone at different times of the day or year, and various crimes are committed with greater frequency than others by offenders in a particular age group. Nevertheless, no segment of our society is immune from criminal attack nor free from generating criminal deviance.

**Limited Accountability**. The impact of the prison on offenders is widely acknowledged as being generally negative and counterproductive. It is unreasonable and inappropriate to expect the prison to correct social problems resulting from the criminal justice process or, indeed, from the larger society. The most that can be expected from a reform of the prison is the lessening of the negative effects of the prison experience.

**Conflicting Objectives.** The prison cannot fulfill concurrently all the purposes assigned to it. Some, if not all, of the objectives (punishment, deterrence, incapacitation, rehabilitation, reformation, retribution, and vengeance) are in opposition to one another. The prison cannot be all things to all prisoners nor to all members of the society.

**Inmate Control.** Penologists generally agree that inmates are relied on extensively for institutional maintenance. Some wardens have stated that the prison could not be operated without the inmates' cooperation or permission; however, most authorities abhor letting the "lunatics run the asylum." The "evil" of power is inherent, not in its existence within the inmate group, but in the illegitimate manner in which it is customarily manifested.

**Common Irresponsibility.** Although crimes and criminals vary greatly in many ways, offenders have one thing in common; they all have violated social norms as defined by the dominant culture.

**Rejection of Totalitarianism.** The Sahara Desert is an unlikely site for instruction in swimming; as members of a democratic society we have selected an equally inappropriate training model to correct criminal behavior. We have created an authoritarian regime in the prison which, in some mystical manner, is supposed to foster positive change in the individual. Presumably, this change will equip him to function in a democratic society where he has a wide range of choices and freedom to make decisions. It seems logical that one way to learn appropriate decision-making techniques which influence one's destiny is to have the opportunity to make responsible decisions. An administrative structure designed to encourage the development of responsibility through decision making should be more productive than the current structure which relies almost exclusively on paternalism.

**Rejection of the Medical Model.** Not all inmates are "sick," and any single treatment model designed to eliminate the incidence of criminality is simplistic. If, as most criminologists contend, criminality is a result of multiple factors, then a multifaceted treatment approach generally would seem more appropriate. A variety of treatment programs, or no formal treatment program, would provide a spectrum of resources from which the staff and inmates could choose to meet the inmate's needs, if any.

**General Applicability**. Although most inmates can profit from participating in the management of the institution, some cannot. Inmates who suffer from mental impairment, have severe psychological problems, reject society's value system, or are accidental offenders may not benefit greatly from experiences such as shared decision making; nor are they likely to be further disadvantaged by the experience.

The proposed model may not work for the draft resister (who sees himself acting responsibly toward himself), for the political prisoner (who sees himself acting responsibly toward society), or for the professional criminal (who acts responsibly toward no one).

## A Model of Responsibility

**Theorem**. If inmates are allowed to participate in decision making, they will tend to act more responsibly toward themselves, others, and the prison society.

**Corollary**. If inmates develop a sense of responsibility while in prison, they may tend to act responsibly after release by committing fewer or no crimes.

## Definition of Terms

*Participation* is defined as the involvement of the inmate in self-rule. Participation may be listening, speaking, serving on committees or councils, or other active or passive reactions to the participatory management process.

*Decision making* implies the right of the individual to determine for himself his amount (or lack) of participation within the range of options. The term implies the authority to implement changes through representation and not merely to make recommendations.

*Responsibility* in this context means demonstrating attitudes and actions toward self and others that are not destructive but which serve collectively to enhance the cohesiveness, stability, and evolution of the society—either the prison or the free world.

The *responsibility model* is defined as individual and group experiences in responsibility which permeate the entire environment and constitute the context within which all activities take place in the prison community. The model encompasses interactions between staff and inmates as well as a context for maximizing decision making.

*The Treatment*

Participatory management is the treatment tool—not group therapy, not individual counseling, not charm school, nor any of the other programs that proliferate in the institution. The shared decision-making philosophy must pervade the entire facility and establish the context within which other feasible components of treatment might succeed, if the prison community perceives a need for them.

The responsibility model is not a treatment program in the usual sense, but it provides the administrative mechanism within which a variety of experiences may emerge. From a research perspective, the variables of interest are power and representation: power to make real decisions affecting one's own destiny, and representation to assure equity in arriving at decisions.

The effects of the experiences within the institution can be assessed by evaluating changes in the level of violence, the number of escapes of inmates or transfers of officers, and the number and kinds of disciplinary reports filed against both staff and inmates. Effects outside the prison can be measured in terms of recidivism and acculturation to the larger society.

For both types of evaluation, it is assumed that the usual barometers of prison instability and unrest are valid indicators of movement on a scale of responsibility-irresponsibility.


*Predicted Results*

It is predicted that once the participatory management model is implemented, there will be some significant short-range gains: a decrease in institutional violence, fewer involuntary transfers of officers and inmates, fewer requests for transfer by officers and escapes by inmates, and fewer disciplinary reports against both officers and inmates. The administration will experience an increase in managerial effectiveness, and there will be reduced tensions and hostility in interpersonal relationships among staff and inmates. The desired long-range gain may be the reduction of recidivism. The short-range objective is the humane confinement of those being punished. The prison, of course, is only one of many factors that contribute to criminality. Any reduction in recidivism rates cannot rightfully be attributed solely to new techniques of prison management. (Any effort to suggest that there is a direct correlation between institutional and free-world behavior is simplistic. Factors such as race, economic status, social class, and opportunity are variables, mostly or totally beyond the control of the individual offender and the prison.)

The character of confinement precludes the possibility that the prison can approach the free-world model. There is no expectation that councilmen in the prison can be trained to become councilmen after they are released. Only a small portion of the inmate population is directly involved in management; the balance must work through their representatives. For the majority the approximation of participatory management to the free world is more realistic. It is not assumed that society really operates in a purely democratic manner. An ex-inmate's future employment is not likely to include an opportunity to share in the management of the firm that hires him. There is probably little danger in raising the postrelease expectations of the inmate to unrealistic heights. However, unfulfilled hopes could result in disappointment, cynicism, and a reversion to criminal behavior. Care must be exercised in establishing and maintaining the responsibility model so that the goals and objectives are clearly understood by the participants.

Neither the experiences of management nor shared decision making is transferable to the free world. These devices are but the means of developing responsibility within the inmate. It is this responsible view of self and others that should be transferred to new situations after release. If successful, this new attitude will encourage the released prisoner to choose responsibly, thus avoiding criminal behavior and a return to prison.

A major purpose of the prison is to train offenders for successful reintegration into the free world; yet the prison model is antithetical to this endeavor. The reintegration process would be enhanced by the creation of a prison environment similar to that of the free world. This environment should include shared decision making among administrators, staff, and inmates. This method requires inmates to accept responsibility for their decisions and the consequences of their behavior. Whereas they have (as all criminal offenders) acted irresponsibly (as viewed by the lawmakers) toward themselves and society, in the responsibility model they cannot run away. They will be confronted with their behavior and will be encouraged to deal with it. But, as with most innovations, the strategy of implementation is just as crucial as the essence of the innovation.

## Case Studies of Participatory Management in Prisons

The literature review has disclosed four cases in which inmates have participated extensively in institutional management. Each of these cases embodies the principles of participatory managment, although they differ in formal structure.[24]

**Alexander Maconochie.** An innovation in penology was begun on Norfolk Island off the coast of Australia in 1840, by Captain Alexander Maconochie of the British Royal Navy. He was commissioned to study the penal colony and, in the course of his study, made strong recommendations for changing the system.

When Maconochie became superintendent of the colony in 1840, he set about establishing his social management theories of prison administration. He rejected the harsh, brutal, oppressive practices of previous administrations and substituted one built on trust and responsibility. Maconochie is well known in the literature for his mark system, his graduated release programs, his development of what is now called parole, and his humane practices. What is often overlooked is the character of his changes.

The only formal organization to involve inmates in their destiny was the creation of small, six-man groups of inmates who were mutually responsible for one another's conduct and, consequently, release from the prison. Although the method was not described in detail, it was stated that inmates chose their own group members. (The selection procedure for group composition was modified after some inmates complained that the group was being punished unjustifiably for the negative behavior of one recalcitrant prisoner.) Maconochie considered these small groups to be moral units of mutual caring and concern for themselves and others. All other activities of the institutional programs were focused around these units.

The inmates were allowed plots of ground on which to raise food to sell to the free people on the island, and they were allowed to retain their earnings. When the group had earned twelve thousand marks, they were paroled to the mainland.

In a less formal way, Maconochie opened up the administration of the prison to include inmate involvement. He allowed inmates to observe court actions that he held inside the prison; inmate testimony and advice were sought on disciplinary matters, although his plan to allow inmates to sit as jurors was thwarted because of a prohibitive law.

Maconochie delegated custodial power to inmates appointed to an inmate police force. They patrolled the island day and night and provided general law enforcement functions for the prison. As Maconochie later observed:

> And my Police [force] was composed of men selected by me from the general body of prisoners, furnished only with short staves . . . instead of a large free and probationer force armed with cutlasses, and in some cases pistols, that has since been maintained.
>
> If, then, with this inferior physical force, I was able to preserve perfect order, submission, and tranquility, it seems to me to follow incontestably either that my measures were most singularly adapted to attain their end or, as a general proposition, that restraints founded on self-interest, persuasion, exhortation, and other sources of moral influence, are in every case more stringent than those of brute force, even in dealing with the worst of men.[25]

Maconochie's plan combined inmate selection for reorganization into small groups with his own intuitive selection of inmates for responsible positions to assist in managing the institution. Ninety days after his appointment, Maconochie allowed the total prison population out of the prison for one day as a holiday. Contrary to dire predictions by the staff, the eighteen hundred prisoners returned to the prison at the appointed hour, no accidents occurred, the jail was unoccupied, "no theft or disorder had disgraced the day," and inmates, to a man, lived up to the responsibility attributed to them by Maconochie.

During the four years of Maconochie's regime, only 3 percent of the 1,450 prisoners discharged were ever reconvicted. Of 920 doubly convicted inmates, only 2 percent were reconvicted of a crime. Inside the prison during this same period, there were only one killing, four escapes, and no uprisings.

Maconochie's impact on the penal colony is best summarized in his own words:

> I found the island a turbulent, brutal hell, and left it a peaceful, well-ordered community . . . the most complete security alike for person and property prevailed. Officers, women, and children traversed the island everywhere without fear. [To which Judge Barry added, "all reliable evidence confirms his statement."] [26]

Maconochie was fired and the subsequent administration was one of partial regression to the conditions that had existed prior to his intervention.

**Thomas Mott Osborne.** Following a series of riots and fires and the subsequent resignation of the warden, Thomas Mott Osborne was appointed warden of Sing Sing prison in 1914. He believed that an inmate's permanent reformation would occur only if he were able to exercise meaningful decision making within the prison. Thus, as warden, Osborne set about developing an environment in which inmates could develop a sense of responsibility through self-determination.

In order to achieve his objective, Osborne established the Mutual Welfare League. All inmates automatically belonged to the league. Every six months, two delegates from each shop were elected by secret ballot. From the board of delegates, an executive board was selected. The executive board selected a clerk and a sergeant-at-arms.

Osborne created a judiciary committee to handle all disciplinary infractions. The warden's court, composed of the warden, the principal keeper, and the prison doctor, handled appeals. Inmates' responsibilities increased and inmate morale improved greatly when Osborne replaced shop and mess hall guards with civilian foremen and delegates elected from the league, respectively.

In addition to creating the league, Osborne set up committees to handle every aspect of prison life.

. . . sanitation, athletics, entertainment, dietary, kitchen, finances, ways and means, reception of visitors, religious services, reception of new prisoners, employment, fire company, prison grave yard, a bank and a parole board.[27]

The impact of Osborne's reforms was reflected in the inmates' attitudes towards themselves and the institution:

Since the League started, these men find it easier to be law-abiding; they find their self-respect restored as their belief in their own manhood grows stronger; they feel responsible for the acts of the community as well as for their own individual acts.[28]

During his tenure, the proportion of wounded inmates treated by the prison hospital dropped from 25 percent to 9 percent. In each of the three years prior to Osborne's administration, an average of thirty-five inmates had been committed to Dannemore State Hospital; during his administration, only nineteen inmates were committed.

Industrial production increased 21 percent. In the first thirteen months of Osborne's administration, there were three escapes. In previous years, there had been ten escapes in 1913, six in 1912, four in 1911, seventeen in 1910, and nineteen in 1909.

According to Osborne:

In Auburn prison for more than two years, in Sing Sing prison for more than a year, the new system had been in operation and *the thing works*. The truth of that fact no reluctant official and no stupid politician can argue out of existence. It is a rock which affords a solid foundation for the future of prison reform.[29]

Osborne's appointment was short-lived. Following indictment by the Westchester County Grand Jury, he resigned because of political pressures. Despite his own professional demise, Osborne's innovations had demonstrated successfully that inmates afforded the opportunity to make meaningful decisions would do so responsibly.

**Howard B. Gill.** Howard B. Gill was appointed superintendent of a new prison at Norfolk, Massachusetts, in 1927, and given a free hand to design the facility to create a new prison environment. Gill espoused what he referred to as the small-group principle. Fifty inmates and two officers were housed together in what he called his community prison.

Although Gill did not believe in inmate government as such, he did create an inmate council with numerous committees which advised the superintendent on all aspects of the prison, including construction. Gill saw this as joint participation and joint responsibility. Eventually there were sixty inmates and thirty officers working on twelve committees.

After discovering corruption within the council on one occasion, Gill decided that candidates would have to be cleared for their positions in advance by the superintendent. The council was recalled by the entire population and subsequently councils included staff members.

> [T]he real and most crucial accomplishment of the council system lay in the intangibles. It was a spirit of armistice where the two factions of social warfare forgot the gun and the instruments of vengeance to live together in amity to think out and put into practice a plan that would reduce the need for these conflicts.[30]

Construction of the new facility proceeded quickly under the joint committee on construction, and inmate foremen were involved in supervising the work. During the five years of construction, only thirty-five of about seven hundred inmates ran away from the minimum-custody facility, even though there was no security perimeter.

Movement into the new facility removed the personal contact between the inmates and the superintendent, and the homey atmosphere of the construction stage was eliminated. Simultaneously, there was a rapid expansion of population and staff.

> Like the early Christian church which was truest and noblest in the days of its adversity, the council system of Norfolk was at its best when it was diligently forging the new plan, and the men involved in its creation were called upon to make sacrifices.[31]

Gill believed that his principles applied to a select, tractable, cooperative segment of the population rather than to all prisoners. He chose these tractable inmates to build the new institution. Gill was unconcerned with reducing recidivist rates but emphasized changing prisoners. He demonstrated that his methods reduced tension and disciplinary incidents and increased production.

Later Gill commented on the effectiveness of inmate participation in prison management:

> Instead of letting it become the means whereby men can achieve anything they want, it is to be the means of teaching them what they should have. We have got to have certain standards of decency, order, quietness, industriousness, and patience which we must insist be the standard of the meanest, the most undesirable men in the place.

> On the other hand, with the proper plans, I think it has been demonstrated that the whole tone of an institution can be raised by this kind of participation, of exchange of ideas, of expression as contrasted with repression. We see men's faces light up and become normal, and that very atmosphere becomes a part of our therapy, because unless we meet that normal human feeling on the part of our men, we cannot

do good case work with them. We cannot do the thing which we have set out to do . . . that is, to help them to help themselves.[32]

Gill was fired on April 5, 1934, following a political fight that had lasted five years.

**Tom Murton.** In February 1967 Tom Murton was hired as the warden of Tucker Prison Farm in Arkansas by Governor Winthrop Rockefeller who had been elected on a prison-reform platform.[33] Murton's first acts were the abolition of corporal punishment and torture and the removal of sadistic guards.

During the first few months of his tenure there was a rash of escapes. Inmates, with whom Murton had established a relationship of confidence, suggested that he reactivate the position of inmate sheriff. In addition, Murton used inmate talents in the creation of the farm council.

Murton's belief that the democratic process was far more important than the product impelled him to take special care in educating inmates for the council:

> This process would have made all subsequent decisions suspect, and there was no assurance that the superintendent could select the proper inmates. Moreover, such a method would have negated an essential ingredient of the council: the inmates had to become personally involved in the process if they were to have any commitment to the outcome. Finally, since the representatives were chosen by the inmates, they had credibility, were accountable to the inmate body and indirectly the general population was thus required to share the responsibility for managerial errors in the future.[34]

The first council dealt with creature comforts, but subsequent councils devoted their efforts to classification and discipline. To make the operation more efficient the council was split in half: three inmates and the warden composed the classification committee; the other three inmates and the warden composed the disciplinary committee. Although Murton retained veto power, he never used it.

The classification committee determined job assignments and custody grades. Because inmates made up the guard force at Tucker, job assignments included deciding which inmates were to carry weapons. With inmate input about job assignments, erroneous decisions were often avoided. For instance, although Murton favored a job change for one inmate, the council unanimously denied it because they knew the inmate would attempt to escape to solve a domestic problem.

The disciplinary committee met weekly to hear rule infractions and complaints filed by both free-world and inmate staff members. Very often inmates were acquitted due to a lack of evidence. Committee members were also personally interested in many cases. One sixteen-year-old youth who had spent much of his sentence in the hole was "paroled" to an older inmate who believed that he could alter the inmate's attitude. The older inmate had a personal interest in the youth's performance because he had agreed to forfeit his job as a barracks orderly should the plan fail. As Murton suggested, "Commitment without personal jeopardy is a meaningless intellectual exercise." The plan succeeded; the youth was eventually paroled and has stayed out of prison.

Following the creation of the farm council, there were no assaults, no fights, and only one escape (from a homosexual assault). No inmate classified as minimum custody every escaped from the farm during Murton's last five months at Tucker. No condemned prisoner ever attempted to escape even while outside the prison. Women and children mingled freely with the inmates and were never threatened or assaulted.

However, as Murton observed:

> The most significant change was in the attitude of the inmates. Fear had disappeared, a new community had been created and despair had been replaced by hope.[35]

Murton's reflections on the involvement of inmates in meaningful decision making in the institution provide an assessment of the experience:

> In review, it should be noted that the first requisite for change was that the superintendent did not consider himself omnipotent. Second, the idea for change had to emerge from the inmates. Time was devoted to really involving the inmates in a legitimate self-help effort. Success fostered success and confidence. A byproduct of the farm council was the re-direction of traditional hostility from the superintendent to the inmate body. The sharing of decision-making with the inmates carried with it the implicit collective responsibility for the decision made.

> Confidence was established through meticulous procedures and credibility. Flexibility was the custom. I did not last long enough to test the final phase wherein the superintendent becomes an advisor and relinquishes the veto power. The true success of inmate government can only thus be validated. The correlation with recidivism would require additional experimentation beyond the insitution.[36]

Despite successful efforts to involve inmates in meaningful decision making in the institution, Murton was fired on March 7, 1968.

**Summary of the Four Case Studies.** Several similarities mark the efforts of these four men to involve inmates in self-determination. Each of them possessed the vision and the power to implement his innovations. Each placed the inmates' welfare above his own and thus jeopardized his personal tenure. Their beliefs that permanent reformation cannot be imposed but emanates from within led them to create an environment in which the inmate's self-respect and sense of responsibility could be cultivated. They believed that the first step in breaking down traditional hostilities between the administration and the inmates must be taken by the warden. Extending trust to the inmates establishes respect, credibility, and a vested interest in the person in power. However, this move might also increase the chances that inmates will act irresponsibly in learning to act responsibly. Enabling the inmates to become actively involved in meaningful decision making also forces them to share the responsibility for the decisions made. Thus the inmates had a vested interest in the election process and in the decision of the councils.

Each man's attempts were successful. Fights, escapes, and general institutional unrest decreased. In some cases recidivism was reduced. The only problem with the statistical evidence is that no research was undertaken at the time of the experiments to validate the results scientifically.

Perhaps the only disadvantage of their innovations was to the reformers themselves, for each man suffered personally for his efforts. Revolutionary attempts to overthrow oppression and to inculcate honesty and genuine concern were rewarded in all cases with the dismissal of the reformer. Although none of the four reformers implemented the full participation model completely, some of their efforts include various aspects of this hypothetical model.

In terms of representation (structure), Gill was the only reformer who involved both staff and inmates in his committee system. On the other hand, staff members did not elect representatives to the council. In terms of power (function), Gill, Osborne, and Murton had councils with real decision-making powers.

More specifically, Maconochie did not have a formal council or committee system, but he involved the inmates in making decisions affecting their own destinies in terms of release from the institution and disciplinary matters. Gill did not believe that inmates should have power over institutional policy matters, but he involved both staff and inmates to advise him of all aspects of institutional life. Osborne allowed inmates to assume some staff responsibilities and to handle classification and discipline matters. Murton allowed the farm council to handle classification and discipline matters. However, neither Osborne nor Murton gave their councils the power to determine institutional policies on a broad scale.

The reformers differed in style, although their conceptualizations of the essence of reform were similar. Nevertheless, each man individually, and all of them collectively, came closer to the pure model of full participation than any other examples found in the literature. If we can measure their successes in these limited ventures, we can project with some accuracy that the full participatory model would indeed produce significantly better results in the management of institutions and the treatment of offenders.

**An Alternative Correctional Regime**

Alternatives should reflect a real change in policies as well as in physical structures. A philosophical renaissance in penological thought should precede innovations in structural changes if inmate behavior is to be modified positively.

*Personnel*

A primary consideration in the reform of the prison should be personnel selection, not new construction. This dictum conflicts with the traditional notion that the failure of prisons to rehabilitate is primarily the result of inadequate facilities.

The major personnel criteria should be that the correctional workers have personal integrity, concern for others, and sincere commitment. Integrity is the glue that binds the substance of reform movements and is essential in this proposed demonstration project. Without it noble and meaningful programs and activities become nothing more than insignificant gestures.

A deep, personal commitment to the reform movement allows no compromise of integrity. In addition, it requires a willingness on the part of the officer to subordinate personal goals of tenure, promotion, retirement, recognition, and other indicators of professional success for the welfare of the inmates if necessary and thereby for the welfare of the larger society as well.

*Organizational Structure*

The foregoing emphasis on human attitudes and relationships should not be misconstrued as viewing the prison as if it exists in a vacuum. Nor is it intended to discount the importance of broader considerations for bringing about societal changes. The democratic institutional model can flourish only within the context of a larger, coordinated correctional system which will provide a supportive environment and a philosophy of continuity of treatment with a variety of alternatives in the correctional spectrum. (Such rhetoric has been espoused under contemporary but diverse models. Nonetheless, it is an essential element of this alternative model; and in both instances it is of no significance if this suggestion is not implemented.) The coordination of probation, institutional, and parole services in a single, statewide agency with a consistent (but flexible) correctional philosophy and policy will provide a supportive context for the experiment.

This system can be envisioned as one that exercises only the amount of control necessary for it to function. The services provided within the correctional agency should be modifications of the currently accepted services of probation and parole. But they should also include many other community institutions as well as the supervision of all state correctional or penal institutions and the support of local innovative programs. Institutionalization would generally be a last resort by which is meant that imprisonment should be justified by a demonstrated or valid prediction of the physical dangerousness of the offender after other alternatives have failed to control him. On the other hand, if one rejects the treatment model as a justification for imprisonment, then offenders can be confined legitimately for punishment. The diversity of offenders thus sent to prison would not, as some argue, result in a congregation of the worst offenders in the prison. Dangerousness in the free world is not necessarily equal to dangerousness inside the prison. The crime of homicide is but one example. The nonpsychotic killer (the majority of murderers) constitutes little or no threat to either prisoners or staff. Institutionalization would provide wider environmental flexibility, such as treatment of males and females, juveniles and adults within the same facility. The option of contracting with the private sector of business for the care and custody of state wards would be available.

*An Alternative Correctional System*

There should be little valid dispute that private industry (which is based on a profit motive) would be more efficient and, probably, more effective than governmental bureaucracies (which are organized for self-perpetuation) in the correctional enterprise. The evil of the chain-gang contract system is not inherent in the system of private enterprise but rather in the exploitative motivation of the contractor. Contractual arrangements with private industry would minimize the inhibiting influences in the areas of finance, building, personnel, purchasing, and, in some cases, law.

Any administrator who works within a governmental structure is painfully aware of the vagaries of budget considerations. He must make his annual pilgrimage to the mecca of money to beg for funding. Thus to a large extent programs and activities are contingent on the whims of the legislators as well as those of superiors in the executive branch. As the Wizard of Id said, "He who has the gold makes the rule." To be sure, it would be necessary to maintain fiscal accountability even under a contractual system. However, a flat daily rate for the care and custody of wards for a period of five years, for example, would provide flexibility within that amount of time to expend funds without approval from some other bureaucrat.

If the contractor was unable to reduce recidivism or demonstrate some other tangible improvement over the state-operated system in terms of the factors subject to measurement, then the contract would not be renewed. Thus there would be a financial incentive to produce a better product—a condition that does not now exist in state systems. In fact, a reduction in the prison population is antithetical to the objectives of state personnel for tenure, promotion, and retirement. Such a trend would threaten their employment which is dependent on maintaining a large, incarcerated criminal population.

One of the slowest areas of change in corrections is the domain of facilities designed to enhance a specific ideology because of the long process involved in taking an idea from conception to fruition. After a need is presented to the legislature, debated, and finally approved, much time has passed. Subsequent delays are a function of the imposition of notions of state architects who are often unenlightened and expensive. In a private system the administrator would have the flexibility of renting, leasing, buying, or building to provide the best facility at the earliest time for the intended programs.

In personnel selection private industry is far more efficient than governmental agencies. In general, employment is contingent on producing a product that will increase the financial rewards to the organization. The civil service system, which controls state employment in most jurisdictions, is probably the single greatest inhibitor of change in any system. Conceived as protection against political influence and as a vehicle for proficiency, civil service has become what it sought to correct—a vehicle that inhibits professionalism.

In the correctional field most job descriptions assume a correlation between requisites and duties. Unfortunately these correlations have never been demonstrated. While certain tests do eliminate the assumed inferior candidate, they may at the same time remove from consideration those who might be the most effective.

Similarly civil service is no guarantee that one cannot be removed arbitrarily. The end product is a system that fosters mediocrity and punishes innovation.

A civil service system cannot provide protection for the reformer who may be removed for political expediency. It does not assure that the best employees will be hired, and it is likely to entrench the incompetent. In a private system, on the other hand, there would be sufficient flexibility to hire and fire as the needs of the organization dictate.

State purchasing requirements have been designed to eliminate the kickbacks, to obtain a high-quality product for the best price, and to enhance the free enterprise system through competitive bidding. Frequently, however, the bidding procedure is so slow and cumbersome that needs must be predicted as much as a year in advance. Such anticipation is not always possible when one is operating an institution with a fluctuating population. Also, the competitive bidding system does not preclude the possibility of collaboration among the bidders. Furthermore, items often cost more on bid than they do on open purchase. The private operator can make purchases as needed, take advantage of low prices by selective buying, and obtain the most suitable product. Here, and elsewhere in this section, it is not assumed that individuals in private enterprise have more integrity than civil servants. Nor is it presumed that private industry is more honorable than a governmental bureaucracy. However, it is suggested that given the same level of integrity and honor in both groups, private industry has the inherent capacity to be more productive and efficient under usual circumstances.

There is more legal flexibility in the regulation of privately operated facilities than in their state-operated counterparts. Since many offenders have an alcohol problem, some administrators have suggested that alcohol consumption be allowed in halfway houses, for example, in order that the inmates learn to deal responsibly with their problem. State-operated facilities, however, are prohibited from this option because of laws governing state institutions.

Similarly other restrictive regulations promulgated by departments of correction probably contribute to the adverse environment of the traditional institution. Restrictions on housing opposite sexes in the same facility, combining juveniles and adults, allowing conjugal visits, and lessening custodial considerations are common in state facilities but could be minimized in private operations.

Community control of the criminal offender by private citizens is hardly new. Initially probation was under private supervision. In the Scandinavian countries probation and parole are largely the responsibilities of private citizens. Prior to the creation of the police force in London in 1829, law enforcement was the responsibility of the citizenry.

There are also more recent precedents for the private care of state wards. Litton Industries was awarded a contract in the mid 1960s to establish regional centers in various parts of the United States for the care and treatment of juvenile offenders. The project was less than successful, not for lack of business management techniques, but because the contractors established a treatment model patterned after the official system.[37]

Minnesota provides for the commitment of offenders to the commissioner of corrections rather than to the department of corrrections. This distinction enables the administrator to contract with private groups for correctional services. However, the department has been reluctant to release control and retains sufficient managerial influence to obviate the advantages of a private, alternative system in spite of the fact that the department is ostensibly committed to transferring state wards to private control.

While a private correctional system should not be considered a panacea for present conditions, there is little question that its organizational structure would provide great advantages for implementing innovative programs. It remains debatable whether the private programs would be different from or would take on the characteristics of existing models. Nevertheless, the idea seems to have merit, is within the realm of feasibility, and should be tried—

if for no other reason than that it cannot possibly be worse than what now exists, excluding, of course, a return to the brutal exploitative convict-leasing system which, I suspect, our contemporary society would not tolerate.

## The Institutional Design

The suggested model for the principal institutional complex can be described best as a village. Whether it is based on the town square or some other concept, the village plan would be a product of the design, concepts, and energies of those who would inhabit it—the inmates and the staff.

Consider a town square concept for purposes of discussion. The design might concentrate group activities in the center while reserving the periphery for residential and industrial activities. The town square might consist of a complex that could serve as a courthouse, town meeting hall, and auditorium, surrounded by a park for less structured activities. Most of the group social activities would take place here.

Adjacent to the square would be the central business district, consisting of individual establishments providing the usual variety of goods and services. A clinic would provide medical services and drugs. Other facilities might include a barber shop, beauty parlor, public library, laundromat, restaurant, cinema, and bowling alley. A public-safety complex housing police, fire, and sanitation personnel, as well as a schoolhouse and a general store, would also be necessary. Vocational training programs would be located in facilities near the school. Ideally most of these enterprises would be operated by inmates.

A jail would be constructed for those who pose a physical threat to the free prison community. Alternatives to the jail system might be explored; in fact, alternatives to incarceration could be devised.

The next district might include prison industries housed separately according to their function. These industries would provide full employment at wages competitive with those in the free world. From his earnings the inmate would be expected to contribute to his own support and self-improvement, to support any outside dependents, to pay fines imposed by the court, and to make restitution to the victim(s) of his crime(s).

The implications are obvious. An inmate would be rewarded financially for his efforts, thus reinforcing the work-ethic value system in the free world. That is, in our society being a productive, contributing member is equated with good citizenship. Also, work is the only generally legitimate route to the traditional goals of acquiring material goods and upward mobility. He not only would be reducing the costs of his incarceration but would be compensating for his crime by making restitution to the victim(s) and thus possibly becoming involved psychologically in undoing the act.

The "suburbs" would be the residential areas where youthful and adult offenders would be housed separately for the most part, but the sexes would be integrated in as many activities as possible, both there and throughout the town.

Farther out might be minimum-custody facilities in the form of single-family housing units, because at some point in the program it might be mutually beneficial for the inmate's family to join him. The inmate would be required to pay for rent and utilities for this housing as well as for maintenance of the premises. The design and construction of new housing, as well as all other facilities within the complex, would be done jointly by inmates and staff.

It is probable that a certain percentage of the village community might pose a physical threat to it. For those persons the traditional response is likely to take the form of demands for a prison. Such a facility would be warranted for those who show a high potential for escape or violence. This prison unit might be a small maximum-custody facility in which a variety of industrial and other activities would occupy the inmates. It should be possible to develop new alternatives or techniques for the reintegration of the convict into the prison village.

Some foreign ventures in prison design merit examination. The Swedish prison officials acquired a lumberjacks' village as an experimental home for prisoners and their families in 1972. This institution is located in a forest twenty-five miles from the nearest town. The cost of the village, Gruvberget, was $100,000, and another $100,000 was spent on refurnishing the homes. An additional $10,000 was used to clear away undergrowth to improve the esthetic appearance of the site.

The focus in rehabilitating the inmate at Gruvberget is on his total family. Each family has its own fully equipped, three-room house for use during the inmate's one-month stay in the village. A grocery store, a variety store, and a library are in the village. Job-training courses are offered during the mandatory three-hour morning study sessions.

According to Claes Amilon, an assistant administrator of the Swedish National Correction Administration:

We believe in this idea of bringing the inmate, his wife and children together in something resembling normal everyday life. . . . While the inmate and his family live at Gruvberget the idea is that they will learn more about the way our society functions.[38]

The Swedish program, which began in the spring of 1972, was designed to accommodate twenty inmates during its first year. Only inmates who have returned successfully from prison furloughs are eligible.

If the inmates—or guests as we might call them—want to leave the village for visits to the town nearby or something like that, the warden will give them permission unless there are very special reasons to deny it.[39]

Authorities in India report an even more innovative program for dealing with some four thousand prisoners who, reportedly, are housed in unwalled institutions. The largest, Sitargani, contains fifteen hundred inmates on a forty-five-hundred-acre farm, while an unspecified number of inmates live and work virtually without supervision on ten acres of ground at Jaipur.

When sent to the institution, each prisoner is given a portion of land and food rations for fifteen days. To meet farming expenses the inmate can borrow money which must be repaid after the harvest, from a "prisoners' council." Prisoners are allowed to market their produce in nearby villages and can sell their labor on other farms. The inmate's family may live with him on the farm and work in the fields if they choose.

Sixty percent of the inmates selected for this program are serving ten or more years; yet escapes reportedly have been very few. Only one of four released prisoners gets into further difficulty with the law, a recidivism rate that is lower than that for those inmates released from the traditional Indian prisons. Officials concede that an evaluation of the experiment has been conducted on an unscientific basis, but observe that in addition to reduced escapes and less recidivism there is "an improvement in the health, work habits and general behavior of the prisoners."[40]

In Illinois the Vienna Correctional Center is a minimum-security institution designed on the village concept to foster trust and responsibility.

> The hub of the Vienna complex of 19 buildings is the Town Square around which all the center's activities revolve. Surrounding the square are residential dormitories, the library, the dining hall, twin chapels, and a cluster of one-story buildings . . . which house the commissary, the barber shop, classrooms and the music room.[41]

The Vienna institution was conceived as a maximum-custody facility. After one of seven housing units was built in 1966, Vernon Houseright, then associate warden, was able to halt further construction and obtain a commitment for creation of a community prison. The philosophy of the community prison is not the formation of a coalition between staff and inmates in a prison society, nor the integration of inmates into the free-world community through education, work release, or furloughs. Warden Houseright sees the function of the prison as a community center that can be used by free-world people as well as corrections personnel.

Thus he encourages free-world people to attend church services in the prison chapels along with the inmates. The local junior college offers classes at the institution for both inmate and free-world students. Inmates work with free-world medical technicians in operating a rescue ambulance service. An umpire school at the institution prepares inmates to umpire little league base-ball games. Through joint participation, learning, and exchange of services, Warden Houseright hopes to break down barriers between inmate and free-world groups, to maximize the use and value of the institutional facilities, and to develop responsibility on the part of the inmate by having him contribute to the well-being of others. In mid 1974 the Vienna institution became coed, which should give the facility an even more normal environment.

Construction costs for this kind of facility should be reduced considerably because of less reliance on concrete and steel to restrain the inmates. Although it cost $24,000 per man to construct the twenty buildings at Vienna to house and serve a population of five hundred, no new facilities would be required if an abandoned town could be used. The town inmates could conduct business, attempt to attract industry, and organize the prison community as a functional unit of the larger free society.

This kind of physical setting would probably be more conducive to family habitation than artificially designed facilities. There would be minimal need for further aid in the inmates' transition to the community because they will have been living in a similar community—from an organizational standpoint—through-out their period of incarceration. It must be noted, however, that this assump-tion is not valid for those who return to the ghetto. Diversion to a nonghetto area, including the option of remaining in the prison village as a free person, would be a desirable consideration.

Patterning an institution after the design and operation of a corresponding free-world community is not a particularly new idea. The Bolshevo Colony in Russia and the Davao Penal Colony in the Philippine Islands purportedly ap-proximate their counterparts in their respective societies. Howard Gill speaks of such a prison community existing in China three thousand years ago.

An intriguing institution, a model maximum-custody prison built in 1966 near Tuleco, Mexico, encompasses a women's unit, facilities for conjugal visiting, inmate-owned and operated industries, and a minimum-custody unit that is totally self-governed. According to the warden the tranquility of the institution is attributable to the soothing effect of classical music played throughout the institution all day. More unusual is the reported recidivism rate of 1.78 percent, a figure startlingly lower than the estimated United States average of around 50 percent. The only known low failure rate that approximates this one is that demonstrated by Maconochie 130 years ago. Certainly this and other foreign institutions must be examined in greater depth for possible significance and implications for American prison management.

Voluntary commitment to the village model could be accomplished by a parolee who feels the need of closer support simply by driving to the town and reestablishing residence. In some ways such a town could be a city of refuge where the criminal offender could withdraw from society temporarily, without suffering the negative effects of criminal sanctions, until he is ready to cope with the free world once again.

It is conceivable that a system of probation, community sanctions, and suspension of privileges would be valuable. Perhaps suspension from work status (and thereby pay status) would provide economic sanctions not unlike those in the free world. But regardless of the solution to criminality within the village, the important thing is that the community would be forced to deal with deviance internally because the possibility of exile from the prison community would be limited by law.

As is the case in society in general, it can be anticipated that deviance will arise as a function of the different value systems of both staff and inmate members of the new prison community. One can expect the model to manifest some criminal exploitation in the form of violence, gambling, and abuse of sex and alcohol. The corruption of the town council is also possible if the inmates are allowed to govern themselves. Such an eventuality may, however, provide inmates with practical experience and more realistic assumptions about governmental frailties in the free world. The likelihood of corruption of the town council would also provide an opportunity to observe deviance in a new (to the inmate) form and a chance to deal with it responsibly.

*Programs*

The key to the successful operation of the prison village community would involve minimizing the traditional "we-they" syndrome common to existing institutions. This plan would require the maximum use of inmates in the process of community management. Perhaps initially officials would want to retain the authority usually vested in a city council (or in traditional prison administration) to serve as a check on inmate control. But inmates should be on the city council and should operate the facilities, including such services as the police department. We know from the Arkansas, Louisiana, and Mississippi prisons that inmates are capable of exercising far more responsibility than is generally acknowledged. The inmate sheriff and tower guards seem to function quite efficiently and more effectively than free-world guard personnel. Both Gill (Massachusetts, 1927) and Maconochie (Australia, 1840) had inmates serving on police forces with no reported negative side effects. However, one should not infer an endorsement of a system of inmate guards which may create negative side effects. The key is whether the motivational purpose of the use of power is exploitative or responsible.

Those who deviate from the rules established for the prison community by the citizens of that community would probably be dealt with in the usual fashion: a complaint would be filed with a magistrate of the prison community alleging an offense, an arrest would be made by the staff-inmate police force, and a determination of guilt or innocence would be made by a staff-inmate tribunal. New approaches to dealing with criminality would probably occur. But then again, the elite might revert to traditional concepts of the use of power experienced in the free world and respond from that traditional role, thus visiting the same kinds of degradation on their fellow convicts as was done to them by the criminal justice system. See George Orwell's *Animal Farm*. If this were to occur in the context of "friendly village," traditionalists would probably be justified in referring to the reformer as the "village idiot."

In such a village the inmate would live in a residential area, go to other areas for school, for vocational training, for recreation and work during the day, and return to the residential area in the evening. For special evening or weekend events and for public forums, movies, or other activities, the inmate would gravitate toward the village center. Such a plan would provide some sense of territorial rights as well as some freedom of movement. The process would approximate that in the free world and would give the inmate a feeling of choice, mobility, and experience in decision making.

A limitation to the village model is the quite obvious fact that the inmates will not be returning to a small, country friendly village on release. Many will return to an urban area, and some will return to the ghetto. Nevertheless, the village would provide experiences that could be transferred to a larger community, although it is recognized that their value would be lessened. It could be argued that such training and subsequent return to the ghetto would be dysfunctional and frustrating to the offender. This factor could be averted either by societal efforts to remove the necessity of his returning to the negative environment or by changing that environment.

Often those in power excuse their inaction by arguing that their efforts may well be neutralized by those with greater power or by their successors in office. The argument lacks the same logic as suggesting that the physician quit "wasting his efforts" on healing because man is destined to die eventually anyway.

Both male and female officers would work with inmates of both sexes as they usually would in a nonprison setting. No unnecessary distinctions would be made based on sex or age in either institutional or noninstitutional treatment of the offender except in housing assignments.

The inmates' use of money, free time, and personal resources would be monitored, as in the free society, by the indigenuous legal authority. Varying degrees of responsibility would be granted to the offender as he is able to deal with them.

The free-world staff members would wear civilian clothing appropriate to the assignments they perform in the prison community. They would be indistinguishable in dress from the inmates. Obvious exceptions would be the medical staff, police, and firemen. As the inmate population becomes more confident, however, it is hoped that traditional attitudes toward the necessity of uniforms would disappear, as in Denmark.

Views regarding the directions in which the community might shift in attitudes, policies, and activities must remain speculative because the possibilities are almost limitless. It must be recognized that the village is the treatment program. It constitutes the milieu within which the diversity of the needs of both staff and inmates can be met by using different methods. The village as a total concept fosters whatever change takes place within the individual. All other programs are peripheral to the central, fundamental bedrock of the new community design and organization. In such a context correctional energies will no longer be dissipated on fruitless efforts to reform part of the organism, part of the time, in part of the institution.

## Reflections on Reform

In view of the depths of depravity evidenced in the Arkansas prison system over the past one hundred years, one can only speculate on the degree of degradation required to ignite a penal slave revolt. If systematized brutality, torture, and murder of inmates are not sufficient to provide the impetus for revolution, it is difficult to envision what would be.

A new dimension has been added to prisons during the past few years which could contain elements for violent change. Although the average prisoner has only a junior-high-school education and has been a product of the poor and powerless groups, these characteristics do not always hold for the political prisoner. In recent years college students—some with financial means—were sent to prison for burning draft cards, opposing the selective service system, refusing to submit to the draft, or for commiting other acts of civil disobedience. For the most part these appear to be sincere acts of opposition to what are defined as serious defects in the American way of government. The activist who goes to prison may be highly intellectual and something of a philosopher. He enters the prison with a concern for the alienation, frustration, and lack of power felt by the masses. But if he felt disadvantaged on the street, the activist is in for a rude awakening when he is subjected to the degradation and the arbitrary imposition of control that permeate the prison community. If his commitment was sincere on the street and not merely a popular intellectual exercise, he will probably direct his efforts to change the prison society once he becomes a member of it.

The activist is not hampered by a lack of education or the inability to communicate. Trained in leadership, he is able to articulate the depravity in analytical terms. He brings to the prison the skills of organization, slow-play, sabotage, interruption, and defiance; thus he may know how to bring the prison machine to a screeching halt.

The activist may finally succeed in interpreting for the inmates what Pogo meant when he said, "We have met the enemy and he is us." Inmates are beginning to realize that they are participating in their own degradation, and many are refusing to perpetuate this destructive relationship. In other words, they are now beginning to understand that "a system of oppression can exist only with the tacit cooperation of the oppressed."

As Martin Luther King, Jr., once observed, "Freedom is never willingly granted by the oppressor; it must be taken by the oppressed!" A historical evaluation of prisons certainly affirms the validity of the first half of that statement, and the characteristics of recent prison disturbances indicate the effectiveness of the latter.

Once the activist comprehends that inmates directly or indirectly run all institutions and that the institution cannot function without the permission and assistance of the inmates, he may then conceive a plan for revolution. He can provide the charismatic leadership that has not generally been available because the natural screening process of our criminal justice system has usually excluded the thinker from the prison. A combination of commitment, power, and expertise poses a formidable threat to any power structure.

Prison officials are aware of this potential. At the Wardens' Association of America meeting in Cincinnati in the fall of 1970 one of the priority items on the agenda was the discussion of how to deal with the political activist. Wardens long ago learned to isolate leaders who could foment disorder within the institution. Most reported that they keep activist prisoners segregated from the rest of the inmates by placing them in single cells for fear that if the dissidents are allowed to work or associate with the general population they could cause problems. The penologists are right!

But the activist, too, will be released from prison one day. Even though he may have been incapacitated successfully inside, later he will be able to communicate his observations and critical analyses of the prison experience to the larger society. The dawning of a new age of reform may come as a result of oppression by those administrators who seek to eliminate opposition to the existing prison system. However, thus far there has been no observable, significant impact on reform by the released activists.

Efforts to silence the activist by subjugating him within the prison may, in fact, provide information about the prison that, when coupled with personal outrage, may give impetus to the life-or-death commitment required to sustain a revolt. The political process may be inadvertently creating the very catalyst for change in the prison that has been resisted successfully so far.

Joining the activist will be dissidents spawned by the prison system itself. Since there is no real opportunity to attack the system, dissidents isolate themselves from the prison community by dividing into factions and dissipate their energies by discharging hostilities on their fellow inmates. The militancy and politicization in California prisons in recent years are considered to be the most difficult management problems facing prison administrators.

Because the political prisoners reject the right of the larger society to incarcerate them, they are the most difficult to involve in the responsibility model.

In fact the greatest opposition to implementation of such a model might well come from inmates who have been radicalized and who constitute the greatest threat not only to themselves and the prison, but also to the reformation of that prison. What may be a reform to one inmate may be a placebo to another.

General reform runs the gamut from rather mundane, easily-implemented changes to the more esoteric, risky innovations. In both categories it would appear that several things could be done rather quickly without additional funds or changes in the law.

The notion that all inmates are amenable to—or indeed are in need of—rehabilitation is absurd. Why not abandon the hypocrisy of demanding both rehabilitation and punishment from the prison? A more profitable venture would be to acknowledge that some offenders are sent to prison simply for punishment or incapacitation and not rehabilitation. Probably the white-collar criminal, the hired assassin, and the political dissident will not benefit from efforts to change their belief systems through the responsibility model because they may perceive crime as a way of life. These individuals could be sent to a humane but restrictive facility for the admitted purpose of punishment. Their right to nontreatment should be an option.

Incarcerated offenders who constitute no physical threat to the public could be introduced to the prison system by being placed in a minimum-custody honor camp first instead of—as is now the uniform practice—in the maximum-custody prison. Such a change would to a large extent abrogate exposure to the depredations of the prison and lessen the need for a transitional adjustment experience, such as a halfway house, for the offender to adjust to the free world. In fact, incarceration should be permitted only when it has been demonstrated that it is necessary for a specific offender.

Changes requiring a bit more courage might include the abolition of the parole board. Release from the institution might be accomplished more effectively by involving the inmate's peers in his release from prison. It is more difficult to con another convict than it is to con the parole board. Peers, whose own releases will be dependent on a continuation of the peer parole procedure, are going to be especially careful in ascertaining that the prospective releasee is not just dissembling but has really changed his attitude toward society. According to Orville Pung, deputy commissioner of the Minnesota Department of Corrections, an institution for juvenile offenders in Red Wing, Minnesota, has demonstrated the efficacy of this notion at least within that setting.

For those who wish the prison to be a self-sufficient institution, the idea of employing all inmates to generate revenues for the prison should be appealing. But instead of retaining the past model of exploitation for the benefit of the state, prison labor models should be modified. There may well be some merit in reinstituting the contract system of prison industry management.

Profit sharing by the inmates or the operation of inmate-owned industries certainly would increase production and provide full wages from which each inmate could make restitution to his victim, pay his court fines, support his family, and pay for his room and board at the prison. At the same time he could enjoy some dignity in knowing that his work is not slave labor that benefits only the state.

The concept of indentured servitude for making restitution to the individual or the state is an idea worth exploration In lieu of institutionalization some judges are now ordering participation in public works projects for offenders.

Although the concept of restitution generally has been reserved for losses resulting from property crimes, it need not be so. The American Indians had a system of compensation for human life in terms of a number of blankets. A Florida judge has considered placing a man convicted of murder on probation on the condition that he support the widow of the murdered man and provide a college education for each of the victim's children.

Holding the offender personally liable for the injury to the victim is a thirteenth-century idea which should perhaps be revived. Some psychologists would also argue that undoing the criminal act is an essential ingredient in the concept of restitution that could dissuade the offender from continued criminal actions.

Requiring a little more boldness from administrators would be changes such as making the institution coed, allowing babies to live at the prison, providing conjugal visits, and other innovations that would make the prison approximate the free-world situation more closely.

For the prison reformer who has his suitcase packed there are more exciting ideas that should be tried. There might be some merit in family prisons, such as the Davao Penal Colony in the Philippines, where the offender can take his family to the open prison with him. The Bolshevo Colony experiment in Russia, which is reportedly self-operated by the inmate population, should be replicated in the West. Some two-thousand inmates are under the supervision of less than a dozen staff who serve only as administrators. The deterrence to escape is the certainty of not being allowed to return to this open institution and the equal certainty of being sent to the Kara salt mines if caught.

In 1973 courts in Great Britain began sentencing felony offenders to 40 to 240 hours of community service work on weekends. The work consisted of painting and repairing the houses of old people and deprived families, helping youth clubs, constructing playgrounds for children, restoring canals, doing clerical work for a conservation agency, and working at an outdoor museum on industrial archaeology. In October 1974 a San Francisco judge sentenced an offender found guilty of transporting illegally killed big game to spend one day a week for a year treating zoo animals. A Florida white man was convicted of shooting into the home of an interracial couple. The judge placed him on probation on the condition that he attend Saturday morning breakfasts in a black church and perform voluntary work for a black charity. An artist convicted for possession and sale of cocaine was ordered to teach art to mentally retarded children. These judges must be commended for being innovative in a profession not usually devoted to change and for devising alternatives to incarceration.

The reform penologist who does not own a suitcase and is independently wealthy may suggest the purchase of a ghost town and negotiate with the prisoners of this facility for joint private operation by private industry on a contract-for-services basis. Although this idea is not likely to be implemented in the near future, the notion is an intriguing one and can be tested only in reality. Perhaps prison conditions must worsen considerably before state administrators will be willing to risk such an innovation.

Some steps have been taken toward contracting for private services for state offenders. In 1973 Connecticut contracted with a private agency to operate a halfway house for adult female offenders. Minnesota also has done the same with both male and female offenders. The precedent was set decades ago in the treatment of juvenile offenders.

A private firm has contracted with prison systems in Maine, Indiana, and North Carolina to provide counseling and job-finding services for prison inmates. In Maine officials claim a $280,000 savings in one year through the early release and employment of 85 percent of the paroled inmates under the contract system. These figures are difficult to verify because the Maine Department of Corrections has no research division.

Whatever direction reform or change takes in the future, it is essential that a research component be included in order to demonstrate the effectiveness of the proposed change. Thus far the innovations in corrections have been based more on political expediency, desperation, or beliefs than on empirical evidence.

## Evaluation

Correctional fads have been the rule in prison administration since the first prison was built. We can trace management practices through punishment, penitence, hard work, education, reformation, rehabilitation, and reintegration. We have observed large prisons and small ones, bastilles and honor camps, sophisticated institutions and decadent ones. We have built halfway houses, diagnostic centers, reception centers, prerelease centers, cottages, and community correctional centers—all instituted with no prior evidence or valid reasons by which to predict any changes in recidivism or behavior.

Between 1969 and 1974 the Minnesota Governor's Commission on Crime Prevention and Control (GCCPC) awarded $6 million in LEAA funds to the Department of Corrections and local government units to establish and operate forty residential, community corrections projects. An eighteen-month assessment of projects that had been operational for at least eighteen months was conducted by the evaluation unit of the GCCPC and the results were made public in April 1975.

By project type, only 28.3% of the halfway house clients [those on parole] . . . [and] 38.5% of the P.O.R.T. clients [those on probation] . . . successfully completed their programs. . . .

In each project type, approximately 50% of the residents fail to complete the programs because they abscond, fail to cooperate with the program or engage in criminal activity.

The fact that so few clients successfully complete the programs suggests that residential community corrections programs, for a variety of reasons, are an inappropriate form of rehabilitation for a large percentage of persons for whom these programs are now being used. . . .

There were only slight differences between the recidivism rates of halfway house [or P.O.R.T.] clients and the comparison group in terms of arrest, felony convictions or total convictions and revocation of parole. . . .

After an initial start-up period, P.O.R.T. projects' occupancy rates . . . averaged 77.4%. Halfway houses had the lowest post start-up occupancy rates with 48.3%. . . .

All halfway houses and P.O.R.T. projects operated at a cost greater than the Prison at Stillwater. . . . One halfway house and all four P.O.R.T. projects operated at costs less than the Reformatory at St. Cloud.[42]

These dismal findings stunned the commissioners, who had expected that the applicants' predicted results would be realized. In summary, the director of the evaluation unit concluded that:

Present data indicate that the majority of persons sent to these programs are not amenable to the rehabilitation programs offered by the projects. Further, evidence suggests that success in the program is not related to lower rates of recidivism. Finally, the data indicate that in terms of recidivism, the programs do no better, but no worse, than the traditional methods of incarceration and parole.[43]

After much recrimination, self-examination, and pleas for support from applicants the commission reluctantly imposed a moratorium on the funding of new residential community corrections programs for a period of one year until further evaluations could be made.[44] If past experience is a predictor, however, Minnesota will continue to lead the nation in community based corrections; pilgrims will come from afar to view this mecca of treatment and return to their jurisdictions to perpetuate the mythical efficacy of community corrections.

Some research projects have demonstrated that no prison treatment program has had any effect in reducing recidivism;[45] consequently the administrator is forced to defend any new program with arguments rather than with empirical evidence. Hence it makes sense to evaluate programs wherever possible to determine their feasibility before they gain large-scale acceptance in the field of penology. It could be argued that the warden has an obligation to the profession to prove (or disprove) the worth of any program under his control.

For the warden a more important reason for research is the simple fact that with evidence of a good program his selling job is made much easier. Positive results from an evaluation will justify implementing it elsewhere in that system or in other systems. If the results of the evaluation should prove to be negative, then a service will have been performed by demonstrating that to our colleagues. That is, if as a result of exposure to the responsibility model there was an increase in violence, escapes, or recidivism, the result would be considered negative.

Another use for research is the education of those individuals both inside and outside the system. If the research is conducted scientifically and the results warrant positive conclusions, the warden should not hesitate to use the data for public relations purposes. Although this should not be the motivation for the research, no reluctance should be demonstrated in capitalizing on this by-product.

We have some clues about what works, but little evaluation and no rigorous research designs have ever been used in the few examples of participatory management that have occurred in the history of penology. (Even so, the warden has better evidence for implementing shared decision making than any other program.) Those who have experimented in corrections thus far have done so intuitively. There have been some overall plans and assumptions, but the practices have not been subject to valid measurements based on a research plan.

## Observations

It has been nearly two centuries since the concept of incarceration for criminal offenders was employed by our forefathers for the purpose of modifying human behavior. It has been at least 150 years since the paternalistic-dictatorial-autocratic model of prison management was adopted. It has been over 50 years since the medical-sickness model of treatment was introduced into the prison.

One need not be a scholar or a person with keen insight to deduce that if an idea has any merit, then 200, 150, or even 50 years should be ample time for it to achieve its objective. There has been an abiding faith in the correctional doctrine which holds that given sufficient time and ample resources (and a great deal of luck), the prison model will eventually fulfill its rehabilitative function.

However, there is abundant, irrefutable evidence that the prison has not achieved success in performing its rehabilitative function. Since the evidence runs contrary to the expectations and beliefs of the proponents of the present model, there might be some value in attacking the problem from another perspective.

## Conclusion

We have some evidence of what has been successful in prison management in terms of benefits to the inmates and society. Logic and common sense can teach us the need for an entirely different system of criminal justice. We can even envision a system with no institutions as we now know them.

The preponderance of evidence that the essential elements of prison reform—human interactions between staff and inmates—do not require additional funding is convincing; some innovations discussed in this treatise would even reduce the costs of incarceration while they are benefiting the prison community.

If we possess the intellectual capacity of reform and have some evidence of what has worked, why has reform never really been achieved? The answer is neither palatable nor optimistic. In addition to the usual skills the essential ingredients in a real reform movement are intuitiveness, moral courage, and integrity. Confusion often arises over the distinction between the compromise of strategy and the compromise of integrity. Integrity, which is more easily recognized than defined, is an illusive trait which means different things to different people.

Systems are designed for stability, order, and control, not for change, flexibility or self-improvement. The managers of the existing systems are not evil men; they are weak men. They are not willing to risk failure in order to achieve success. Most significant changes in the course of human development have not been evolutionary; they have been revolutionary. Those who were unencumbered by traditions, those who dared to deviate from the norm, those who refused to allow historical antecedents to determine future events were the men who opened the doors to new worlds.

Correctional administrators have the power to effect reform; history has given them some clues as to what will succeed. Perhaps they need the added ingredient of courage exemplified by Robert F. Kennedy who said:

Some men see things as they are and say "why?" I dream of things that never were and say "why not?"[46]

## Notes

1. Tom Murton, *The Dilemma of Prison Reform* (New York: Holt, Rinehart and Winston, 1976), p. xii.

2. Alexander Maconochie, *Australia. Thoughts on Convict Management, and Other Subjects Connected with the Australian Penal Colonies* (West Strand, London: John W. Parker, 1839), pp. 13-14.

3. Gustave de Beaumont and Alexis de Tocqueville, *On the Penitentiary System in the United States and Its Application in France* (Carbondale, Ill.: Southern Illinois University Press, 1964), p. 79.

4. See generally Harry Elmer Barnes and Negley K. Teeters, *New Horizons in Criminology* (New York: Prentice-Hall, 1959); Ronald Goldfarb and Linda Singer, *After Conviction* (New York: Simon and Schuster, 1973); Orlando Lewis, *The Development of American Prisons and Prison Customs, 1776-1845* (New York: Prison Association of New York, 1922); and Frederick Wines, *Punishment and Reformation* (New York: Thomas Y. Crowell, 1923).

5. "New Prison at Eagle River," *Anchorage Daily News*, October 26, 1972.

6. *Report of the Grand Jury*, Superior Court, Third Judicial District, Anchorage, Alaska, November 8, 1974.

7. *Holt* v. *Sarver*, 309 F. Suppl 362-385 (E.D. Ark. 1970).

8. *The Pine Bluff Commercial* (Ark.), January 20, 1971.

9. Ibid., October 12, 1974.

10. *Delta Democrat-Times* (Greenville, Miss.), April 13, 1971. Subsequently an order by the federal court has resulted in the elimination of inmate guards and some impetus for change (but not reform) of the prison system.

11. *Corrections Digest*, Washington Crime News Services, Annandale, Va., January 8, 1975, p. 3. As with many other innovations in corrections, change does not usually come about through new insight or humanitarian concepts; it usually occurs as a result of economic arguments—so long as staff are not disadvantaged in the process.

12. William G. Nagel, *The New Red Barn: A Critical Look at the Modern American Prison* (New York: Walker and Co., 1973).

13. Ibid., p. 176.

14. Ibid., pp. 48-49.

15. Ibid., pp. 47-48.

16. Ibid., p. 10.

17. Norval Morris, *The Future of Imprisonment* (Chicago: University of Chicago Press, 1974), p. 10. Copyright © 1974, University of Chicago Press.

18. Ibid., pp. 27, 36.

19. Ibid., pp. 39, 55, 19, 90, 112, 101.

20. Ibid., p. 105.

21. Ibid., p. 117.

22. Ibid., pp. ix, 121.

23. Ibid., p. 89.

24. The material in this section is reprinted with permission from "Shared Decision Making as a Treatment Technique in Prison Management," *Murton Foundation for Criminal Justice*, Minneapolis, March 15, 1975, pp. 32-42.

25. John Vincent Barry, *Alexander Maconochie of Norfolk Island* (London: Oxford University Press, 1958), p. 166.

26. Ibid., p. 167.

27. Frank Tannenbaum, *Osborne of Sing Sing* (Chapel Hill, N.C.: University of North Carolina Press, 1933), p. 130.

28. Thomas Mott Osborne, *Society and Prisons* (New Haven, Conn.: Yale University Press, 1917), p. 230.

29. Ibid., pp. 222-223.

30. Carl R. Doering, ed., *A Report on the Development of Penological Treatment at Norfolk Prison Colony in Massachusetts* (New York: Bureau of Social Hygiene, 1940), p. 86.

31. Ibid., p. 86.

32. Ibid., p. 182.

33. The Arkansas experience with participatory management is reported here reluctantly, not for the aggrandizement of the author, but because it is the only other reported example approaching the full participatory model and because it is contemporary.

34. Tom Murton, "Inmate Self-Government," *University of San Francisco Law Review* 6 (1971):94.

35. Tom Murton, "One Year of Prison Reform," *Nation*, January 12, 1970, p. 14.

36. Murton, "Inmate Self-Government," p. 101.

37. These comments on the Litton Industries project are based on personal investigation by the author in 1965.

38. "Sweden Tries Family Living for Prisoners," *Atlanta Journal and Constitution* (Ga.), April 2, 1972. Reprinted by permission of United Press International.

39. Ibid.

40. "Open Jails Give Convicts Right Climate," *Los Angeles Times,* May 28, 1972. It is worth observing that there may well be advantages to such innovations that are evaluated in terms of worthy aims other than recidivism.

41. *Pontiac Flag News*, Illinois State Penitentiary, Pontiac, Ill. April, 1975, p. 5.

42. "Residential Community Corrections Programs: A Preliminary Evaluation, Summary, and Recommendations," (Mineapolis, Minn.: Evaluation Unit, Governor's Commission on Crime Prevention and Control, April, 1975) pp. 3-6.

43. Ibid., p. 10.

44. Ibid.; emphasis in original.

45. Robert Martinson, "What Works? Questions and Answers about Prison Reform," *Public Interest* 35 (Spring 1974). Yet recidivism should not be the only, or indeed necessarily the primary, measurement of the success of the institution.

46. Edward Kennedy, "A Tribute to Robert F. Kennedy," *Representative American Speeches*, vol. 40, no. 5 (New York: H.W. Wilson Co., 1968), p. 178.

# 2

# Restraint and Incapacitation: An Analytical Introduction

*Robert Martinson*

A void has been created by the inability of treatment to control crime by re-habilitating offenders. This has led to a revival of interest in deterrence and has fostered attempts to estimate the incapacitative effects of imprisonment. As always the critical source of intellectual confusion is the prison. This institution has such a variety of purposes that every important idea in penology is implicated. Retribution is as much a function of the prison as are deterrence (both individual and general), rehabilitation, criminalization, recidivism, punishment, and incapacitation. This confusion of functions makes it difficult to think about and plan for crime control.

The idea of incapacitation has long been taken for granted, yet any introductory text will confirm that this assumed function of the prison (sometimes called isolation) is uncharted territory, untouched by theory as if it were unworthy of thought. Elementary statistics about incapacitation are unavailable. For example, the relationship between numbers incarcerated and crime rates is not known currently or historically. This information might supply an upper bound to the incapacitation effect although it would not determine precisely its independent contribution to crime reduction. Despite the lack of statistics on incapacitation, claims are made for its obvious utility as a method for reducing crime.

We view incapacitation as an *effect* that can result from applying *restraint* to identifiable persons. This useful distinction helps to identify a family of measures—handcuffs, shackles, banishment, prison—by which persons can be restrained; it draws attention to the degree of restraint attained by each of these measures and permits thinking of the effect (incapacitation) as problematic, something to be investigated, not taken for granted. Finally this distinction helps in isolating the causal process common to measures of restraint so that their effects can be disentangled from other criminal justice measures.

*Restraint* here is defined as any deliberate interference with the accomplishment of a criminal act or other undesirable behavior. Deterrence (reaction to legal threat) and treatment (induced behavioral change) seek to prevent crime by inhibiting the motivations to engage in it. Restraint presumes such a motivation but seeks to prevent (or make difficult) the carrying through of the criminal

I have been saved from many errors by the critical assistance of Johannes Andenaes, Stevens Clarke, Gilbert Geis, Solomon Kobrin, and Judith Wilks. I also thank Daniel Nagin, Morris Silver, and Ernest van den Haag.

intent. To restrain implies that someone has been apprehended, but restraint is as distinct from apprehension as the use of a straitjacket is distinct from the discovery of the behavior it is meant to control.

## Restraint and Its Direct Effects

The reduction in criminal behavior due to restraining an individual will be called *direct individual incapacitation.* If restraining Smith by any means prevents Smith from accomplishing one criminal act, then direct individual incapacitation gets a score of one. Hence the total direct incapacitative effect of restraining a number of persons is the sum of their scores. We refer to this quantity as $D$ (for an individual) or $D_{Tot}$ (for any number of individuals). For any individual $D$ can vary from zero (restraining Smith prevented no crime since none was intended) to a large number (restraining Jones prevented twelve robberies by Jones, or restraining pickpocket Adams prevented Adams from lifting 123 wallets).

Later it will be necessary to distinguish $D_{Tot}$ from the net preventive effect of restraint $P$. Quantity $D$ is the subject of this section and the basis for all that follows. We begin by asking what sources there are for the widely held belief that restraining criminals is certain to reduce crime. Our aim is not to indict common sense but to reveal its considerable limitations. Throughout this chapter, restraint is being compared with deterrence—its only realistic alternative for controlling crime.

Imagine a small community. The residents are well acquainted, and criminal behavior is visibly a product of this or that person. What are the controlling assumptions about restraint?

### *Crime as an Activity of Particular Persons*

Certain identifiable persons are, for some reason, prone to commit dangerous, offensive, or bizarre acts, although these may be done only occasionally. Neighbors or bystanders can often predict and prevent an altercation by applying restraint during its initial stages, for example, by separating two incipient brawlers. It is folk knowledge that restraint works. It seems tolerably effective for everyday use, since it can be done quickly and because the person restrained can help provide clues to determine when it is no longer needed. Some persons (lunatics or idiots) make this decision more difficult by supplying ambiguous clues.

The implied scheme of cause and effect is simple. No extended inquiry into motives, rationality, or criminal responsibility is needed to successfully shackle anyone—petty  thief, murderer, maniac, enemy soldier. Restraining a person is like restraining a vicious dog; it is successful if one can prevent the threatened behavior.

The efficiency of restraint seems obvious since an episode may be over in a few minutes; nevertheless, this efficiency is an illusion. To prevent one particular act in progress or about to be committed, one restrains the whole person. With even the best of intentions this cannot help interfering with a variety of innocent or valuable acts that the person could perform. We regard this inherent inefficiency as the most striking attribute of restraint and give it the name *overkill*. Though barely perceptible in folk restraint, this inefficiency is present in every form of restraint.

Restraint is not necessarily punishment. There seems to be no punitive intent, at least in most folk restraint. This is clear when a parent restrains a child having a tantrum. However lovingly applied, restraint is experienced as a painful loss of freedom by humans, the painfulness increasing sharply as overkill increases and becomes more apparent.

When parochial forms of restraint are left behind, overkill increases dramatically. Assume that a car thief requires six hours to steal, strip, and sell the parts of an automobile. Chaining this thief to a post for one year will prevent ten such acts. If direct individual incapacitation were the sole purpose, one measure of its efficiency is given by the fraction 60 hours/6,664 hours, or approximately 0.001.

In general, the efficiency of restraint varies directly with the degree of correspondence between restraint periods and crime periods, both measured as historical events. Restraining a tantrum is efficient because the parent knows the approximate lengths of the two periods and is willing to expend the attention required to make the two periods coincide. But for the car thief the case is hopeless. The increased efficiency of his restraint demands the ability to predict when ten separate historical events (totalling sixty hours) will take place in the course of a year. If we knew this we could attach the chain at the appropriate times, permitting the thief to ply an honest craft the rest of the time.

There is less overkill when criminal behavior is part of a person's daily life. For example, restraint is more efficient when it is used to prevent robbery, theft, begging, prostitution, numbers running, vagrancy, and, perhaps, transmitting a communicable disease. Note, however, that it is a change in the type of behavior restrained that results in the increase in efficiency. Given the type of behavior, little can be done to adjust restraint to fit it. For instance, devices such as the brank—an apparatus that fits over the head and holds down the tongue—attempted to restrain only the sanctioned behavior, scolding, but the tendency toward overkill is still apparent.

Restraint is plagued by rigid inefficiency when it is used to prevent events that are rarely committed. In addition, it is known that a very large proportion of criminal events are committed by persons who do not engage in crime on a daily basis.

## Restraint as Public Protection

To restrain a person is to define and locate the source of a danger that may be broadly social. We assume that the person is not a witch or demonic spirit who can transmit the danger elsewhere. He is an ordinary person who is to be crippled, hobbled, or caged for the protection of others. There is a general danger from persons of this sort, and he is one certain source of it. Then common sense takes a leap: the best way to deal with the total danger is to be sure to remove a major source of it. If criminology is to be a science, it must not follow common sense blindly. The effectiveness of restraint varies widely, as will be shown later; but in any community, restraint should be compared with available sanctions. Devices such as alarm bells, high walls, locks, or well-lit streets may be more effective (and less costly) than restraint, but they are measures taken against unknown persons. Apparently locking away burglar Smith is a balm and a certainty; the alternative protective device is an unknown probability.

If a scowl is sufficient to halt a bit of misbehavior, why restrain? The overwhelming proportion of human behavior is kept within tolerable boundaries by such sanctioning techniques. When persons are in each other's immediate presence, these techniques are extraordinarily precise. To misuse one of them in the smallest degree is to invite the possible embarrassment of being labeled a less-than-competent person. In comparison with the delicately calibrated world of sanctions, the barbarities of restraint are gauche and unsuited to the human condition. But as societies become complex and stratified, informal methods of social control give way to an apparatus of law enforcement and a system of legal codes. Sanctions give way to punishments that are roughly graduated to make the punishment fit the crime. At times legal codes have provided a dreadful catalogue of retribution—execution, mutilation, branding, whipping, banishment. These measures are more barbaric than restraint; however, the source of this ferocity is not overkill but vengefulness. There is nothing inherent in a formal punishment that makes it peculiarly inappropriate for human beings. It is the misuse of punishment—not its use—that is ineffective, while overkill inheres in the very use of restraint. For humans, punishment is the norm and restraint the measure of last resort.

## Characteristics of Restraint

It is difficult to abstract what is essential to restraint from a variety of symbolic meanings (degradation, shame) that may be attached to its use. In its crudest and most dramatic form restraint overpowers by physical means such as binding and shackling or inhibits by interfering with bodily functions, for example, maiming, prefrontal lobotomy. More subtle and costly forms are widely used, although they are not as easy to identify. The assignment of the duenna to supervise unmarried girls in many Latin countries is a form of restraint, as is close supervision of very young children in general. There is reason, then, to distinguish between the speed-reducing effects of highway signs on all drivers who pass them and the dramatic effect of driving in the vicinity of a marked highway patrol car. Overcautious driving stops when the patrol car disappears, but drivers still take the speed limit into consideration. Overcautious driving is a result of an element of restraint in the situation.

Note that the restraining device or agency achieves its preventive purpose only when it is present (active) but ceases to do so entirely when it is not. In contrast the threat of punishment may be internalized and need not be present on every occasion. Whatever else they accomplish, ropes, chains, handcuffs, prison cells, shackles, stocks, brands, straitjackets, duennas, and highway patrol cars all share this quality. They work (incapacitate) only at the precise times that they are used. Seen in this perspective, imprisonment is a crude form of restraint—like a set of shackles welded shut.

The restraint of a straitjacket is almost total, yet it is easily removed. Severing the right hand of a pickpocket is permanent, yet the incapacitative effect may be partial since the wretch may proceed to steal with his left hand or even his teeth. (Maiming is not purely restraint; it includes a strong punitive intent.)

Exile and banishment are extreme forms of what we shall call ecological restraint. This includes expelling a person from a community; forcing a person to reside in a remote, sparsely populated area; or even temporarily hindering a person from visiting his favorite haunts. An obvious example is the military policy of placing an establishment off limits. Probation or parole agents may individualize this policy by warning persons in their charge not to frequent particular areas or associate with particular persons. Like all forms of restraint, ecological restraint presumes a criminal intent and incapacitates, to some degree, by making it difficult to carry out this intent. At times the incapacitative effects of many forms of banishment may be illusory; a person may undergo the temporary inconvenience of being expelled from one community only to continue his activities in the next. This situation is called pseudoincapacitation. For example, the apparent drop in overall crime rates during World War II in the United States may be attributed in part to pseudoincapacitation.

## Fitting Restraint to the Person

Restraint is universally used to control young children. The simplest procedures are to walk hand-in-hand, remove the forbidden object, or place the child in a penned enclosure. (The use of a leash for a child might be an example of overkill on this level.) Older children may be confined to quarters, forbidden entrance to places, or simply kept in sight. Direct supervision can be quite effective in preventing mischief, but it is time-consuming. A parent or guardian can arrange to make this restraint unobstrusive and therefore relatively painless.

The painfulness of restraint increases sharply after the age of direct supervision. A person who needs restraint when most persons of the same age are controlled through sanctions is humiliated, shamed, or reduced in stature. (The special painfulness of overkill—being restrained when there is no need for it—is always present.)

Most attempts to fit restraint to the person illustrate how inappropriate restraint is for the human adult. The bars of a cage are indifferent to the captive and treat alike the petty thief, the murderer, or the philosopher. Rough distinctions can be made for the sexes: the chastity belt for the female and castration for the male. For the most part degrees of restraint are adjusted to the likelihood of escape and take into consideration physical strength, determination, or cunning—characteristics that man can share with the beasts.

When attempts are made to fit restraint to the person, a rationale is required to justify the different treatment. The force needed to contain a person must be estimated. His biography may provide evidence: Does he have enemies in prison? Has he attempted escape? How dangerous is he? Signs of past dangerousness need not determine the degree or kind of restraint. One may deliberately release a murderer who has reformed or unshackle a psychotic who has been cured. The potency of restraint may be altered in either direction—by transferring a convict from minimum- to maximum-security confinement or vice versa. Penology has developed special types of restraint for various categories of persons such as females, juveniles, or the mentally disturbed.

If there is a rough proportionality in fitting restraint to persons, it is not necessarily congruent with the proportionality demanded by retribution or by rehabilitation and may even conflict with them. For example, measures to restrain an escape-prone petty thief could be more drastic than those taken to control a killer now thought to be harmless. Similarly evidence of reformation may be useful in estimating restraint measures, but persons are normally restrained as an adjunct to treatment. The restraint itself is not thought to rehabilitate. If, by chance, a person reforms while under restraint, restraint would be relaxed not tightened.

However rough the calculation of proportionality, deviations from established standards excite feelings of injustice for individuals or groups so treated. Indeed, the limited means of restraint are likely to conflict with the fine distinctions persons come to make about their need to be restrained. Strain may be reduced by attempting a nicer fit, but this is difficult since the technology of restraint is so devoid of options. In principle, indeterminate sentencing is open to fine adjustments—months, weeks, even days—but the idea of a sentence is a category of punishment not restraint. A hypothetical sentence of five years may run from February 3, 1970, to February 3, 1975. There is no provision for distinguishing between restraint periods and crime periods. Temporary custody is sometimes used by field supervision agents to prevent an anticipated crime, but the accuracy of such judgments is unknown.

## Categorical Restraint

If police cordon an area, all persons (however law-abiding) are prohibited from entering. A curfew applies to all citizens (or all juveniles), not merely those likely to commit offenses. Much "target hardening" is restraint applied to citizens or consumers. For example, if bus drivers no longer carry change, all bus riders are inconvenienced; barred windows may increase fire hazards; closing subway stations during certain hours may force some to take other routes where muggings are more likely to occur; closing streets, parks, or routes of travel in the interests of crime reduction may restrain freedom of movement.

Categorical restraint is used sparingly, usually as a temporary measure to control riots and other forms of collective disturbance. Additional imprisonment for multiple recidivists appended to a punitive sentence, should be classified as categorical restraint. The use of categorical restraint dramatizes overkill. We ask why we and not the criminal should be inconvenienced. Citizens will resist such measures, considering them unfair. They do not realize or care whether convicted criminals suffer from overkill.

A brief summary is necessary before we analyze restraint within complex systems of criminal justice. Direct individual incapacitation $D$ is the reduction attributable to restraint in the criminal behavior of identifiable persons. This effect is present in all deliberately imposed restraint. Its efficiency as a social policy depends on the ability to predict who will commit offenses and when. Prediction becomes more difficult as the threatened behavior is observed less frequently and as restraint is applied by persons unacquainted with the offender. In comparison with sentencing, restraint is grossly inefficient.

## Incapacitative Effects of Criminal Justice

There are no pure forms of restraint in criminal justice. A number of complex networks have evolved and have been transformed under various pressures; and incapacitative effects, some intended and others inadvertent, are mixed with other effects. To identify its independent effects restraint must be taken as an analytical dimension.

## Penal Restraint

Historically, maiming, execution, banishment, and imprisonment have been important forms of punitive sentences normally imposed after finding an offender guilty of behavior defined as criminal. Unlike penal sentences, such as fines or whipping, these measures contain a strong element of restraint. It does seem awkward, if not absurd, to classify execution as a form of restraint. Execution is the only completely irreversible criminal justice measure, although most forms of maiming are also irreversible. It would be considered unjust to execute solely to restrain, yet execution clearly achieves an incapacitative effect similar to milder measures and thus must be included. If penal sentences are viewed simply as various means of exacting retribution from offenders, all these measures need be graded only on degree of punitiveness. However, to focus on the crime-reducing effects of various punishments requires factoring our different causal effects so that they can be measured independently. Restraint as a social policy for reducing crime always appears in the form of penal restraint and is thus simultaneously and inescapably both a deterrent to the public and a means of incapacitating some offenders (which may also help to reduce crime rates).

A few rough distinctions will help in distinguishing the mixed effects achieved by penal restraint. For example, deliberately dreadful methods of penal execution (burning at the stake, immolation, garroting, drawing and quartering) achieve precisely the same incapacitative effects as the so-called painless methods of today (electric chair, gas chamber). It is difficult to say whether these dreadful methods ever achieved an additional (or longer-lasting deterrent effect beyond that achieved by execution. The punitive element in banishment varies when it takes the form of a judicial order to leave a country instead of the once-popular American custom of tarring, feathering, and riding the offender out of town on a rail. Maiming can be accomplished by lopping off a hand with an axe or by the "painless" surgical procedures of castration or prefrontal lobotomy. Imprisonment in the galleys or at hard labor is more punitive than the simple isolation from the community achieved by house arrest or minimum-security confinement. Prison reformers have fought to eliminate from prison such additional brutalities as hanging in chains, electric shock, the treadmill, and standing at attention for long periods. They invented a slogan to highlight this struggle: Persons should be imprisoned *as* punishment rather than *for* punishment. Although politically useful, the slogan is ambiguous and misleading and should read: Convicts should be sent to prison *as* punishment but not for *additional* punishment. Imprisonment is a penal sentence, so a person is sent to prison *for* punishment; that is, whatever unpleasantness is incident to the fact of his imprisonment is an aspect of his punishment. Thus penal restraint should be broken down into punitiveness and restraint so that varying mixtures of effects can be traced back to their proper sources.

We have argued that even the purest forms of restraint are painful (except perhaps for small children). When persons are restrained under the authority of a penal sentence, restraint can be used as a convenient disguise for additional punishment. Examples readily come to mind. Suppose that a military officer confined to quarters was stripped of all his clothing to prevent his easy escape or that balls and chains were attached to the ankles of youths in a juvenile hall. These punishments-in-disguise would further restrain; but since their further restraint would achieve no more incapacitation, they would be glaringly in-efficient. Even those who accept overkill as a fact of life would denounce this uncalled-for extension as inappropriate and unjust.

It is difficult to discover cases in which the painfulness of mere restraint is the official punishment for an offense. The branks and the pillory might seem to fit the bill, but these devices were primarily means of public humiliation similar to the Nazi policy of forcing Jews to wear the Star of David except that the Jews had done nothing to merit such humiliation. In small American com-munities two hundred years ago miscreants were identified and made infamous by the use of the scarlet letter. The crimes punished by such devices were minor, as was the degree of restraint and its duration. The public identification of miscreants made it possible for citizens to shun such stigmatized persons, per-haps making it more difficult for them to commit further offenses. (Police can use the mild and momentary stop-and-frisk restraint as an unofficial punishment for members of delinquent gangs, loiterers, prostitutes, or tramps.)

*Inadvertent Incapacitation*

Arrest, booking, pretrial detention, and appearance in court may have inad-vertent incapacitative effects. The direct individual incapacitation, incident to being arrested or appearing in court, is trivial. In the past most legal punish-ments required only the incidental restraint needed to put them into effect. Criminals were punished severely but swiftly. Illegal delay in the booking process is less trivial.[1] But the term inadvertent might be abandoned in the case of pre-trial detention which is widespread and which incapacitates as effectively as does imprisonment imposed as a punishment. The controversial notion of pretrial pre-ventive detention explicitly recognizes and deliberately strengthens this in-capacitative effect. It cannot be argued that preventive detention does not, in fact, have some incapacitative effect on those detained; it can only be argued that this effect is not worth the constitutional price. A rough guess is that the direct incapacitative effect of pretrial detention in the United States today is at least one-half that of imprisonment and is probably much more.[2]

The legal objective of pretrial detention is to assure appearance at trial, not to incapacitate or punish. Bail studies indicate that release on bail or on personal recognizance is often effective in assuring appearance, and prevailing bail prac-tices discriminate against the indigent. The conditions of pretrial detention are frequently more painful than imprisonment, and this situation is not lost on the lower court judges. "Even in many lesser cases the magistrate seemed to be imposing high bail as punishment on the assumption that the defendant was guilty."[3] That pretrial detention is largely a cheap system of justice for the indigent does not make it less incapacitative in its immediate effects. However, if feelings of rank injustice lessen one's commitment to conventional society, the long-term effects may be criminalizing.

The inadvertent incapacitation visited on groups of arrested or accused persons typically includes a small proportion (perhaps 3 percent) who are found innocent and a larger proportion whose charges are dropped. If one assumes that all these persons are legally innocent, then at least restraining the remainder temporarily incapacitates.

## Execution

Execution, no longer important as a means of incapacitation, has also come under strong attack as a deterrent (when compared with the alternative of life imprisonment). Its usefulness as a concept is also impaired by stubborn errors in thinking about it; the most common is the assertion that execution accomplishes total incapacitation. A little thought will convince one, however, that the execution of an innocent person will accomplish total restraint but zero incapacitation, as would the execution of the most dangerous killer on the day he was to die anyway by natural means. In contrast, temporarily binding the arms of a protagonist in a lovers' quarrel could totally prevent the disaster that might have occurred. The root of the error may be semantic, since the term *incapacitation* is often used to refer to both a means and a consequence. The final result is that the overkill—inherent in all forms of restraint and carried to its ultimate in execution—is confused with the actual effects achieved by applying various degrees of restraint to various categories of persons.

In estimating the incapacitative effects of restraint, long-term criminalizing effects (recidivism) frequently complicate the problem. If all convicted offenders were executed, however, recidivism would be impossible for them, not merely by definition, but as a fact. For this reason, it will be useful to use the concept of execution as a benchmark or polar concept, despite the growing insignificance of execution as a social policy.

## Incarceration: Partial, Temporary, Intermittent

The central restraining measure of modern societies is caging or corralling. Typically the body of the prisoner is left unhampered, and he is free to move within a much-reduced physical space. He may be under constant surveillance, although this is rare; but he is not crippled, hobbled, or bound. Extreme forms of caging such as solitary confinement with no social interaction that may induce psychotic behavior have been abandoned. The most drastic segregation generally used permits some individual activity and considerable opportunities for social interaction. Hence caging in principle is always partial restraint; and the most closely caged prisoners frequently engage in destruction of prison property, suicide, assault, rape, and rebellion. Incarceration in congregate prisons combines caging and corralling and is less efficient because it regularly permits—or even induces—a wide variety of criminal and deviant behaviors during the prisoners' sojourns.

Modern incarceration is notoriously temporary. The number of people who serve life sentences is small. Average prison sentences in the United States today range from about twenty months to about five years. Increases in life expectancy over the last centuries have resulted in an increase in the amount of time an offender will be at large even if the length of prison sentences has not declined. The result is that at present in the United States, two out of every three convicted offenders are supervised in the community. In addition, for the typical offender incarceration has become more intermittent. Periods of confinement, community supervision, and reconfinement are spaced irregularly in the course of his life.

The limitations on direct individual incapacitation are the product of different factors: restraint is *partial* due to both the increasingly humane care of prisoners and the exigencies of prison administration, *temporary* because of the requirements of justice, and *intermittent* because of high recidivism rates, lengthy criminal careers, and the increasing use of probation and parole.

## Restraint in the Community

A suspended sentence without field supervision serves only a deterrent purpose. Compliance is induced by the threat of more severe punishment, usually prison, should the offender return to crime; he is not restrained at all. But field supervision is a complex bureaucratic system that may achieve a number of effects depending on the mix of indeterminacy, client characteristics, and the supervision and services delivered or offered.[4]

A *deterrent* effect is possible due to variations in either agent surveillance or revocation policy across jurisdictions, regions, or even district offices. Compliance is induced by the threat of revocation and the certainty with which this threat is applied, and it depends on the vigilance and firmness of agents.[5] A rehabilitative effect is possible from efforts by the agent to treat or help the offender, although at present this is seldom achieved.[6]

A decrease in the direct costs of punishment to the state has been an important aspect of the shift to field supervision. This benefit declines as field supervision is enriched with expensive programs and smaller case loads. The hidden cost of increases in crime due to the shift to field supervision has increased considerably as higher-risk categories of offenders are shifted from prison to field supervision. This hidden cost cannot be estimated by comparisons of recidivism rates alone, since a larger number of offenders may account for a larger total volume of crime even if there is a decline in the recidivism rate.

An *incapacitative* effect is achieved (whatever the intention) when a probationer or parolee is held for investigation in a jail or other facility or is incarcerated temporarily as part of a treatment regimen. Halfway houses often have prisonlike characteristics including twenty-four-hour surveillance, sign-out procedures, obligatory counseling sessions, and punishment for AWOL residents. Intensive forms of supervision (including gatherings for Nalline testing or group supervision) may restrain partially and temporarily whatever additional effects they may have. The elements of restraint in these situations are obvious and are used consciously by policymakers and individual agents.

But there are inadvertent or at least unremarked partial restraints involved in a wide spectrum of treatments in field supervision. Foster parents, group homes, and the special duenna gang worker often assigned to delinquent gangs use some elements of restraint. Often just engaging in treatment activities can result in more intensive surveillance than occurs in most prisons. Indeed, any interference with the free movement of the supervised offender may increase the difficulty of committing crime and result in partial incapacitative effects. Requiring a parolee to reside in a remote rural area could reduce his capacity to commit crimes, independent of the deterrent effect of the threat of return to prison. Parole or probation rules that limit or regulate residence, driving, and association may have partial incapacitative effects.

In many cases it would not be easy to distinguish between the incapacitative and deterrent elements of a policy or agent decision. Compliance with the orders of field supervision agents is at present more a matter of threat than restraint, but this may be because restraint has not been a legitimate and deliberately cultivated policy of field supervision. It exists behind the back of criminal justice, and bringing it into the light raises the questions when and where it should be used and with what type of offender it is appropriate. The partial incapacitative effects of existing methods of supervision may be small in comparison with those of incarceration, but in principle they need not be.

Field supervision has a profound superiority, largely unrecognized by its theorists, to the total institution. It can be divided and subdivided in a way that prison cannot. It has flexible walls which can be changed by bureaucratic fiat. It creates no inmate subculture by mere propinquity. It knows no riots, gang rapes, or injuries from escapees "hitting the wall." It can shift its operations quickly as crime ebbs or flows and is not rooted to one spot like the prison, that mastodon of inflexibility and futility. These qualities account, in part, for the expansion of field supervision.

Yet field supervision has been the most conservative and unchanging entity in criminal justice. It expands but does not change its structure. There is a cry for smaller case loads; but the idea of the case load, borrowed from the alien field of social work, is almost as fixed a unit as the cell is in biology. This is primarily due to the predominance of the treatment ideology and the failure to recognize the possibilities inherent in this mode of social control. Revolutions in human practice frequently grow slowly beneath the surface for centuries before they surface. Field supervision has become the central mode for coping with crime in modern industrial society. It can outlast the conditions that were associated with its establishment and could be made much more determinate.

Field supervision must undergo searching criticism and profound reorganization if it is to slough off the excrescences that followed its birth and are now crippling its potentialities. The rhetoric of community treatment must be abandoned in favor of realism and honesty. Indeterminacy must be reduced and what remains of it justified by evaluating its actual effects in reducing crime. The case load idea must cease to be applied indiscriminately to all; it should be the exception, not the rule.

Functions of field supervision should be factored out so that what is needed for one offender is not forced on all. Field supervision should be divided into three distinct parts—policing, restraining, and helping—corresponding roughly with deterring, restraining, and rehabilitating.

The central device of policing is the Damocles sword of special legal threat, a legal threat directed at persons convicted of crimes and sentenced to the status of probationers. If they offend again, they receive the normal punishment for their new crimes plus a special punishment for having betrayed the trust of the community while probationers. The aim should be to maximize the deterrent effect and minimize any other interference in the life of the probationer.

The second speciality of field supervision should be close supervision for those who might be called restrainees, in open recognition of the aim which assumes a criminal intent and takes restraint measures to the degree necessary to prevent this intent from being carried out. This would be a kind of prison in the community but with infinitely more flexibility than a prison. The aim is not to change the offender but to prevent him from committing crimes.

The helping functions should be removed entirely from the criminal justice system. It should be given to a variety of specialized agencies that have no responsibility for crime and are therefore free to aid the offender who seeks this help.

Some day, people will wonder at the absurd fixation on the cage as a means of restraint in this age of space exploration. They will note with astonishment that each cage could have been replaced by the simple expedient of hiring a fellow for the sole task of constantly keeping a restrainee in sight as if he were a small child who could not be trusted. All this would cost far less than these rigid structures of cement and steel, and could be relaxed, expanded, or abandoned when deemed necessary.

Restraint used in the community would not be a return to folk restraint. It could be used only for those convicted by due process of law and accomplished only by a recognized agent of the state. It is a difficult and unfamiliar idea but in no way utopian or incapable of being tried today. It would damage the offender less, interfere with his movements less, and could adjust quickly to his moods and changes of intentions. Some historical forms of restraint in the community may have been effective in preventing certain kinds of behavior. The nineteenth-century czarist system of internal exile to remote villages was an effective means of limiting if not extinguishing the political activities of urban dissidents. By using such measures, the czarist regime could rely on the lethargy of the Russian peasant community and the hostility of rural folk to intellectuals and city people.

### Measuring Direct Individual Incapacitation

$D$ was defined as the reduction attributable to restraint in an individual's criminal behavior. Viewing restraint as an analytic dimension of criminal justice highlighted the problem of accurately measuring $D_{Tot}$ for any sizable number of convicted offenders. As offenders are detected, arrested, booked, detained, tried, sentenced, and processed, they are subjected to widely varying degrees of restraint. This restraint is frequently inadvertent and always partial, the more so as security is relaxed and as detention is a breeding ground for crimes against fellow prisoners, state property, and officers.

For most offenders crimes are rare events spaced irregularly in the course of life. Each of these events takes very little time from the inception of the criminal intent to the accomplishment of the criminal act. Criminology knows little about the frequency, sequence, spacing, duration, and seriousness of criminal events in general. A cohort of persons in detention or in prison in any given year is a mixture of every type of offender. Persons of all ages, races, and socioeconomic conditions are represented. To measure $D_{Tot}$, one needs to know what this conglomeration of persons would have done had they not been detained at that particular time. It would be more difficult to trace the variation in incapacitation over time as a cohort of offenders progresses through the criminal justice process.

Measurement is a technical problem, and perhaps these intricacies can be resolved. If this were done, $D_{Tot}$ for a particular cohort would still be a hypothetical quantity that could never be measured directly. Confidence in such mathematical extrapolations can seldom be strong and becomes weaker as the string of assumptions on which they depend grows longer. To gain confidence in the as-if of $D_{Tot}$ would require experiments of a complex nature using the crime rate in a jurisdiction as the dependent variable.

If more were known about the unimpeded criminal career, more accurate estimates could be made of the average number and seriousness of crimes per criminal per unit of time. But it is unclear how the ponderous instrumentalities and legally proscribed rhythms of criminal justice could be adjusted to take advantage of this knowledge. These intricate processes now ignore such considerations. At present a decision about a particular burglar is not based on a prediction of the average number of crimes that burglars of this type are likely to commit nor on the amount by which this average number would be reduced by various types of restraint. In this sense the incapacitative effects of criminal justice will remain a by-product of primary objectives such as retribution, punishment, and simple fairness.

Recent estimates of the effects of incapacitation must be viewed with caution.[7] These estimates depend on a number of confident assumptions about the unimpeded criminal career. They equate restraint with prison, ignoring detention and field supervision; they seem unaware that restraint is always partial and that imprisonment breeds crime; they leap to policy recommendations that do not follow from their estimates; they exude an air of naive enthusiasm that is unfitting given the little that is known with certainty. But the most serious difficulty in estimating $D_{Tot}$ arises from the assumption that restraint has no further effects—either rehabilitative or criminalizing—on the person restrained. If the brutalities of imprisonment were diminished, the prison sojourn would still damage the person restrained by interfering with normal life chances.[8]

Such criminalizing effects might be reduced by rehabilitation or individual deterrents. The institution of penal restraint inextricably mixes the effects of punishment and restraint on the offender. Controlling for sentence length, one might demonstrate that an additional increment of restraint, for example, as opposed to minimum-security confinement, could have an additional detrimental effect on recidivism rates. The effects of sentence length are so overpowering, however, that such an effect would be difficult to detect. This fact of life cannot justify ignoring the joint effect of punishment and restraint in estimating direct individual incapacitation ($D_{Tot}$).

Direct individual incapacitative effects are partial, temporary, and intermittent, but the costs (criminalization) of attaining such effects may be lifelong. The conclusion is that the net effect of restraint on those restrained can be measured accurately only by using some estimate of the lifetime pattern of offending. Rough estimates of short-term incapacitation effects can be computed through the use of imprisonment statistics. On any current day in the United States there are about 360,000 persons behind bars (detention plus prison). $D_{Tot}$ for the nation would then be 360,000 times the average number of crimes per criminal per day.

To estimate $D_{Tot}$ for any large, varied group of offenders, information would be needed on the following:

Unimpeded lifetime patterns of offending by type of offense (with various levels of general deterrence assumed)

Additional crimes committed due to the criminalization incident to punitive restraint or prevented due to a combination of rehabilitation and
individual deterrence

Intramural crimes committed during prison sojourns at various points in
the course of life by type of offense

Partial incapacitative effects of field supervision restraint by type of offense

If more information is collected so that $D_{Tot}$ can be estimated accurately
for any number or mix of offenders and for patterns of restraint, then the
essential question for public policy still has not been approached. What is the
efficiency of restraint in reducing crime *compared with available alternatives?*
This question is important since restraint is, on the whole, inefficient in preventing most criminal behavior, especially that which is rarely engaged in.
Restraint, as a general social policy, presents further and more intricate difficulties.

### Restraint and Public Protection

What overall protection is provided to society by the restraint of convicted
offenders? The question is unanswerable in the abstract, since the restraint of
some offenders reveals nothing about the reactions to this restraint by those
(offenders or members of the public) who are not restrained. No society has
restrained all offenders, and most societies restrain only a small proportion of
them. To estimate the net preventive effect of restraint, we will vary $D_{Tot}$ and
ask what further effects this could have alone. In the absence of firm knowledge
hypothetical situations are imagined based on various assumptions about the
nature of criminal behavior.

### *The Criminal as Beast: A Limiting Case*

Let us deprive criminals of human nature and imagine that all crimes are committed only by a fixed stock of tigers. The capacity of a tiger to commit a crime
is limited by his appetite. Tigers are indifferent to the execution of their fellow
tigers, which is the sole social defense policy used by the society. First, let us
offer the tigers an unlimited supply of victims.

We wish to determine the net preventive effect $P$. Let $D$ be the reduction
in crime achieved by the execution of one tiger. Since there is an unlimited
supply of victims and since all tigers stop committing crimes when satiated, the
execution of one tiger can have no effect on the behavior of the survivors. In
this situation $P = D$; that is, the execution of each additional tiger reduces the
crime rate by the fixed capacity of a tiger to commit crime.

Now let us reduce the number of victims to the point where the tigers are competing for a limited number. Some tigers are capable of committing crimes but are prevented from doing so by the unavailability of victims. Now the execution of each additional tiger creates an opening for another tiger who would otherwise be unable to commit a crime because he could find no victim. $D$ would not change; but the net preventive effect $P$ of this second type of execution would be less than $D$. Let $O$ be the crime that results from creating an opening for another, previously deprived tiger.

A general expression for the preventive effect of restraint can then be written $P = \overline{D} - O$ or $\overline{P} = \overline{D} - \overline{O}$, averaging over the fixed stock. The constant $\overline{D}$ is the average amount of crime prevented by the execution of a tiger. The variable $\overline{O}$ depends on the degree to which the removal of one tiger creates openings for other tigers. The constant $\overline{D}$ is fixed by the capacity of the average tiger, and $\overline{O}$ can vary from zero (victims are unlimited) to $\overline{D}$ (as a limit). If the availability of victims in relation to a given fixed stock of tigers is assumed to be fixed for a particular time period, then $\overline{D}$ and $\overline{O}$ are constants for that period.[9]

We have removed some of the complexities that bedevil an analysis of restraint for human beings. There is a fixed stock of offenders not subject to incentives, no deterrent effect, and tigers are dangerous so overkill is irrelevant. Executing the tigers instead of penning them brings restraint to a pitch of efficiency. But crime is not savage behavior in the abstract; it is a damaging event involving "criminal" and "victim." At this apex of efficiency the net preventive effect of restraint $P$ will be less than direct individual incapacitation $D$ except when the number of victims is virtually unlimited in relation to the number of tigers. If one could imagine a world in which restraint is the sole effective policy of social defense, the effectiveness of restraint in this world would approach zero as the ratio of offenders to victims became very large. Imagine attempting to protect a field of grain from being eaten by a swarm of locusts. Killing one (or even a larger number of locusts) simply makes room for the others: restraint is completely useless.

## The Human Criminal: Restraint and Opportunity

Human criminals do not commit crimes at a constant rate but are subject to incentives. (Retain the previous assumptions: fixed stock, no deterrence, overkill is irrelevant, and execution is the policy.) Imagine that the sole variation in incentive results from restraint—executing smaller or larger numbers of the fixed stock—and set a sufficiently large number of criminals so that there is considerable competition for victims.

The execution of one tiger provided an opening for another tiger, implying that tigers (unlike humans) do not adjust their criminal activities. Given the opening they commit the crime, otherwise they do not. On the assumption that crime is subject to incentives, it is important to determine whether a member of the fixed stock will commit a crime because (and only because) an opening is available. To do this let us create two radically different kinds of openings by dividing the crimes into organized crime and traditional property crime, executing a number of criminals who commit each type. The survivors in organized crime are lured by impressive opportunities and rapidly expand their criminal activities; those in traditional property crime are less impressed. With only restraint operating one would expect organized crime to return to its previous level after a time. Traditional property crime would take longer and might be reduced permanently.

The incentive to engage in criminal acts is never supplied solely by such openings. It is a complex product of personal characteristics, the skill and training needed, the type of crime, the risk of apprehension and punishment, and other factors. Variations in such factors create incentive structures that probably vary widely by type of crime. If crime were a fixed personal attribute, incentives would not matter. If they do matter, it is an open question how much variation is due to incentives in general and how much to that special incentive opened up by removing an active criminal from the field. Given an incentive structure, the net preventive effect of restraint $P$ will be less than $D_{Tot}$ because there is more competition among criminals.

The majority of criminal acts occur within a local framework in which propinquity plays a decisive role. Hence it is an error to dismiss the possibility of competition among offenders on the grounds that modern societies have created a plethora of dwellings, commodities, and densely packed humans to prey on. Criminal markets occur in neighborhood contexts dominated by locally generated incentive structures. Communication and experience may establish a locally shared criminal "map" in which certain streets, parks, or establishments are preferred as recognizable sites for victimization (at particular times) and are given precedence as criminal targets. One index of the degree of competition among criminals might be the degree of concentration of patterns of victimization; the more random the patterns, the less competition among criminals. Competition among offenders for the disposal of stolen goods with criminal fences is a more orthodox economic problem.

An increase in the number of dwellings in New Hampshire cannot be said to enter into the criminal calculations of a delinquent in Philadelphia. Indeed, this delinquent may pass hundreds of people in his neighborhood before settling on one well-dressed woman walking alone. We say that the restraint of criminal competitors can sometimes create an opportunity ($O$) to commit a crime where none was perceived to exist before.

If we relax the assumption of a fixed stock, we must decide whether the opportunity effects of restraint will cause a marginal person to enter crime as well as cause active criminals to expand their activities. Suffice it to say that active criminals will feel some pressure from marginal criminals and may take a contemptuous view of the disorganized criminal. Restraining the more active and least cautious may crowd the field with the untrained, the bunglers, those who use violence when none is needed.

### Incapacitation and Historical Change

The degree of restraint has declined over the last century in most Western societies as fines, probation, parole, conditional release, and community treatment have been expanded to ever-larger proportions of the convicted criminal population.[10] Combining this fact with recent increases in reported crime, some see an obvious causal relation; because restraint declines, crime rates increase. But the restraint in question—imprisonment—is the major punishment for offenders, and therefore crime could increase because deterrence was relaxed. The apparent causal relation may be real and yet may have nothing to do with restraint per se. Economists and systems researchers make similar yet opposite errors in dealing with the confounding of restraint and legal threat. The former seek to dispose of restraint quickly so as to grant deterrence a major role; the latter sweep deterrence under the rug and seek to have restraint account for the variance.

Can we say anything more about the historical relationship between restraint and incapacitation? Assume that $D_{Tot}$ is achieved solely by execution, that criminals are not a fixed stock, and that the sole crime is robbery. The execution of one robber can deduct no more from the crime rate than the person's yearly rate of commiting robberies; so, other things being equal, the younger the robbers are when executed, the lower the crime rate. Imagine, then, no change over time in the average age at execution.

Would the execution of a typical robber in the year 1600 have a direct incapacitative effect $(D)$ any different from such an execution in 1900? The physiological makeup of men is likely to be invariant over such time periods. Criminal techniques can improve and life expectancy has increased. Men benefit from urban anonymity and increased mobility in ways that tigers cannot. Societies have become more complex; wealth has accumulated and is more fluid; and victims are tied less to fixed domiciles and friendly neighbors. A case could be made that $D$ has increased and that the amount of trouble (crime) one man can produce in his lifetime has gone up. This proposition seems self-evident for crimes such as political terrorism, skyjacking, and certain forms of arson, sniping, kidnapping, and bomb threats in which a person's potential for doing damage is raised dramatically by some technological multiplier. But one should not underestimate the troublemaking capacity of the devoted criminal in the past.[11] If this amount really had increased for most crimes, then a given amount of restraint would result in a historical increase in $D_{Tot}$.

What has been the effect of social change on $O$ (opportunity effects)? Two distinct but interrelated types of change must be examined: changes in the incentive structures of various types of crime and changes in the effect of restraint on competition among active criminals and in the entry of marginal criminals into each particular criminal industry.

This is a complex problem. First, the distribution of persons among the law-abiding, marginal, and active categories is subject to the restraints of socio-logical factors such as sex, age, urbanization, and ecology. Only as persons are freed from these restraints will they transfer from law-abiding citizens and become engaged in the choice process investigated by economists. The larger the proportion of calculating persons, the more economic factors will account for variations in criminal activity. But the more that mere opportunity to commit a crime causes criminal behavior to occur, the more removal of any group of offenders will lead others to take their place; hence the more useless restraint will be. The degree of competition required for this to be true is not known. One way to avoid these complexities is to assume that the opportunities to commit most of the common crimes—robbery, burglary, theft, assault—are virtually unlimited and always have been. As evidence there is the profusion of homes, goods, consumer durables, and unguarded persons that abounds in industrial societies. This is a solution by fiat. It shuts off inquiry into the way objective opportunities become actual criminal opportunities.

Little more can be said without supporting data. Recent discussions of the political economy of criminal industries are interesting but speculative[12] and are marred by the idea that crime is comparable to legitimate industries. Societies actively resist crime in a way that they do not resist increases in the production of sofas or bicycles.

The case against restraint does not depend on the existence or size of opportunity effects. Overkill is sufficient. But it seems fair to suggest that the possibility of additional reductions in efficiency may be disregarded entirely only by assuming that for crime as a whole and for each of its subtypes, criminals are indifferent to the activities of other criminals in deciding whether or how to commit a crime. Those who make such an assumption should justify it.

## Why Has Restraint Declined?

If $D$ has increased in the last centuries, why not restrain more? Why has the use of restraint declined? Overkill is not the answer. This has been a cost incident to restraint throughout its history. It is such a high fixed cost that it can increase little as crime becomes less a daily or frequent professional activity of criminals. High and increasing, recidivism would seem to argue for a greater use of restraint for chronic violators. Has society been irrational, then, in succumbing to the century-long movement to release the convict from prison and substitute fines, probation, parole, halfway houses, and other forms of community control?

The close historical relation between restraint and recidivism has been recognized. One seems to grow and feed on the other. Clearly restraint is appropriate for the recidivist offender, and it "needs" this offender or it will wither. But deterrence needs the one-time offender or it cannot prosper. It is easy to see how restraint in the form of imprisonment could help produce what it needs by the damage it does to the life chances of those restrained. Could it also be that increasing reliance on deterrence could help produce the one-time offender?

The imprisonment-equals-recidivism insight fueled generations of prison reform. Historians too often attribute changes in criminal justice to broad changes in popular sentiments about rehabilitation, humanitarianism, punishment, and their proper balance.[13] These ideas are important, but people are practical also. They pay attention to how efficiently (or inefficiently) social institutions accomplish their purposes. They can hardly help noting that recidivism seems to increase with the number of prisons.

Recidivism has been denounced with monotonous regularity since the first prison opened. An industry of scholarship has been expended on it. In contrast, incapacitation is a Johnny-come-lately, a strangely unexplored subject. This being so, opportunity effects could give only a slight additional impetus to decarceration sentiments although overkill should be obvious enough. Let us look at the history of the prison in these terms.

Imprisonment was substituted for punitive measures such as execution, banishment, maiming, and public humiliation early in the development of commercial and industrial society. Human labor (and the individual) became valuable so that citizens, who were potential victims, were nevertheless willing to erect and maintain expensive new structures to punish, restrain temporarily, and perhaps reform miscreants instead of eradicating or expelling them. In the villages and towns of that day isolating notorious malefactors by means of temporary removal to distant penitentiaries appealed to common sense. The immediately visible drop in local crime that followed rounding up and disposing of an active gang or other known group of criminals provided common sense with ample evidence of the soundness of this policy. That crime seeped back to its previous level passed unnoticed, especially if ex-prisoners resettled elsewhere.

Inducements to crime were also limited. Businesses were small, local, and nonbureaucratic. The commercial classes faced the common folk, and there was no permanent underclass disposed to preying on their neighbors. There was no bulge of unguarded working-class or middle-class homes with attractive consumer durables and no supermarkets with goods begging to be lifted. Crime was limited and local; recidivism was not an obdurate problem; the risk of punishment was high. Under these conditions successful criminals probably required some skills. There were fewer born losers and more professionals. (The day of the delinquent, the housewife shoplifter, and the joy-riding auto thief had not yet arrived.) The more skill and enterprise were demanded, the more difficult was the process of recruiting and training replacements for those hauled away to prisons.

A viable setting for restraint might occur if inducements to crime are not widespread, skill requirements high, criminals engaged full-time, and the risk of punishment considerable. It is difficult to think of a better situation. For this reason we advance the hypothesis that the net preventive effects of imprisonment have declined since the prison was introduced. As this became more apparent, movements for prison reform grew, and societies responded by using the prison less and by seeking alternatives to it.

The net preventive effects of restraint cannot be observed directly. This fact has contributed to the prison's long tenure by camouflaging factors undermining its effectiveness. Causal effects between $D$ and its unintended consequences $O$ operate in one direction, from $D$ to $O$. An increase in the number of persons restrained in a locality could have immediately visible effects on local crime which gradually level out. Variations in the speed with which this happens are not noticeable, and none of this has any discernible effect on the fixed efficiency of the walls, bars, or security arrangements of prisons. The prison visibly embodies security from victimization. The forces that undermine it are invisible and work on a time scale of centuries, not years, altering with changes in commercial practices, the growth of urbanization and affluence, and the decline of criminal specialization. These facts help explain why the prison persists despite the feeling that it is now ineffective.[14]

### Searching for Realistic Assumptions

Common sense is not always the best guide to public policy. In discussing restraint there is a danger of falling into the one-to-one fallacy, that we can reduce crime as we lock up more offenders. Three unrealistic assumptions must be made for this idea to be true: a fixed stock of criminals in society exists, it consists of individuals who commit crimes at some constant level, and those restrained are not less criminally prone than those who are not restrained.

These are unreasonable assumptions. The skills and resources needed for criminal activity, except for a declining minority of professional crimes, are not hard to come by, so there is less reason to assume a fixed stock of criminals than a fixed stock of bricklayers, coal miners, or beauty parlor operators. Acts that are rarely committed take place at a variable rate, and offenders are not compulsive so they adjust crime to opportunity, risk, and need. The third assumption is conceivable but unlikely. Those imprisoned are likely to be more criminally prone than those in the free society, fixed stock or not. To combine these three assumptions is to create an unrecognizable world.

Suppose a utopian regime were determined to extirpate crime. By a combination of genetic and welfare policies it has induced citizens to become law-abiding but has been unable to settle affairs with bands of gypsies roaming the countryside. The regime is faced with an unlikely but theoretically interesting fixed stock of rational criminals. If there were no deterrence, a sufficiently determined regime could reduce crime to zero but apparently only at the cost of restraining the entire stock. Unlike the tigers, these criminals are subject to incentives, so higher returns could induce survivors to commit more offenses as restraint thinned the ranks. Curves graphing the extirpation of crime would look different in these two cases.

As one relaxes the three unrealistic assumptions, singly or in concert, opportunity effects can increase, and the net preventive effect $(P)$ can decrease. If active criminals are unskilled, marginals are straining to enter the industry, competition is fierce, and criminal justice is incarcerating more or less at random, then one can imagine a state of equilibrium in which the net preventive effect of restraint is close to the vanishing point. In this unhappy situation, for every burglar locked up an equally crime-prone substitute appears to take his place. This is not the real world either.

All modern societies expend scarce resources (police, courts, jails, prisons, probation, and parole systems) to control crime. A good portion of the jails and prisons are designed for restraint in addition to any deterrent or rehabilitative functions they may perform. These resources have multiple effects, and it would be erroneous to suppose that they are arranged rationally to reduce crime maximally. Improvements are possible if the right balance of effects can be achieved.

Criminal justice is not a random process. There are a priori reasons for believing that convicted criminals constitute a distinctive subgroup of the population with an above-average "criminal propensity."[15] There is also empirical evidence.[16] This means that those who are incarcerated are, for the most part, those who ought to be. The mix can be improved; but proponents of radical alterations in the proportions of offenders in prison and in field supervision should provide more than rough estimates based on unstated or untested assumptions.

Restraining more persons varies the use of restraint, but can anything be done to make restraint more effective for any given number of those restrained? Apparently this cannot be done by improving the prison which combines the maximum of overkill with the maximum of damage to life chances. More personnel might reduce intramural crime, especially in jails and detention facilities where even the nonconvicted are shamelessly abused, raped, or driven to suicide. Escapes could be reduced, and many criminologists and public officials point proudly to the small escape rate as evidence that prison effectively incapacitates.

From our perspective, escape is like placement in field supervision; primarily it relaxes restraint for those who escape. (Of course, escapees commit the crime of escape and may injure others in the process.) Carrying this thought further, absconding is to field supervision as escape is to imprisonment, since it relaxes restraint for the absconder. It seems best to regard escape (or absconding) as the cost of maintaining effective supervision over those who do not escape (or abscond). (Some correctional wits regard successful escape—where the escapee evades capture and takes up a new life—as one of the few effective treatment programs available.) For example, a minimum-security facility is easy to manage and may reduce intramural crime, but the cost usually manifests itself through a larger number of walkaways. This should be seen as a system problem, since escape from prison could probably be reduced by providing the escape hatch of field supervision. Since escapes are few in number, variations in escape rates are not a serious problem in estimating $D_{Tot}$.

If restraint takes place within field supervision, supervisory efforts can be made to maximize the incapacitative effects achieved. Restraint in the community would be less certain and more risky since absconding will be easier than escape, but overkill would be lessened drastically and damage reduced.

### The Incapacitation-Deterrence Conundrum

Recent econometric research has provided the impetus for this discussion.[17] These studies raise questions about traditional criminological assumptions. They begin by specifying a crime generation function (CGF) and employ non-experimental data to estimate the CGF parameters (correlation coefficients and elasticities). The data are the natural variations in crime rates and other variables discoverable among jurisdictions (precincts, counties, states, regions). One study employed time-series analysis; all others used cross-sectional data for geographic units.

All the studies assume that criminal activity is subject to incentives that may vary by type of crime (homicide as opposed to petty theft). They also tend to assume that at any point in time criminal acts are committed by a finite number of individuals, the criminals. It is not assumed that this finite number is a fixed stock. Standard economic analysis is then applied to the crime industry. For example:

> If the stock of criminals is reduced by incarceration, higher returns may induce the survivors to commit more offenses but total criminal activity must decline: the decline will vary directly with the stock reduction. Population growth or the lure of higher returns will tend to bring new "suppliers" (from the "marginal" category) into the "industry" and thus restore the level of criminal activity.[18]

These studies provide evidence of the impact of the objective probability and objective severity of punishment on crime rates. The economists control for "taste," that is, for a number of factors identified as causally important by sociologists, psychologists, and demographers. We quote Silver's conclusions about these studies not knowing whether all these variables have been properly identified and controlled. As for probability of punishment, "the evidence convincingly demonstrates that crime rates are reduced by higher probabilities of punishment." He continues:

> In all but two instances the coefficients of probability of punishment . . . are negative and, typically, they are also statistically significant. This is the pattern not only for broad offense groupings (all felonies, crimes against property, or against persons) but for more narrowly defined felonies. These results appear despite the biases toward "no effect" noted in the report, and regardless of whether they are estimated according to single equation or simultaneous equation models. [Hence] . . . the negative relationship cannot be attributed to the possibility that unanticipated increases in the crime rate, by spreading law enforcement resources more thinly, cause the probability of arrest and conviction to decline.[19]

The findings for severity of punishment "point in the same direction as those for probability of punishment but not as convincingly." Silver concludes: "In the event . . . that new studies continue to produce weak or unstable results, a possible explanation would be that criminalizing effects of longer sentences roughly balance general prevention-incapacitation effects."[20]

Almost all these studies fail to distinguish between the incapacitative effects of restraint and the deterrent effects of legal threat. The importance of the distinction is recognized, however, by Isaac Ehrlich:

> an increase in the probability and severity of punishment by imprisonment might reduce the total number of offenses even if it did not have any deterrent effect on offenders, because at least those imprisoned are temporarily prevented from committing further crimes.[21]

Ehrlich has submitted mathematical proofs of a method for indirectly determining whether there is an independent deterrent effect; we leave the proof to the mathematicians.[22] Silver, in contrast, has suggested incorporating an additional variable into the crime generation function as a means of directly estimating the independent effects of restraint and controlling for them. This variable (%INC) would reflect the proportion of offenders currently incarcerated in a jurisdiction and might be one means of estimating the net preventive effects $(P)$ of restraint. Up to now, however, no direct estimate of the extent, significance, or even the sign of the coefficient of this critical variable has been made.

This variable masks the distinction between $D_{Tot}$ and $P$, thus avoiding the question of whether stock reduction would be less efficient for one type of crime than another and whether to attribute differences in observed inefficiencies to overkill or opportunity effects. Arguments are raging over whether decarceration increases crime. But it is important to know how decarceration might increase crime. What would be the effect on crime rates of flooding a jurisdiction with a higher than usual number of offenders? (This happened quite dramatically in California after the passage of the probation subsidy program.) Would this larger number share more equitably a given level of opportunities? Would some offenders become less active or be forced out into legitimate occupations? Answers to such questions are critical for the evaluation of a number of programs—probation subsidy, pretrial diversion, early release, work release, and closing of juvenile institutions.

The confounding of the effects of threat and restraint is the Achilles heel of the econometric perspective. It is a critical problem for any research into incapacitation or general deterrence. Until an acceptable method is found for resolving this conundrum, only the joint effects of penal restraint will be known, and thus the efficiency of various combinations will be unknown. To leave this matter in the dark is to transform overkill from an invention of man into a fact of nature and to hinder the search for a means of restraint in the community.

## Partial Confounding of Effects

We argued earlier that it is difficult, if not impossible, to isolate a purely incapacitative form of penal restraint when incarceration is both the sole significant restraining measure and the major punishment for serious crimes. In general, there is no restraint that does not impose some pain, but there are forms such as convictions, fines, and whippings in which the element of restraint is so trivial that it can be disregarded.

To understand more clearly how mere conviction can deter regardless of the sentence, it is helpful to abandon the narrow legal focus. This focus views deterrence as the net reduction in crime attributable to the inhibiting effects of the legal threat of punishment. In law and criminology punishment is regarded as pain purposively inflicted or threatened and justified by the value that it serves. Punishment is defined in terms of the legal intent rather than the perception of the person who undergoes it or is threatened with the action of some legal agency. The term *sanction* is preferable. Sanction may be positive or negative and brings the inadvertent pain of restraint and the deliberately imposed pain of legal punishment into the same conceptual framework.

From this perspective the effects of criminal justice sanctions are broader than those of formal legal punishment and far broader than the narrow ambit of restraint. These sanctions, whether carried out or threatened, begin with surveillance and arrest. They include booking, indictment, pretrial detention, court appearance, trial, conviction, and sentence—whether fine, probation or prison as well as parole.

A recent study introduced the concept of sanctioning patterns to reflect variations among jurisdictions in the use of at least some of these sanctions.[23]

A companion concept—restraint patterns—might help pin down variations in measures that restrain among jurisdictions. These twin concepts make confounding more apparent.

The problem is simplified somewhat by the fact that the incapacitative effects of restraint are now largely limited to two stages in criminal justice—pretrial detention and imprisonment. Reductions in crime due to deterrence are confounded only partially with reductions due to restraint. Unconfounded deterrent effects are discoverable in principle. This can be done by noting the effects on offense rates of variations in surveillance, arrest, conviction with suspended sentence, conviction with fine (always assuming no pretrial detention), and similar measures. But the converse is not true. Unconfounded incapacitative effects are not discoverable in principle because both major forms of restraint are severe sanctions, and any restraint is painful.

The measures involved in pure deterrence (arrest, fine) are mild sanctions at present, and it may be improper to conjecture the dimension of severity. Arrest and conviction will also be correlated with imprisonment. Something could be learned about deterrent effects by studying such mild sanctions, and the fine is capable of indefinite expansion as a sanction in the service of deterrence.[24]

### The Two Efficiencies of Restraint

Restraint has both an individual and a social efficiency. The individual efficiency of restraint varies with overkill, which is a high and relatively fixed cost dependent on offense patterns that cannot be altered easily by criminal justice. The social efficiency of restraint is currently tied to the prison and varies with changes in caging, corralling, and escape. In the future, it could vary with critical changes in the restraint-producing features of field supervision.

If $D_{Tot}$ was as high as possible (no escape, no intramural crime, no criminalization due to restraint), then $P$ would be at a maximum. This maximum would vary depending on the offense patterns that exist and on the level of opportunity effects $O$. But these two efficiencies vary inversely. Increasing the social efficiency by tightening security might reduce escape and intramural crime but at the cost of an upward shift in overkill. This can be ignored by those who have no conception of the painfulness of maximum-security caging, but it is a lively topic among convicts. Some convicts volunteer for such maximum-security caging because they fear other convicts, and some profess to enjoy the peace and quiet of these gravelike conditions. But such caging is used as a punishment for infraction of prison rules.

It would simplify things further if variations in caging could be disregarded in estimating the deterrent effects of incarceration. The deprivations that are part of prevailing methods of incarceration are fixed firmly in the public mind, and knowledge about changes in such methods is so imperfect that an assumption of no effect seems reasonable. Sharp increases in the efficiency of caging such as opening Alcatraz-like prisons might be perceived as more punishment, but this is more likely to happen when the caging involves punishment in disguise.

Sensitivity to changes in caging is very high among ex-offenders as well as those on probation or parole. Here knowledge is far from imperfect, and active criminals may shift their field of operations with the intent of avoiding the risk of being caged in a notoriously noxious state penitentiary. This is one aspect of the general problem of the displacement of crime because of the variation in punishment.

If the size of displacement effects is found to be trivial for active offenders, then an assumption of no effect would be reasonable. This would help because it would mean that deterrence is independent of variations in caging, that is, variations in the social efficiency of direct individual incapacitation. Of course, an increase in social efficiency comes at the price of an increase in overkill. In this discussion of efficiency we are not varying the numbers of persons restrained but asking how a given number might be more or less efficient in reducing crime and at what cost. Society could disregard all considerations of efficiency or cost and simply "lock 'em up" on the assumption that $D_{Tot}$ must be substantially larger than zero.

### The Interaction between Restraint and Threat

The effects of two variables may be confounded in a number of ways. The finding from the econometric studies that crime rates are reduced by higher probabilities of punishment is a statement about the joint effects of restraint and legal threat. In theory, if the opportunity effects of restraint were extraordinarily high, the net preventive effect would be quite small, and it would be safe to attribute to deterrence alone the negative relationship found. If there were no deterrent effect, then the negative relationship could be attributed to the net preventive effect of restraint (which could be no larger than $D_{Tot}$, although it could be smaller). The theoretical limit $D$ to the maximum crime-reducing effects of restraint is an aid in studying deterrence. If crime reductions in excess of $D$ are found, they provide evidence that deterrence is operating if other possible sources of the reduction are controlled.    The combination of deterrent and incapacitative effects is most likely. On the commonsense assumption that both effects can work only to reduce crime (if either or both are active), the effects of the two are additive.

It would not be surprising if different combinations of threat and restraint have different overall joint effects. These interacting effects may also differ from one time period to another depending on the level of opportunity effects.

These speculations about interaction effects can be verified only by empirical inquiry. They warn against models that estimate the preventive effect of imprisonment by one set of assumptions and then enter the results into a model based on a different set. For example, in estimating incapacitative effects, Ehrlich assumes that offenders constitute a "non-competing group that does not respond to incentives, the constant proportion of which . . . is determined by nature."[25] In the rest of his work he assumes that those who engage in illegitimate activities respond to incentives, including illegitimate opportunities.

## Scope and Communication as Critical Differences

The sanction is the essential mode of controlling behavior. Why is it superior to restraint? One reason is the absence of overkill; punishment is not inefficient at face value. We will discuss two more reasons: the scope of these methods and the process of communication through which the scope is achieved.

Restraint is applied to particular persons, but there is no such limitation on legal threat, a remarkable contrivance since those who do not need it may ignore it entirely and those who do need it will find it present as the intent to commit crime becomes a reality. Increasing the sanction threatened for criminal behavior or the risk of apprehension necessarily affects those unlucky or unskilled enough to be the exemplars, along with those who are active but unapprehended and an unknown number of marginals. The threat of punishment does not, in any case, come to an end when someone is punished; on the contrary it is made realistic. Enforcement gives the threat a wide potential scope.

If legal threat were similar to a bill of attainder (directed at a particular person), then the scope of threat and restraint would be the same. A threat directed only at John Smith is a psychological restraint for him. It would cause him to refrain from committing the prohibited act but would have no implications for others. It would be similar to the physical restraint of burglar Jones that restrains him alone and only as long as it is active. When legal threat is directed toward particular groups or persons, it becomes similar to restraint.

Totalitarian justice breaks down the boundaries between legal threat and restraint by directing "legal" threats at groups (Jews) or categories (Kulaks). During the Great Terror in the Soviet Union, the population of Russia was in a state of psychological restraint as though everyone was in a severe form of conditional release. Terror may be likened to overkill in that persons refrain from innocent and valuable acts (friendship, conversation, group activity) and not merely crimes. This is why it may be misleading to regard terror as an extreme form of deterrence. The Gulag Archipelago could be described as indiscriminate restraint of minorities used in part to impose a state of terror on the majority.

Modern legal codes are universal in scope; no one is immune. A legal threat is addressed to anyone who might wish to engage in a form of forbidden behavior. The universal character of the threat is established in the very language of the code and buttressed by the expectation of citizens. It is not a function of the degree to which the sanction is enforced. In practice, legal threats deter as they are widely enforced, so that few feel immune as this wide enforcement is communicated. In the rare case of new laws, the existence of the law itself must be communicated.

While law is universal, a penal sentence is directed solely at individuals found guilty by due process of law. If restraint is part of this sentence, the communication incident to carrying it out is sufficient. Restraint is dumb justice, since its effects on those restrained can be fully active whether communicated or not; and possible opportunity effects of restraint are not critically dependent on the process of communication. If there are opportunity effects $O$, then completely unpublicized restraint would still create an objective opening. A lag in entry might be reduced, however, through publicity. False publicity might even create the temporary illusion of such openings.

In contrast, legal threat is communicated or it ceases to exist. Indeed, it has been shown that the mere communication of a new law will deter temporarily.[26] Let me concoct an illustration that highlights the differences between restraint and threat in regard to communication. In this example we deliberately created a situation where the incentive to commit a crime is strong and competition among offenders for limited opportunities is brisk. This artificial example is no proof of opportunity effects for crime in general or for other kinds of offenses.

Imagine that within a certain area the streets must be cleared of parked cars immediately and that the police are not inhibited by ethical standards. The owner of every fifth illegally parked car is located, and his car is towed to a lot. Each owner is ordered not to speak of this to anyone for reasons of national security. Since parking spaces are in short supply, the empty spaces soon fill up because increased opportunities have been created by the restraint of some drivers. Having failed to clear the streets, the police announce a policy of whipping illegal parkers. After the seventh whipping, say, the streets are noticeably empty of parked cars. This began to happen when the new law was announced. Whipping seven persons has produced a result that could not be achieved by removing every fifth car.

Restraint is limited in two ways in this example. At most, it could reduce illegal parking by one-fifth, although this was not at all the case in the example, since parking spaces were in such short supply. Communication played no role although it is central for deterrence. Are there no limits to the effectiveness of deterrence aside from the outrage of whipping traffic offenders?

Note that the deterrent effects accomplished by whipping one person do not vary with the criminal propensity of this person. Beyond the fact that he is one person, his attributes are irrelevant. He is primarily a digit, a punished unit to be added to other units to make up the objective probability of being whipped. (The police carry out the law, so this is not exemplary punishment that requires an exceptional deviation from the law.) He is unlucky, a fact that would be apparent to his neighbors who made use of his suffering to aid them in becoming law-abiding. This inevitable unluckiness of the exemplar is the minimum cost entailed by deterrence. The exemplar's punishment is not unjust, but that he alone is punished, is.

The unluckiness of the exemplar could be reduced—even eliminated—if the mere announcement of the threat of whipping had cleared the streets. Additional exemplars added their suffering to the first to convince the public that the legal threat was realistic, that it could happen to them. If only one widely publicized whipping could have achieved this, communication would have been that much more critical.

One additional point: by making the severity of the punishment very high in relation to the incentive to commit an offense, an extraordinary degree of effectiveness is achievable via deterrence. Why would a person take the risk of parking illegally in such a situation? Something more is communicated in this example. There is a variable present in addition to the trio of deterrence theory (certainty, celerity, and severity). An observer from Mars might wonder why such a tiny increase in the risk of punishment for the majority of persons could have such a profound effect, as if each additional whipping in the series is not a digit of one but a large multiple of this digit.

The implacable determination of the regime to clear the streets at any cost is being communicated. The law is severed from just retribution and becomes an instrument of policy. The proportionality of human sanctioning gives way to intimations of terror, and persons may stop driving altogether for fear of the regime rather than to comply with a law.

The philosophers of deterrence worked within the context of Western civilization in which state power is traditionally limited. They took this context for granted, but unfamiliar forms of tyranny and their unique systems of justice no longer permit this.[27] We need a comparative criminology and therefore a notion of the context within which variables such as certainty, celerity, and severity may operate or cease to operate in the expected manner. Such a contextual variable should be specific to criminal justice and should be capable of variation. A good name for this variable would be *lawfulness*. One symptom of its decline (or absence) would be the prevalence of the sense of injustice in a population, not as a general feeling about a society as a whole, but specifically in relation to criminal justice measures that are threatened or encountered. When a code of law, a network of criminal justice facilities, or a specific measure violates the sense of justice of the majority, the usual relations among celerity, certainty, and severity of punishment might be distorted.

**Deterrence or Restraint**

This chapter has been an extended argument in favor of deterrence as opposed to restraint. In addition, we have suggested that to some unknown degree restraint in the community might take the place of confinement in prison if it is necessary at all. We see no benefit in restating all these arguments.

Restraint and legal threat now operate jointly in controlling crime. Rehabilitation aside, these two great methods are alternatives, staying within the retributive limits imposed by lawfulness as we know it. One can be used instead of the other. The human invention of the prison, not the vagaries of social science, confounds their effects. Which one will prevail is not simply a matter of measurement of efficiency or cost, nor will a slight change in the balance with which they are used be sufficient to destroy the lawfulness that is a product of an entire society and all its political and social institutions. They are alternatives, and there is room to choose between them. To advocate "locking 'em up" in our present state of knowledge is to acquiesce to the barbarism of confinement and to treat the overkill inherent in restraint as a fact of nature and not an invention of man. In other words, we choose evil instead of having it forced on us. A democratic and prosperous society will seek ways to reduce this evil and crime as well, for caging a human being to protect society seems to be a confession of impotence in the face of crime.

**Notes**

1. American Civil Liberties Union, "Illegal Detention by the Police," in *The Sociology of Punishment and Correction,* ed. Norman Johnston, Leonard Savitz, and Marvin E. Wolfgang, (New York: Wiley, 1962), pp. 12-17.

2. "According to a Law Enforcement Assistance Administration census, American jails hold collectively, in an average day, a population of over one hundred sixty thousand. . . ." E. Flynn, "Jails and Criminal Justice," in *Prisoners in America,* ed. Lloyd Ohlin (Englewood Cliffs, N.J.: Prentice-Hall, 1973), p. 55. About half these persons were unconvicted and therefore presumed innocent. The total prison population on any given day is about two hundred thousand.

3. Caleb Foote, "The Bail System and Equal Justice," in *Sociology of Punishment and Correction*, p. 21.

4. Robert Martinson, Gene Kassebaum, and David Ward, "A Critique of Research in Parole," *Federal Probation* 28 (September 1964):34-38.

5. For a more thorough presentation of these dimensions of field supervision, see Robert Martinson and Judith Wilks, "A Static-Descriptive Model of Field Supervision," *Criminology* 13 (1975):3-20.

6. Douglas Lipton, Robert Martinson, and Judith Wilks, *The Effectiveness of Correctional Treatment* (New York: Praeger, 1975).

7. See Benjamin Avi-Itzhak and Reuel Shinnar, "Quantitative Models in Crime Control," *Journal of Criminal Justice* 1 (1973):185-217; Stevens Clarke, "Getting 'Em Out of Circulation: Does Incarceration of the Juvenile Offender Reduce Crime?" *Journal of Criminal Law and Criminology* 65 (1974):528-535.

8. Robert Martinson, "The Paradox of Prison Reform," in *The Philosophy of Punishment*, ed. Gertrude Ezorsky (New York: State University of New York Press, 1972).

9. See Isaac Ehrlich, "Participation in Illegitimate Activities: a Theoretical and Empirical Investigation," *Journal of Political Economy* 81 (May-June 1973):535. Apparently Ehrlich assumes that the commission of offenses by survivors is independent of the opportunity to commit offenses or that opportunities are unlimited and offenders are committing offenses at some physiologically maximum (and constant) rate. In either case no provision is made in his model for the possibility of the opportunity effects of stock reduction.

10. See Nils Christie, "Changes in Penal Values," in *Scandinavian Studies in Criminology*, vol. 2: *Aspects of Social Control in Welfare States* (London: Tavistock, 1968), pp. 161-172; see also Alfred Blumstein and Jacqueline Cohen, "A Theory of the Stability of Punishment," in *Crime and Justice, 1973* (Chicago: Aldine, 1974), pp. 96-105. Blumstein and Cohen argue that punishment of crime tends to be stable; but they ignore the dramatic decline in imprisonment reported by Christie over the nineteenth century and focus solely on that part of the curve that supports their idea of stability.

11. For a witty example, see R. Head, *The English Rogue: Described in the Life of Meriton Latroon, a Witty Extravagant; Being a Compleat History of the Most Eminent Cheats of Both Sexes* (Boston: New Frontiers Press, 1961; originally published in London in 1665).

12. For a discussion of the effects of monopolizing one part of crime on the remaining "parts," see J.M. Buchanan, "A Defense of Organized Crime?" in *The Economics of Crime and Punishment*, ed. S. Rottenberg (Washington, D.C.: American Enterprise Institute for Public Policy Research, 1973). Buchanan says: "If we should assume that potential criminals constitute a noncompeting group of persons, distinct and apart from the rest of society, monopolization of one or a few areas of criminality may actually increase the supply of resources going into the remaining and nonorganized activities" (p. 127).

13. See Leon Radzinowicz, *Ideology and Crime* (New York: Columbia University Press, 1966); David J. Rothman, *The Discovery of the Asylum* (Boston: Little, Brown, 1971), and "Of Prisons, Asylums, and Other Decaying Institutions," *Public Interest* 26 (Winter 1972): 3-17. Narrative historiography is a poor instrument for grasping the billions of undated events that make up crime, recidivism, or arrest. For a more adequate historical method, see H. Goldhammer and A. Marshall, *Psychology and Civilization: Two Studies in the Frequency of Mental Disease* (Glencoe, Ill.: Free Press, 1953).

14. "Those in charge of the prisons, from wardens and corrections

commissioners to state legislators, also share an incredibly high degree of self-doubt, ambivalence, dismay, and even guilt over prison operations. They are no longer secure in what they are doing" (Rothman, "Of Prisons," p. 14).

15. "If the sole objective in expending scarce resources were to rehabilitate or incapacitate, there would be no point in singling out convicted criminals unless . . . they constitute a distinctive subgroup of the entire population with an above average 'criminal propensity'" (M. Silver, "Punishment, Deterrence, and Police Effectiveness: a Survey and Critical Interpretation of the Recent Econometric Literature," report prepared for the Crime Deterrence and Offender Career Project under a grant from the U.S. Office of Economic Opportunity, New York, February, 1974).

16. Marvin E. Wolfgang, Robert M. Figlio, and Thorsten Sellin, *Delinquency in a Birth Cohort* (Chicago: University of Chicago Press, 1972).

17. See the nineteen studies summarized in Silver, "Punishment, Deterrence, and Police Effectiveness."

18. Ibid.

19. Ibid.

20. Ibid.

21. Isaac Ehrlich, "Participation in Illegitimate Activities: a Theoretical and Empirical Investigation," *Journal of Political Economy* 81 (1973):535. The statement should read "temporarily and partially prevented from committing further crimes."

22. Ibid.

23. Solomon Kobrin et al., "The Deterrent Effectiveness of Criminal Justice Strategies" (Los Angeles, University of Southern California, Public Systems Research Institute, September 1972).

24. Ernest van den Haag, in *Punishing Criminals* (New York: Basic Books, 1975), has proposed using the fine more often, increasing the amount of the fine, and making it more fair by multiplying it by some estimate of the person's income.

25. Ehrlich, "Participation in Illegal Activities."

26. H.L. Ross, "Law, Science, and Accidents: The British Road Safety Act of 1967," *Journal of Legal Studies* 2 (1973).

27. Robert Martinson, "Solzhenitsyn, as Criminologist," *Federal Probation* 38 (September 1974):71-73.

# 3

# Sweden: The Middle Way to Prison Reform?

*David A. Ward*

Discussions of prison problems by American journalists, criminologists, and prison administrators often involve references to Sweden—the land where so many of the problems that plague American prisons seem to have been solved. This notion of Sweden as *the* model prison system for Americans is supported by extensive literature.

A number of American colleges and universities, for example, offer summer study tours of prisons in Scandinavia; and many Americans have become interested in seeing for themselves, usually as part of a vacation-study trip to Europe, what Sweden's prisons look like.

This chapter first examines the appealing picture of the Swedish correctional system that has been presented to Americans by Swedish government agencies and American journalists and scholars. Since these reports tend to focus on innovative features that usually apply to only small numbers of inmates, correctional policies and practices that apply to all prisoners in Sweden will also be described. At least one innovation—the effort to establish prison democracy—has not succeeded and, despite all its efforts, Sweden's recidivism rates are not low. Some new directions in Swedish penal policy will be described, and these are similar to trends in two American states, Minnesota and Wisconsin. Finally, the principal question for this essay will be, To what extent can Sweden really provide a model for American correctional systems?

## The Swedish Penal System as Seen from the United States

### Swedish Information Service and Swedish Institute Reports

Sweden's international reputation as a leader in prison reform has been enhanced by a continuous flow of reports, pamphlets, and news announcements released

I wish to express my appreciation to Norman Bishop, Swedish National Prison and Probation Administration; Ulla Bondeson, University of Lund; Phillip Bush, University of Minnesota; Thomas Ekbom, Assistant to the Director, Stockholm Correctional Region; Gilbert Geis, University of California, Irvine; Gunnar Marnell, Director, Stockholm Correctional Region; and Annika Snare, University of Oslo, for materials and for their helpful criticisms, comments, and suggestions on an earlier draft of this chapter. Deficiencies that remain are in spite of their efforts.

through the Swedish Information Service Office in New York and by the Swedish Institute in Stockholm. During recent years, reports such as "Prison Democracy," "Labor-Market Wages for Prisoners," and "Opening Up the Prisons" have conveyed the picture of a penal system committed to reforms that would be considered radical in the United States. There are also articles on this subject in the magazine *Sweden Now*, published by the Swedish Engineers' Press, Ltd., Stockholm. One article, "In for Repairs," declares that "penal experts from around the world travel today to the north of Europe to acquire stimulation for the modernization and humanization of their own prisons back home." Then follow descriptions of the furlough or home-leave system, prisons without walls ("more than half the rooms in open institutions are 'nearly in the class of a hotel,' as the correctional authority describes them . . ."), the "treatment plan" designed for every inmate, and the payment of wages equal to free-market wages at Tillberga Prison. If prisoners are workers, then there is the matter of allowing them to receive the minimum twenty-four days of vacation each year to which all Swedish workers are entitled. The article quotes former prison director Torsten Eriksson to the effect that inmates should have this right and reports that "as of two years ago, a west Swedish lake resort has been open to inmates. Several groups have spent three-week holidays there, fishing, swimming, sightseeing, making side excursions and going to the night clubs."[1] The article concludes with the famous Eriksson credo of Swedish penal policy:

> deprivation of freedom is enough punishment in itself. *One comes to prison as punishment, not to be punished* [emphasis added]. Everything in the realm of possibility must be done, therefore, that can ease the adjustment of the criminal back into society.[2]

A more recent *Sweden Now* piece, "Where Prisoners Are People," describes Sweden's prison village, Gruvberget. The concept behind the prison department's purchase of twenty houses and stores that had been vacated by a lumber company represents a radical departure from established penal practices in other Western countries since the village is intended to provide a facility for inmates taking a vacation from prison

> either as a break in a long sentence or to provide orientation to life outside toward the end of a sentence. They may bring their wives and children, or fiancees, if they like, to live everyday lives, attend courses, do a bit of skiing and fishing.[3]

The author enthusiastically describes the "Stockholm-restaurant" quality of the food served in the prison dining room, the friendliness of the villagers toward the inmates, happy prisoners going cross-country skiing with boots and skis provided by the prison (track suits and bicycles in the summer), and inmates sitting around roaring fires, roasting sausages, and complaining about KRUM, the prison reform organization which "stirs up trouble" for inmates like themselves who have managed to obtain special privileges.[4]

To its credit, the Swedish Institute in 1972 began a series of reports called *The Swedish Dialogue*, which contain excerpts from newspapers, magazines, books, and reports on a variety of topics. An issue of *Dialogue*, published in 1973, was devoted to criminal welfare. Edited by Svante Nycander, a political scientist who had written *Abolish Forensic Psychiatry* and who is a reporter for Sweden's liberal newspaper, *Dagens Nyheter*, the *Dialogue* contained short, critical statements about government penal policy by the chairman of KRUM, as well as by a sociologist, and by a law professor. Other authors included the minister of justice, the director of the National Correctional Administration, a prison guard who appealed for friendly relations between guards and inmates in a piece entitled "We Don't Hate Anyone—We're Scared," and a female novelist who criticized conditions at the women's prison. Other selections offered differing perspectives of a sensational escape in 1972 of fifteen prisoners from the security wing of Sweden's maximum-security prison at Kumla. Twelve of the fifteen escapees were quickly recaptured, but two others called *Dagens Nyheter* while still at large to give their reasons for escaping. The escape and the reporting of the inmates' views set off a debate in the press which is well reported in the *Dialogue*. The excerpts included opinions to the effect that the escapees were really not dangerous and that the escape "is a sheer and absolute scandal" for which the prison department must take responsibility.[5] The following editorial from *Svenska Dagbladet*, a conservative Stockholm newspaper, indicated that there was no consensus among all Swedes about the treatment of offenders:

> Minister of Justice Geijer has visited Kumla Prison in the company of Director General Martinsson of the National Correctional Administration, and has also held a press conference at which nothing of any great importance was said. This is understandable enough. To begin with, the mass exodus from Kumla is so embarrassing that it can be wisest to say as little as possible. Secondly, it is naturally impossible, as Mr. Martinsson says, to consider, until the present inquiry is completed, what measures must be taken to prevent further escapes.

> But if the ultimate authorities have very little at present to add, those associated with KRUM are still presenting their grand procession of inanities on the occasion of the escapes. Most recently, Maja Eklöf, known as the authoress of *Report from a Bucket* (primarily a piece of social reporting), has been brought forward to testify to her correspondence with one of the most prominent fugitives from Kumla, Tony Rosendahl. . . .

> We are told by Maja Eklöf that Tony Rosendahl is one of the nicest people she could imagine, "gentle, sweet and wise." He is frightened, so

we learn, of being broken down by his imprisonment, and is eager to do a great deal for society. His escape from Kumla was thoroughly considered—he knew what he was doing, and he does not need anyone's advice. A person presenting himself as an old friend of Rosendahl's at Kumla takes the opportunity to supplement Maja Eklöf's testimony with the information that Rosendahl had been assigned to the security wing by reason of his "activity in the field of crime policy"—not, in other words, by reason of his dangerousness or criminal actions, but because he had been concerned to improve the social conditions of prisoners. Tony, by Maja's testimony, is a revolutionary, and so is she. They do not, in their letters, discuss one or another type of reformist policy. No, revolution is the thing.

In the light of all this, it can be of interest to recall something of what the gentle, sweet and wise revolutionary Rosendahl, who is concerned to do so much for society, has achieved to date. He has perpetrated some of the most advanced bank and post-office frauds in the country's history. He holds a probably unbeatable Swedish record in the falsification of remittance cheques, manufactured with great skill by his own hand. His bills were cheerfully accepted by the banks, and if he had not been put under lock and key he would have made millions. We can also recall a dramatic post-office robbery on Vartavägen [Stockholm] the other year, with a major alarm, helicopter reconnaissance and police officers in bullet-proof vests. The masked robbers fired shots inside the bank. And one of the robbers was Rosendahl, the sweet revolutionary.[6]

The "Criminal Welfare" issue of the *Swedish Dialogue* provides some valuable and badly needed critical perspectives on Swedish penal policy for Americans, since most reports by American journalists and academicians, along with most publications from the Swedish Information Service, the Swedish Foreign Office, and the Swedish Institute, convey official government and National Prison and Probation Administration opinions, objectives, and analyses. Critics of Swedish policy and practice include inmates, members of KRUM, and journalists who are less likely to be interviewed by foreign visitors, and their views are rarely given expression through government publications.

It is, of course, not surprising that Swedish government agencies produce materials describing innovative aspects of their country's social institutions. Publications such as "Current Sweden" and *Sweden Now* are intended to provide light, interesting articles that capture the attention of the reader and arouse interest in Sweden. The problem is perhaps not so much with the picture of Swedish corrections presented by the Swedish government agencies as with the uncritical acceptance of these reports by American journalists, prison officials, and criminologists and the equally uncritical reports Americans prepare after their own superficial study tours and investigations of the Swedish correctional system.

## Swedish Corrections as Portrayed in the
## American Popular Press

While Sweden's maximum-security prisons do not feature gun towers or armed guards, they are surrounded by high concrete walls and inmates reside in cells. The inmates in those prisons would have difficulty in recognizing the prison system described to Americans in a *New York Times* story which appeared under the heading "A Prison in Sweden Is More Like a Hotel."

> A new prison unit that opened here has 20 cells with carpeting and telephones. . . .
>
> The unit is primarily for prisoners under temporary detention. Soft lighting floods the cells. Meals are brought in from a nearby restaurant. . . .
>
> The exercise yard has architect-designed "bars" of stainless steel circles with vertical steel stringers. There is a pleasant view over meadows and woods. . . .
>
> Alf Johansson, the head warden, says: "It's wonderful to get away from the usual gray prison atmosphere."[7]

They would wonder whether the author had visited Kumla Prison when Paul Britten Austin wrote, without qualification, of the

> humane, non-moralistic attitude [which] is reflected in Sweden's prisons which, by comparison with most European or American prisons, are almost homes away from home. Just how liberal they are can be inferred from the type of complaints brought before the ombudsman by their inmates: petitions that a prisoner has not been allowed full privacy when visited by wife or sweetheart; has not been given his regular furloughs (if in an open prison); or has suffered from too great a diet of TV and wants more film shows instead. The type of punishment meted out to drivers found by the police to be under the influence of alcohol is probably excellent for such persons' health—a spell of wood-cutting in the forest. . . . The motto when building new prisons nowadays is "build the workshops first, and the prison afterwards." Such prisons as Tillberga, where 120 inmates live what can only be called a normal life, are fully comparable with any ultramodern Swedish factory. In another prison, near the university town of Uppsala, persons with scholastic aptitude can simply continue their education.[8]

Nor would most Swedish prisoners likely agree with the title of Michael Durham's article in the *Smithsonian*, "For the Swedes a Prison Sentence Can Be Fun Time." Durham noted the escape of the fifteen inmates from Kumla Prison, but here they are described as Sweden's "most dangerous criminals." Their cell block in Kumla Prison was, according to Durham,

> positively resortlike. . . . Amenities included private rooms with TV, a spacious dining area also with TV, a pantry where prisoners kept private food supplies, an exercise room, a workshop and a "love room" where men could entertain female visitors privately.[9]

Durham reported that the escapees were soon recaptured and that "public opinion" turned on prison officials for being too oppressive. An unnamed sociologist was then quoted as saying, "The state has an obligation to the primary victim of crime who is, in our view, the criminal."

Another reference in the article was made to Kumla's love room to which fiancees may be admitted. This page was accompanied by a full-page photograph of a young couple kissing while seated on a bed. A second picture showed another young couple—"in for drug dealing"—riding their bicycles near the vacation village where they were spending a month. Durham's article described other features of Swedish penal practices such as the study farm, the work program at Tillberga Prison which permits inmates to receive close-to-market wages, and the modified therapeutic community at Gävle Prison.

Swedish prisoners and other critics of the image of Swedish corrections conveyed to foreign audiences complain that descriptions such as those cited focus on superficial features of confinement in closed prisons and overlook the social and psychological consequences of imprisonment—stigma, lack of opportunity to exercise free choice and individual responsibility, and the impact on family relationships and future employment. Most journalists fail to make clear that the programs and practices they describe apply to inmates in open prisons or to a minority of inmates confined in closed prisons. Furthermore, the reports do not emphasize that most of these special programs are experimental and apply to only a small number of inmates or are available in only one institution in a system that includes more than seventy prisons.

Although difficult to find, there is one somewhat critical report about Swedish corrections written by an American, presumably an ex-inmate. The article, prepared by an anonymous writer who had visited Sweden for six weeks, appeared in the *Outlaw*, which is published by the California Prisoners Union. The author, however, seems caught between his conclusions that "things are certainly better" in Sweden and his suspicion that efforts to improve the lot of prisoners really hide a subtle but effective plan to disrupt inmate solidarity. He cites efforts in the United States to co-opt leaders of antiestablishment organizations and the threat to convict unity posed by inmate participation in "so-called therapy programs which attempt to get them to deny their mutual interests, and to inform on each other."[10] The author then goes on the describe the therapeutic community program at Gävle Prison which supposedly respects prisoner rights and dignity.

The author was impressed by what he saw at Tillberga, the factory prison, but he found inmates in another prison gluing and folding envelopes, tasks that could have been done far more rapidly by machines. Kumla Prison, the author concludes, "is an unmitigated disaster. Walking through its subterranean corridors one is reminded of the sterile, bombproof SAC bases. Although the guards aren't as visible and guns are unseen, the atmosphere is bland and oppressive."[11] The mixture of short- and long-term offenders in prisons (there are no separate jail systems in Sweden) is, in the writer's opinion, "another bar to convict unity." He reports that Swedish prisoners complained that the ombudsman always rules in favor of "the establishment." While noting such problems, the author goes on to applaud other features of Swedish corrections policy:

> The prison and parole system are humanized somewhat by many devices which are almost unheard of in this country: Parole supervision is typically by volunteers with small caseloads who are given stipends; women guards and workers are used extensively throughout the system. Cells seem clear, and the food is usually brought in by outside caterers. Violence against convicts is extremely rare; there are no beatings, gassings and murders, to the best of my knowledge. . . .

> There is also none of the more radical forms of "psychotherapeutic" abuse in Sweden; no psychosurgery, no electroshock, no aversive chemotherapy, even in mental institutions.

> We could certainly use some of the things that are accepted in Sweden but are considered unacceptable reforms here. These include the right of convicts to organize, to communicate between prisons, to publish uncensored newspapers, to get visits from other ex-cons, to get their mail uncensored, to have frequent furloughs and conjugal visits, and to (in a few cases) attend the University.

> The goals of our union, the right of collective bargaining, the restoration of human and civil rights, and the abolition of the indeterminate sentence (which is becoming extinct in Sweden) are already a fact there, and the payment of the going wage has already arrived, to some extent.[12]

The *Outlaw* article is incorrect in one respect: Swedish inmates do not have the right to collective bargaining. They do have the right to organize in behalf of their interests, but this right does not require that prison authorities negotiate or bargain with the inmates over issues that the latter may raise. The problem for both the author of the *Outlaw* article and the author of this essay is that many features of Swedish corrections look good, even remarkable, to Americans. But so many unpleasant aspects of imprisonment still remain in Sweden that Swedish inmates and prison reformers consider the problems they have to be as serious as those of their American counterparts.

*Professional and Scholarly Reports*
*on Swedish Corrections*

Very few American scholars have studied Swedish prisons or prisoners systematically, but references to Sweden based on the stereotype established in American minds by Swedish government and correctional system authorities appear
in criminology and penology books. The following statement in a recent
criminal justice text is typical: "Sweden is considered by many penal authorities as representative of the most progressive, effective correctional system in
the world."[13] Another standard criminology text reports "Sweden has for some
time been regarded as a model country as far as prison treatment is concerned."
The article from which this excerpt is taken provides the usual description of
Swedish prisons, notably features of physical appearance and reports of what
the visitor was told by the prison staff. In the absence of the perspective of those
who must serve time in the prisons, visitors (and readers of the articles) usually
come to the point where they ask, How can criminal conduct be deterred by
such a benign system? This question is answered through the response of a
Swedish official who is accustomed to hearing the question from foreign visitors.
He replies to the effect that if a man is treated kindly, "he then unburdens all
his troubles to us. Which is just what the psychologist wants, of course."[14]

John Conrad's survey of correctional practices around the world also cites
official dogma and, again, those Swedish prison officials who seem so patient
with visitors from the United States and other countries. Conrad supplies the
comments of one inmate, and while it is noted that this man's ringing endorsement of Swedish penal philosophy is not shared by all of his fellow prisoners,
only his views are reported.[15]

Sociologist Louis Bultena reports that he visited ten prisons in Sweden and
that one youth prison demonstrates the traditional view held by Americans of
what a prison is all about:

> [I] raised the question with the prison governor [superintendent]
> whether it would not be well to have a high fence some distance out
> from the buildings, a fence which would not prevent all escapes but
> which might make a youth think twice before trying to escape. Ex-
> treme permissiveness and ease of escape would seem to place too great
> a strain on a youth's self-control, a personal quality in which he might
> be lacking and a basic reason why he was there.[16]

The response of the prison official was that in Sweden the individual must
learn to control himself rather than to depend on control from outside sources.
Bultena quotes a newspaper reporter who was one of the founders of the reform
group KRUM, but the reporter portrays that organization not as a force for
radical reform but as a kind of prisoners' aid society. Frequent references are
made to statements by prison officials, but apparently no inmate comment

merited inclusion, if any was sought. Bultena claims that "Swedish prison authorities estimate the repeater rate of Swedish prisoners at 15 percent"[17] — a figure very far from the truth. He concludes:

> In many respects the Swedish correctional system is probably the most advanced in the world. It meets many of the specifications for prison reform which the United States Federal Bureau of Prisons has been advocating for years. . . .[18]

(Bultena's Swedish and American colleagues will want to see the Federal Bureau of Prisons' plans for holiday prisons, conjugal visiting facilities, recognition of prisoner unions, and market wages for prison labor.)

The type of American correctional journal article that promotes disdain by Swedish inmates, journalists, prison reformers, and even some corrections department officials, continues to appear in the United States. Harvey H. Siegel, writing in *Offender Rehabilitation*, describes Sweden's most controversial prison, Kumla, in a manner typical of visitors who spend several hours touring a prison and listening to a description by the warden of staff-inmate relations:

> It is interesting to note that this maximum security prison has a swimming pool and a soccer field, and the day we visited the director [warden] was wearing a blazer jacket and turtleneck sweater. There appears to be a relaxed atmosphere between staff and inmates, and a prevailing attitude that prisoners must be treated with dignity and respect. Inmates are referred to as clients in the prison, which establishes a positive climate and relationship.[19]

This is the complete description of a prison that has been the focal point of Swedish efforts to modify maximum-security confinement and the site of prisoner strikes and escape attempts in which guards were taken as hostages.

Incredibly, Siegel also quotes the 1971 statement of the director-general of the National Prison and Probation Administration, which was released to Americans through the Swedish Information Service but not distributed in Sweden. This statement, made at a moment of optimism that proved to be premature, claimed that Swedish inmates would negotiate their grievances and demands "on an equal footing" with representatives of the correctional administration and employee union. Siegel somehow missed completely the distinction between a prisoners' union which negotiates all issues of concern to inmates and inmate councils which negotiate only minor concerns such as sports, entertainment, and commissary privileges. Siegel contends that the inmate councils have brought about "many changes in the procedures of the prisons, as well as the roles of the institutions' directors and staffs."[20] However, Sweden's experiment with prison democracy failed in 1972.

Not all articles written by American scholars and correctional workers about Swedish penal practices are as inaccurate, incomplete, and uncritical as those cited. An article by Norval Morris that has been widely read in the United States—because it appeared in a journal that is sent at no cost to corrections workers and academic criminologists—has undoubtedly contributed to the elevation of Sweden's corrections system to the status of a model system for other countries. Fortunately this article is carefully written, and while some of Morris's observations no longer apply a decade after his visit, he identifies some of the key features of Swedish penal policy that distinguish it from policies in the United States.[21] Morris points out that imprisonment in Sweden is much less likely to be used for the confinement of those who violate laws pertaining to morals—gambling, sex, and narcotics. (Drunken drivers, it should be emphasized, are incarcerated for general deterrence, not to punish individual offenders.) Morris applauds the use of shorter sentences, community and media interest in and concern for prisoners, the employment of women in some prisons, a unified system of probation, prison, and parole, the use of citizen volunteers as probation or parole supervisors, and the ability of inmates to take furloughs and to receive visitors in their cells or rooms. The major deficiency in Swedish penology, Morris observed in the mid 1960s, was a lack of interest in research in general and program evaluation in particular—a deficiency that is now being corrected. Morris asked the right question in his article—a question we shall attempt to answer in the conclusion of this discussion:

What practices in the Swedish adult correctional system merit emulation in this country and adaptation to our different correctional problems? Or, put more succinctly, how can the Swedes help us to escape from our correctional cultural cocoon?[22]

In 1976 Richard Salomon sought to update Morris's earlier article. Salomon reviews developments in Sweden related to the abortive prison democracy experiment and its aftermath, notes the demise of "the promise of rehabilitation" in Sweden as elsewhere, and describes the new system of regional prisons along with the usual features of Swedish corrections that Americans find remarkable—market wages for inmates at Tillberga Prison, conjugal visits, home furloughs, the holiday prison, and the greater number of staff than inmates in some prisons. American criminologists may be surprised, however, at Salomon's assertion that Sweden's probation service has a few things "to learn from the United States Probation Service with its far more decentralized organization, well-developed training programs and high staff morale."[23] Empirical evidence to support these contentions and the implication that American probation services are in fact more effective is not presented. In addition, the decentralization argument carries less weight when one considers the difficulty in comparing Sweden's unified criminal justice system for 8 million persons with the United States system for 220 million people which is composed of fifty separate state systems and the federal government system. A more accurate critique of staff training and morale would contrast Sweden and American states of comparable size.

Reaffirming Morris's earlier observation that the amount of empirical research in Swedish penology is limited, Salomon assumes that Americans and others will be more likely to adopt Swedish innovations if evidence of their effects can be provided. Since there is little evidence that the results of empirical research in this country presage significant policy changes in our own correctional systems, there is little reason to believe that research results from Sweden related to conjugal visits, market wages, small prisons, high staff-to-inmate ratios, or short sentences, for example, will assure that these practices will be implemented in the United States. Moreover, Salomon has overlooked the rapid growth of correctional research by scholars including Ulla Bondeson and Eckart Kuhlhorn, the proliferation of studies produced under the direction of Norman Bishop of the National Prison and Probation Administration, and the studies being initiated under the aegis of the National Council for Crime Prevention. The limitations of correctional research noted by Norval Morris are no longer so apparent.

A more sophisticated article by Paul Friday takes a broader sociological review of penal sanctions in Sweden and makes the important point:

> Sweden's penal and legal philosophy has developed out of a general social welfare ideology which tends to emphasize the similarities among its citizens rather than differences. . . . The acceptance of the social welfare policies of the Social Democrats by all political parties is a reaffirmation of the idea that society has a responsibility for the welfare of its members—a tradition more than 200 years old.[24]

Friday identifies trends to criminalize some new forms of conduct—including violations of rights to privacy, hijacking, and terrorism—and to increase the penalties for certain types of white-collar, tax, and corporate crimes along with efforts to decriminalize petty offenses. Such changes in penal policy can have profound effects on jail and prison populations.[25] Friday observes that what is significant about Swedish probation is not the character of probation services but the use of probation in cases where prison might have been used.

An extended review and description of Swedish correctional institutes and programs was prepared for *Corrections Magazine* by Michael Serrill.[26] The day-fine system, the free-market wage experiment, KRUM, and features of the 1974 Act on Correctional Treatment are discussed. In addition to three new facilities, Serrill describes the local open prison at Stangebro, the open national prison at Skenas, and the Stockholm Treatment Center for probationers and parolees which provides a wide variety of employment, housing, medical, and mental health services for three hundred to four hundred persons with drug and alcohol problems. A special supplement to the article reviews the status of institutions for juveniles in Sweden. Serrill's report, unlike almost all previous accounts by American observers, attempts to include some qualifications and dissenting opinions about Swedish penal policy as expressed by KRUM members, inmates, and Swedish social critics. Theoretical and functional differences between Continental and Anglo-American criminal procedures, unfortunately, are not explicated and may lead readers to conclude erroneously that offenders can receive harsher and less fair treatment in Swedish courts and jails than in the United States. On the whole, however, Serrill has provided American corrections professionals with the best general description of Swedish penal facilities and practices to date.[27]

Finally there is one article by Gunnar Marnell, the Swedish director of corrections for the Stockholm region, based on his visits to prisons in Massachusetts, Connecticut, Minnesota, and California.[28] Marnell has a reputation among Americans as the most innovative prison administrator in Sweden, and his view epitomizes to visiting Americans what they see as that country's progressive, benign, and eminently rational penal philosophy. On his visits to prisons in this country, Marnell talked to prisoners, usually seeking out those who were inmate council members, and he insisted on meeting with representatives of correctional officer unions. He was dismayed at what he observed in American prisons with regard to housing and health conditions.

> I think that in both [Sweden and the United States] there is not very much to say of the food in prisons and institutions. But how about the housing and possibilities of getting some fresh air every day? To me your system of keeping human beings behind iron bars, like animals in a zoo, is very disturbing, not only for psychological reasons, but also because I think everybody should have the right to some quiet and rest behind a closed door—some privacy. Most of the prisons I have seen in your country do not give such opportunities, not even the very modern youth institutions in California, with no iron bars but big dormitories with about fifty boys in the same hall. At Stillwater prison in Minnesota, I found environmental conditions in the solitary confinement unit which I think no health official in Sweden would allow to exist: The prisoners were kept behind steel bars, giving out onto a corridor on the further side of which was a bullet proof glass wall. Beyond the corridor was another one, which was screened on its further side by an opaque glass wall. *For months and even years,* I was told, *a prisoner could be kept in such segregation with no time outside at all and without seeing a glimpse of the sky!* At Roslindale, in Boston, youngsters awaiting trial for days and weeks also were refused any periods outdoors. In Sweden the law on prison treatment authorizes the use of isolation. In general such isolation is of short duration . . . [now seven days] but has been severely criticized since isolation has been judged to carry risks for mental health. Every prisoner, however, including those in solitary confinement, has a right to at least one hour outdoors every day.[29]

Marnell identifies several promising developments in the United States—the effort to close prisons for youth offenders in Massachusetts and attempts in several states to hire ex-offenders as probation and parole officers. With regard to the latter, he notes that there would likely be resistance from Swedish probation officers to hiring ex-offenders because the probation staff are "too professionalized." When asked what a Swedish prison administration could possibly learn from visits to American prisons, Marnell's diplomatic reply was: "We have much to learn from your mistakes."

Swedish government reports of penal practices in that country naturally highlight the more innovative features of their correctional system. What is remarkable is that Americans, including many scholars, have accepted so uncritically official Swedish government reports and the characterization of Swedish penal policies, programs, and problems by National Prison and Probation Administration officials. Swedes who visited the United States and used these same sources of information for articles about prisons in America would be considered naive by some of these same authors.

The quality of several recent descriptions of Sweden's correctional system by American scholars has improved over the earlier, completely uncritical reports of holiday prisons and conjugal visiting. The recent articles by Paul Friday and Michael Serrill are cases in point. In these more careful presentations, attention is paid to fundamental aspects of the administration of justice in Sweden and the organization of the entire prison and probation system. It is to some of these basic questions that this discussion now turns. What sentencing options are available to Swedish courts? How is the corrections system organized? Which rights and privileges apply to all inmates and which apply only to special categories of prisoners? Which penal experiments have succeeded and which have failed? How effective are Swedish correctional practices in reducing recidivism? To what extent has Sweden succeeded in reducing the damaging effects of imprisonment on inmates? The answers to these questions taken together will help address the issue whether there are features of Swedish penal policy that might realistically be adopted or adapted by corrections departments in the United States.

## Penal Sanctions in Sweden

To understand the nature of the Swedish correctional apparatus—its size, structure, and the character of its staff, inmates, program services, and physical facilities—the manner in which criminal conduct is penalized needs to be considered. The principal question for this discussion is, Of those persons convicted under the penal code, who goes to prison and for how long? As is the case in the United States, the great majority of convicted persons receive punitive sanctions other than imprisonment. There are, however, some variations in the application of sanctions in Sweden. One is the manner, unusual by American standards, in which most fines are assessed.

## Fines

Although there are several types of fines, the most widely used is the day-fine, a penal sanction best described for Americans by Hans Thornstedt.[30] The argument behind the day-fine, according to Thornstedt, is that financial penalties should take into account the offender's per diem income. These fines are often determined by the public prosecutor, and if the offender accepts the fine proposed, the action is analogous to a sentence by an American court. More than 75 percent of all fines in Sweden are determined by prosecutors. Thornstedt describes the method by which fines are determined under this system:

> In the day-fine system the *number* of day-fines represents the measure of punishment, and the *amount* of each day-fine is estimated in accordance with the financial situation of the accused.

> In Sweden the *number* of day-fines is normally 1-120. If a person is sentenced at the same time for several offences, of [which all] deserve day-fines, he has to be sentenced to a joint punishment, which may not exceed 180 day-fines.

> The *per diem amount* of a day-fine is in Sweden 2-500 kronor. Accordingly, the highest sum which can be imposed in one sentence to day-fines is 60,000 kronor for one offence (120 × 500 kronor) or 90,000 kronor for more than one offence (180 × 500 kronor). A fine with a lower amount than 10 kronor may not be imposed.

> The scale of 1-120 (180) day-fines is intended to fit both petty offences and more serious offences. Only in very exceptional cases do the courts apply the maximum of the scale.

> The normal amount for ordinary traffic offences is 10 or 15 day-fines. On the other hand, the punishment for the less serious type of drunken driving ... may be 40-100 day-fines.[31]

Bultena has also provided a helpful example of how this system works:

> The total fine is arrived at by multiplying the number of day-fines by the amount of each day-fine. The number of day-fines imposed relates to the gravity of the crime, while the size of the day-fine is adjusted to the offender's capacity to pay. The day-fine system is an example of Swedish democracy in operation. If a simple assault is assessed 10 day-fines, then for a wealthy person who earns 300 crowns a day the fine would be 10 times 300, or 3,000 crowns, for a poor man earning 20 crowns a day it would be 10 times 20 or 200 crowns for the same offense.[32]

The financial situation of the accused is a per diem measure of the individual's income which also takes into consideration yearly wages (minus taxes), additional income, debts, and obligations to support children or other dependents. Thornstedt notes that fines may be paid in installments over time, and nonpayment is punishable by imprisonment:

> Fines which are not paid can be *converted* to imprisonment. The conversion is done according to a sliding scale (5 day-fines are converted to 10 days' imprisonment, 100 day-fines to 64 days', 120 day-fines to 70 days' and 180 day-fines to 90 days' imprisonment). The conditions for conversion are, however, rather strict. These conditions, together with the rule that day-fines should be adapted to the offender's ability to pay, as well as an appropriate use of the device of extensions of time, payment in installments, and enforced payment, are intended to reduce conversion of fines to the smallest number which is possible without jeopardizing the preventive effects of the fines. Often the enforcement of imprisonment to which fines have been converted is suspended. The result is that about 130 cases a year of such imprisonment are enforced in Sweden, whereas the number of people punished with fines by the prosecutors and the courts is about 250,000 a year. We do not think that this has injurious effects on the general obedience to the law.[33]

In addition to day-fines, there are specified fines for some minor offenses in the penal code such as drunkenness and disorderly conduct, with a maximum fine of about $125. Fines may be imposed in combination with another punitive sanction. In 1974 some three hundred thousand persons were fined, more than 75 percent under the day-fine system.[34]

## Conditional Sentences

This sanction amounts to a suspended sentence or unsupervised probation and is assessed against any offender whose conduct does not appear to warrant punishment more severe than the warning implied in the sanction. In 1974 some fifty-three hundred persons received conditional sentences.[35]

## Probation

According to Sweden's National Prison and Probation Administration,

> Probation resembles a conditional sentence in not entailing loss of liberty, but differs from it in involving a substantial degree of intervention. Probation is intended to be a form of treatment, and equivalent as such to institutional treatment.[36]

The period of probation supervision was reduced in 1974 from three years to one year with the probation supervisory board having the authority to continue the probation period for a second year. A period of penal confinement of at least one month, but not more than two months, may accompany probation. In 1974 some 291 of the 6,276 persons sentenced to probation were also sentenced to short-term institutional treatment.[37] In 1976 the total number of persons under probation supervision was 13,158, with an additional 3,163 persons on parole.[38] The period of probation supervision has decreased, while the number of full-time probation staff has been increased so that now most probation officers work directly with only ten to twelve clients and indirectly, through the volunteers, with another fifty cases. Some 8,700 persons work as volunteer probation and parole workers, including students, teachers, persons involved in social welfare activities, and even a small number of police officers. Volunteers receive a small fee—about $30 a month—for each person supervised, and no volunteer may have more than five persons under supervision at any one time. Most volunteers work with only one or two persons. When special or complicated problems arise such as making arrangements to pay off debts, the volunteers turn to the full-time professional staff for assistance. The use of volunteers perhaps gives some parolees and probationers a sense of acceptance in the community as well as considerable individual attention. In addition, the direct involvement in the life and problems of convicted persons and ex-inmates can provide a large number of Swedish citizens with direct knowledge of the impact of the policies and programs of criminal justice agencies on offenders.

*Youth Prison*

The age of criminal responsibility in Sweden is fifteen years. However, most youthful offenders up to age eighteen are the responsibility of child welfare authorities rather than the criminal justice system. Sweden's method of dealing with young offenders requires further explanation. Most American visitors are surprised to learn that no juvenile court system is needed in Sweden because delinquent youngsters are referred to the Child Welfare Board. This conjures up in the minds of visitors a nonpunitive system for handling delinquents. Images of American detention homes and training schools—our junior prisons—with all the damage that presumably derives from confinement in those institutions, along with the consequences of being labeled a juvenile delinquent and prisoner, vanish with the assumption that actions by the Swedish Child Welfare Board have consequences different from those of actions by juvenile courts. Few American visitors ask whether supervision by child welfare workers avoids the negative labels given to delinquents who receive probation in Sweden or whether confinement in a youth welfare school is seen as nonpunitive by youths placed in them. In any case it should not be assumed that no action is taken just because Swedish delinquents are handled by a state organization other than the juvenile court system or that supervision and control mechanisms analogous to those used by the juvenile courts cannot be applied to difficult or recalcitrant cases. The great majority of child welfare cases in Sweden are arranged without resorting to removing the young person from his or her home. In one of the few contemporary reports describing the juvenile justice and child welfare systems in Sweden, Richard Sundeen reported that Stockholm's Child Welfare Board in 1973 placed 133 delinquent (as opposed to neglected) youths in private (foster) homes and 63 delinquent youths in youth welfare schools.[39] Actions of the Swedish Child Welfare Board are intended to be nonpunitive, with delinquent or suspected delinquent conduct seen as a symptom of trouble and a signal to the board that the young person needs help. Just as delinquent conduct in the United States covers a variety of acts that are not crimes if committed by adults, the Swedish Child Welfare Board also does not need an official excuse, such as an officially reported crime, to bring a young person under its control.

As in the United States, Swedish youths aged fifteen-to-seventeen, charged with serious offenses, may be prosecuted in the criminal courts and sentenced to a youth prison,[40] although most youth prison admissions are in the eighteen-to-twenty age group. Such commitments are for indeterminate periods, with the term fixed on arrival in prison by the National Youth Prison Board. The standard practice at present is for a youth to serve ten months in prison (barring misconduct), to be followed by two years of parole supervision, although an offender released from a youth prison may be subjected to supervision up to a maximum period of five years from the date of sentence. In 1976, 150 persons were admitted to youth prisons, 90 for the first time and 60 as recommitments or parole violators.[41] In 1975 a special government committee was established with a mandate to find alternatives to youth imprisonment. During the study period, certain existing youth prisons were designated as local prisons—that is, they could receive both adult and youth offenders who lived in that locality.

### A New Penal Sanction: Intensive Supervision

In late 1977 the youth prison committee, which was asked to develop a new method of dealing with young offenders, proposed a new type of probation called supervision order. According to Thomas Ekbom of the Stockholm Correctional Region:

> The new sanction [supervision order] is considered to correspond to at least six months imprisonment. It will last for two years and may be combined with six months of *intensive supervision* with a probation officer as supervisor. . . .
>
> Intensive supervision should imply frequent contacts, in the beginning

once a day and in the end at least once a week. During this period, the sanction above all is directed to control, but the elements of help and support are also important. The chief probation officer should give more detailed instructions about this and may also appoint an assistant supervisor.

Disobedience of the instructions leads to more strict instructions or to a short term arrest [jail] for 1-14 days. These last sanctions are to be decided by a probation supervision board. In serious cases of misconduct a court may decide to transform the order to imprisonment for 1-3 months. A court may also decide to let intensive supervision begin with a period of imprisonment. A court or a probation supervision board may also decide that the client shall stay in a probation hostel or with a family.

The probation supervision board may prolong the supervision at the most 3 months at a time during the sentence period. If new crimes are committed during the sentence the court may reconsider supervision for another 3 month period.

The clientele that is planned to receive this new sanction is the present youth prison clientele and the delinquents who today are placed in youth welfare schools and are over 18 years of age. A group of older persons, who today are sentenced to imprisonment and those who today receive 3 or 4 sentences of probation may also receive this new intensive probation sentence.[42]

Although intensive supervision, as proposed in Sweden, emphasizes the surveillance and control function of probation, it does offer an alternative to imprisonment for young offenders and certain categories of adult offenders who have not succeeded under ordinary probation supervision.

## Imprisonment

In Sweden imprisonment is imposed for a specified (determinate) period. Terms can range from one month to ten years or for life. Parole may be granted after two-thirds of a term or in special cases—youthful offenders, first-termers, and those serving long terms—after serving half the term. In 1976, 9,901 persons were admitted to penal institutions.[43]

## Special Imprisonment or Internment

Internment sentences are a matter of considerable controversy in Sweden. They are indeterminate and are applied to habitual offenders. Members of KRUM and other critics of Swedish correctional administration charge that internment sanctions not only are too severe but the indeterminancy aspect represents a powerful means of controlling dissent. In official language, internment is described as follows:

> This is a sanction involving deprivation of liberty for a period not determined in advance, which may be imposed when a defendant has committed offenses punishable by imprisonment for two years or more. This sanction is intended for recidivists who cannot be deterred from continued serious criminal activity by any less radical measure.
>
> Internment involves care both in and outside institutions. The emphasis is on institutional care. The court determines a minimum period of institutional care varying according to the individual case from at least one to not more than twelve years. On the expiration of this minimum period, care continues outside the institution if it appears probable that the risk of relapse into serious crime is not excessive. The decision on this question is made by a central board called the Internment Board. While undergoing extra-institutional care the internee is subject to supervision. Institutional care may not, without the consent of the court, continue more than a total of three years beyond the minimum period, or not more than a total of five years beyond the minimum period if the latter was three years or more. If an internee undergoing care outside an institution neglects his obligations, the Local Probation Board may direct him to follow certain prescriptions or serve him a warning. The Internment Board also has the right to order recommitment to an institution in case of misbehavior.
>
> Except in special cases, three years shall pass from the internee's last transfer to non-institutional care before the sanction is discontinued. If supervision has continued for five years, the sanction shall be discontinued.[44]

In 1976, 220 persons received the internment sanction; 33 persons were sentenced to internment for the first time and 187 for having committed new offenses during the internment parole period.[45] According to the National Prison and Probation Association, "a significant proportion of the persons sentenced to internment are mentally abnormal."[46]

Other sanctions include the possibility of commitment or referral to special facilities for persons with alcohol problems and to psychiatric facilities or hospitals for the mentally retarded.

## The Organization of the Swedish Correctional System

Americans should regard the Swedish corrections system as they would a state system in which all confinement facilities—local and county jails, workhouses, houses of detention, state reformatories and prisons, hospital facilities for mentally ill prisoners and sex "psychopaths"—and all probation, parole, and community corrections programs and facilities are integrated in a single organization which handles all convicted offenders over the age of eighteen and those between the ages of fifteen and seventeen whose criminal acts are serious enough to warrant their being treated as adults.

The Swedish corrections system is governed by a central office called the National Prison and Probation Administration. Under the Correctional Treatment in Institutions Act passed in 1974, the country is divided into fourteen regions, each coinciding geographically with one or two counties. While the NPPA maintains overall responsibility and operates national prisons for longer-term offenders, each region is governed by a local director. The regional director has authority over the jails, local prisons, and probation and parole operations in his district. In 1976 in addition to the 255 members of the NPPA's central office staff, some 4,170 persons worked in Sweden's remand prisons (jails) and its open and closed local and national prisons; and another 730 persons worked in the probation and parole departments.[47] The Correctional Treatment in Institutions Act authorized doubling the number of personnel working in the noninstitutional care section.

*Number and Size of Prisons*

There are forty-nine local (regional) prisons in Sweden most with a capacity of 20 to 60 inmates who serve sentences of less than one year. Some local prisons are closed (secure), others are open, and some can house inmates in both types of accommodations. The twenty-two national prisons have a combined capacity of 2,791 inmates, with 2,098 of these spaces in closed (secure) facilities. Sweden's largest prison, Kumla, built in the mid 1960s, has a capacity of 390, and there are five other prisons which can hold between 200 and 500 inmates.

*Inmate Population Trends*

Despite a rising crime rate, Sweden's prison population has been decreasing. In 1970, for example, 10,546 persons were admitted to all correctional institutions with an average daily population of about 5,000; in 1976, as indicated, 9,901 persons were admitted to the jails and prisons, and the average daily population was about 2,806.[48]

Given the number of staff working in the prisons and the size of inmate populations, the ratio of staff to inmates is close to one to one. In addition to the use of imprisonment for only a small number of convicted offenders, Sweden's low prison population can be explained by the use of sentences that are short compared with those of the United States (even taking into account that comparisons with states in the United States would have to combine misdemeanor and felony sentences, not just sentences to state prisons). Of the 9,901 persons admitted to Swedish penal institutions in 1976, 69 percent received sentences of less than four months, 20 percent drew terms between four and twelve months, and 11 percent were sentenced to terms of one year or more.[49] (In 1970 the figures for these three sentence categories were 66, 24, and 10 percent, respectively.) The main categories of offenses for which persons were committed to Swedish penal institutions in 1970 and 1976 are shown in table 3-1.

An American state with a population of 8 million that included its city and county jails as part of its prison system might approximate the number of penal institutions found in Sweden. But the resources available to most prison administrators in the United States are sharply limited in terms of number, size, and quality of facilities. Most states have one or two fortress prisons for adult males, a junior fortress called a reformatory for youth offenders, and three or four state training schools for other youth offenders. In Sweden the number and variety of institutions available to prison officials permit matching types of offenders with facilities seemingly appropriate to their different needs for custody and programs. The small size of Sweden's maximum-security prisons is also in sharp contrast not only to the large state and federal prisons such as Attica, Joliet, San Quentin, and Leavenworth, which hold thousands of inmates, but also to the "small" prisons in states such as Minnesota where the average daily population of Stillwater Prison in 1976 was some nine hundred men. With a relatively small proportion of offenders, with all offenders serving short

**Table 3-1**
**Main Categories of Offenses to Receive**
**Prison Sentences**
*(in percentages)*

| Offense Category | Percent of All Sentences | |
|---|---|---|
| | *1970* | *1976* |
| Drunken driving | 37 | 32 |
| Larceny | 23 | 17 |
| Violence | 11 | 12 |
| Fraud | 7 | 6 |
| Drug act | 5 | 3 |
| Refusing military service | 4 | 9 |
| Alien's act | 3 | 3 |
| Other | 10 | 17 |

terms, with almost as many staff to work in the prisons as there are inmates, and with almost all those inmates the same color, most Swedish prison administrators have been able to concentrate on prison problems other than assault and murder among inmates and inmates taking hostages, destroying prison property, and rioting over basic conditions. This is not to say that Swedish prison officials do not have some difficult problems; they must provide secure custody for a small number of international terrorists and professional criminals, deal with drug smuggling in the prisons, and cope with the wide variety of languages and social customs of prison populations that come from many countries outside of Scandinavia. But the problems of widespread violence between inmates, particularly between different racial and ethnic groups, and the violence and continual threat of violence between inmates and staff are not general features of prison life in Sweden.[50]

## Some Special Features of Swedish Penal Practice

Those who inquire about the remarkable correctional policies and practices in Sweden often do not ask whether they apply to all prisoners. There are, for example, differences between correctional regions in Sweden with regard to implementing national policy.[51] Some widely publicized programs in Swedish prisons are experimental and apply only to one institution. Other programs apply only to certain categories of prisoners. This section lists the rights and opportunities that apply to all prisoners. The next section describes privileges or opportunities to participate in special programs that are available only to certain groups of prisoners.

### General Rights and Opportunities for Inmates

1. The right to establish an association that represents inmates' interests and the right to meet with each other to discuss matters of mutual concern. Article 56 of the Correctional Treatment in Institutions Act states:

> Taking into account the limitations which follow from the provisions below and from agreements concerning the operation of the national correctional system, inmates shall be entitled to enter into joint consultations with the management of an institution under some suitable form concerning matters of common concern to the inmates. They shall also be entitled, as appropriate, to meet each other for consultation purposes concerning such matters. An inmate who is being kept separate from other inmates may, however, participate in such consultations or meetings only if this can be arranged without inconvenience.

Hofer points out that while strikes by prisoners are not common, Swedish inmates have no formal right to strike.[52]

2. The right to bring a complaint to the justice ombudsman about any action taken against them by police, prosecutors, or correctional personnel.[53] The office of Parliamentary Ombudsman was established in Sweden in 1809 when a new constitution was adopted. To provide controls over activities of the government, a justice ombudsman (J.O.) was appointed by Parliament to ensure that officials adhered to statutes. The Ombudsman's Office was vested with the authority to prosecute judges and other civil servants who violated laws or neglected their duties. Other Ombudsman Offices have been established: a Freedom of Commerce Ombudsman in 1954, a Consumer Ombudsman in 1971, and a Press Ombudsman in 1969. Since the creation of the office, the J.O. has inspected prisons and received complaints about their treatment from prisoners. The J.O. pays particular attention to the length of time suspected offenders are detained between their arrest and the resolution of their cases in court. The 1969 annual report of the Swedish Parliamentary Ombudsmen reports that in 1969 the J.O. received 390 complaints against prison officials of which 41 were dismissed without investigaion, 43 were referred to other state agencies, 263 resulted in no criticism of officials, and one case resulted in prosecution or disciplinary action.

3. The right to retain all civil rights. (Prisoners may vote in elections while in prison.)

4. The opportunity to communicate by telephone and uncensored mail with family members, friends, lawyers, and newspaper reporters—except in cases where security reasons call for monitoring calls or mail.

5. The opportunity to leave a local prison on "town passes" to work, study, or participate in vocational training or to leave any prison for a special, short furlough at the discretion of the regional director.

6. The opportunity to receive regular furloughs from prison. Inmates in open prisons become eligible for a furlough four months after commitment. Inmates in closed prisons must serve six months, and all inmates with sentences longer than two years must submit furlough applications to the National Prison and Probation Administration. This procedure as well as the one requiring approval from regional directors for short-term town passes from local prisons is intended to reduce the pressure on local prison officials. The change implies that too many leaves were granted by local officials. An inmate's first leave is for forty-eight hours plus travel time. Furloughs may be taken every two months after the first leave, with the time extended to seventy-two hours plus travel time. In 1976, 42,663 furloughs were approved. In 3,402 cases (8 percent) inmates failed to return within the time allowed; and in an additional 1,142 (3 percent) inmates returned to prison under the influence of alcohol or drugs, or they engaged in criminal conduct while on leave. As the number of inmates given furloughs has increased sharply (from 26,377 in 1974),

the number of inmates "on the run" as a result of violating furlough leaves has risen to 300 or more at any given time. Such a program tests the tolerance of the police and the community.

7. The opportunity to have unsupervised visits in prison. There is no regulation allowing conjugal visiting; the policy is simply to allow unsupervised visits in private rooms (in open prisons in the inmate's own room) during which time sexual intercourse may take place if that is the wish of the inmate and the visitor. The prisons at Ulriksfors and Viskan, which are in remote areas of northern Sweden, have taken over nearby hotels where inmates may spend weekends with families or friends.[54]

### Rights and Opportunities Available for Certain Prisoners

1. The opportunity to spend from one to three weeks at a "vacation" prison in the mountains. This facility was established on an experimental basis in 1967 after the National Prison and Probation Administration agreed that inmate workers should have the same rights to vacation days that all Swedish wage earners have. Vacations are also seen as a way of supporting family relationships. The vacation village of Gruvberget is available to about one hundred long-term prisoners each year. This vacation prison has aroused the concern of at least one correctional administration official, who pointed out that caution should be exercised in making available to prisoners a cost-free vacation given that some Swedish citizens, particularly housewives, do not have similar opportunities for a vacation.[55]

2. The opportunity to further their education is available to all prisoners, but only certain inmates may leave prison to go to school. Inmates receive two kronor (about fifty cents) per hour for time spent in studies. The money received for participating in educational activities is intended to provide an incentive for inmates who would otherwise choose work in order to earn money, although the amount that can be earned is less than the wage paid for prison labor. Classes or self-study courses may be taken in both open and closed prisons and are arranged by the local school authorities. Local colleges offer courses at three prisons. Inmates in open or local prisons may attend schools outside the prison. The most widely publicized educational program is the Uppsala Study Center.[56] This institution, consisting of two barracks surrounded by a large recreation area and a fence, is devoted completely to study activities. It is often described as the prison where inmates ride out on their bicycles to attend classes at Uppsala University. At the present time sixteen inmates go to school outside this prison.

3. The obligation to work (or study) includes the right to some pay and, for a smaller number of prisoners, pay at the level offered for similar work in the community. The majority of Swedish prisoners are paid according to piecework

rates, with the average worker making about fifty cents per hour. Since a forty-hour work week is required, most inmates make approximately twenty dollars per week. The opportunity to earn free-market wages, which many Americans assume is available to all prisoners in Sweden, has been tried on an experimental basis since November 1972 at Tillberga, an open prison with a rated capacity of 120 men, and more recently at Skogome, a closed prison near Gothenburg. (A variation of this idea permits inmates to leave the prison during the day to work at normal civilian employment for which they receive regular wages.) Inmates at Tillberga manufacture prefabricated wooden houses and, according to the National Correctional Association, are paid the same wages as workers in the private wood products industry. Inmates work as carpenters, welders, truck drivers, and clerks.

> During the experimental period the prisoners are exempt from income tax. Thus their wage scale corresponds to what a wood products industry worker would earn after withholding tax is deducted. This means that "Tillberga wages" are estimated at 8-10 kronor per hour ($1.70 - $2.10). Deductions for meals are made at the same rate as that for the personnel. After deductions for meals the prisoner is allowed 25% for his personal use. The remainder is set aside for savings and to cover his personal financial problems.

> An important goal is to get the prisoner to clarify his present financial situation and to learn to plan his economy with an eye to the future. Thanks to the higher wages he earns at Tillberga he should be able to improve his situation prior to being released, for example by paying off his debts in whole or in part, or by paying rent on an apartment which he might otherwise forfeit. He should even try to save enough to support himself and his family during the first weeks after his release. The prisoner should plan his budget himself. He will be encouraged and given an opportunity to contact his creditors and, when necessary, make agreements with them on conditions for repayment. The guiding principle is that the prisoner himself should take the initiative and feel responsible for his future. The duty of institution personnel is to gain his confidence and assist him through advice and guidance.

> What is hoped will be the main result of the Tillberga experiment is a reasonably good financial and social situation for the prisoner when he is released. This should have a favorable influence on his readjustment to society and reduce the risk of a relapse into crime.

> Participation in the Tillberga experiment is voluntary. All prisoners in all institutions in the country have been informed of the experiment by means of a specially printed folder. They have been given an opportunity to request transfer to Tillberga, at the same time agreeing to accept the conditions set by the experiment.[57]

In addition to receiving the higher wages that Swedish prisoners may collect each week, inmate workers at Tillberga may take home leaves every fourteen days. They may also receive visitors in their own rooms and have the right to lock their doors. To be selected for Tillberga, an inmate must be eligible for housing in an open prison, have some skills, and agree to the budget plan for his wages. A study of Tillberga inmates reports that about 40 percent of those who apply are accepted. The full-market-wages concept is related to the right of Swedish workers to a paid vacation. It is also related to another employment question for prisoners. Do they have the right of civilian workers to strike? Inmates at Tillberga have participated in strikes, but prison authorities have exercised control over such actions by threatening to remove striking prisoners from their jobs. Inmates at Tillberga can therefore be effectively prohibited from joining in sympathy strikes designed to show support for prisoners at other institutions, and they can be required to work when civilian employees or staff members strike. It might be possible, however, for the Tillberga inmates to increase their leverage in bargaining by virtue of the their ability to withhold their labor. Compared with the labor of other prisoners, the Tillberga prisoners' labor is more valuable in the short run because the prison accepts contracts for private industry which require that production schedules be met. The Tillberga experiment thus serves as a reminder that improvements in prison work programs can generate new complications for inmates and administrators.

## The Sundsvall Experiment

An experimental treatment program for probationers and parolees was instituted in 1972. The intent was to test the impact of substantially increased resources for these groups. The Sundsvall district, when the experiment was conducted, had three probation officers for some 375 clients prior to the start of the project. After July 1972 the number of probation officers was increased to nine; a clinic was established and staffed by a part-time psychiatrist, a psychologist, and a nurse; a hotel with facilities for twenty persons was purchased to provide for individuals needing temporary housing; a halfway house for twenty was provided; and one staff member at the local labor exchange was engaged to deal specifically with the employment problems of the parolees and probationers. Volunteer lay supervisors were also employed for routine direct contact with clients. They were selected by the probationer or parolee and were presumably persons with whom the probationer or parolee had had a good relationship before his arrest. Contact, according to a risk assessment for each client, ranged from once-a-month meetings (normal supervision) to meetings once a week and more frequently.

The program is being studied carefully, with the follow-up period to cover two years after release from the treatment. A matched sample of clients from another district is being used as part of the same study. Clients under supervision in both districts prior to the start of the experimental program are also being followed. Study results will not be available for several years, but a preliminary report by the project evaluator, Eckart Kuhlhorn, has been issued.[58] To date, a number of problems have been observed that suggested to Kuhlhorn that the impact of the enhanced resources on clients will be negligible.

> Can staff reinforcements have positive effects? It is probably true to say that measures intended to steer developments lose some of their force before they reach the client. This problem has therefore been labelled the "absorption" problem. It could be shown at different levels. At the treatment staff level it could be demonstrated that the somewhat complex steering mechanisms were less popular than the elements governed by tradition, such as supervisor training, joint treatment conferences and so on. It could also be proved that a large amount of the reinforcement had disappeared by the time it reached supervisor level. At the client level notable effects of the reinforcement of resources were, in the opinion of the supervisors, no longer visible. It has also to be borne in mind that reinforcement of staff for dealing with probationers and parolees only increases the strategic scope. Practical resources, such as jobs, social assistance, scope for writing off debts or number of dwellings available are not altered by reinforcement of the staff. In such circumstances, assumptions concerning positive effects on clients would seem unrealistic.[59]

Kuhlhorn also reports on supervisor-client relationships from the perspective of groups in both the treatment and control districts. The frequency and content of communication was examined, the needs of clients and the steps taken to assist them were identified, and the implications of the changes in noninstitutional treatment associated with the adoption of the 1974 Corrections Care in Institutions Act were studied. Kuhlhorn describes two types of noninstitutional treatment that might be developed. One would involve normal probation supervision, or preventive supervision, provided by a layman. The second type, open correctional treatment, would call for intensive supervision provided by a trained probation officer and would involve more frequent contact with the client. The purpose of intensive supervision would be to provide an alaternative to a prison term, and "one of the short-term targets should be to achieve the goal set up by society in connection with prison sentences, i.e., the incapacitative effect during the term in prison."[60] This proposal corresponds to the new supervision order (intensive supervision) described earlier. Final data on the impact of the Sundsvall experiment are yet to come, although Kuhlhorn is pessimistic about any important positive effects on the conduct of either probationers and parolees. Like so many other tenets of correctional treatment philosophy, the theory that substantial increases in staff for offenders will assure changes in behavior appears to be unsupported. In the following section one more interesting experiment in Swedish corrections is examined— another good idea that was tried by did not work well.

## Prison Democracy: An Experiment that Failed

During the late 1960s inmates in several Swedish prisons sought to organize groups to bring matters that concerned them to the attention of prison administrators and to effect improvements in prison life. This resulted in the inevitable clash between organized inmate pressure for change and the resistance of prison staff members as described by the director-general of the National Prison and Probation Administration:

> During the 1960's organizations were formed among the inmates of penal institutions. In some cases they were sports associations or hobby clubs. In other cases the organizations more resembled trade unions. The boards of these organizations have taken up discussions with the prison administrations about the problems of interest to the inmates. In many prisons, advisory boards have been set up among the inmates and the boards have regarded themselves as being the representative spokesmen. According to Swedish law, there is nothing to prevent the inmates of penal institutions from forming their own organizations. The general freedom of association applies to them. Likewise there is nothing to prevent them from electing bodies within the institutions to further their demands.
>
> On the other hand, the right of the inmates to meet and discuss their problems is limited by prison regulations. Order and security within the institution must not be jeopardized if such meethings are arranged. Regulations designed to prevent detrimental effects on the inmates might in some cases limit the right of association. It is only reasonable that the correctional authority guarantee a certain amount of security for the individual inmate so that he does not risk being subject to violence or threats from other inmates. . . .
>
> In 1969 a very active advisory council was formed at Hall Prison. . . . The activities of the council caused unrest within the institution and also led to strikes in the workshops on several occasions. In this situation, the region's chief [administrative] officer felt that he had to prevent the council from carrying on its activities without restriction. His decision gave rise to an animated public debate. After careful scrutiny by the highest judicial authority in this field, the Attorney-General, the measure was declared justified.
>
> The debate over prison democracy went on, and in November 1969 the National Correctional Administration, after consulting the Central Works Council, decided to appoint a working committee to prepare a report on increased cooperation between personnel and inmates. The committee consisted of representatives for the Correctional Administration and the four different trade unions in which the personnel of the correctional institutions are organized. Afterwards the committee had been criticized for not including any representatives of the inmates. The deliberations of the working committee resulted in a circular letter in May 1970, in which the National Correctional

Administration also gave instructions as to how the process of consultations was to be outlined. The Administration declared its positive views on the rights of the inmates to form advisory councils. Regardless of what associations might exist among the inmates it was seen as important, however, to find organizational forms for the consultation process through which various personnel categories and inmates could feel shared responsibility for the effects. Even though the warden was still to be the one who made the decisions it could be presumed that participation in institutional councils or other forms of consultation could bolster the inmates' self-respect and responsibility to the benefit of their treatment. Likewise it could give the employees a feeling of their importance in the work of rehabilitation.

An institutional council was to consist of a maximum of six representatives of various personnel categories and a corresponding number of inmates representing different groups within the institution. The warden, or who[m]ever he appoints to substitute [for] him, was to act as chairman.

According to the circular, the institutional councils were to deal with suggestions for improvements and matters of common interest to personnel and inmates. The issues were to be of general importance to the rehabilitation work within the institution, dealing with such subjects as catering, hygiene, health and medical care, sports, entertainment, canteens and visiting conditions.

In some cases the inmates have boycotted these consultations periodically, partly because they have felt that they were not permitted to participate in the formation of the councils, partly because they felt they were in too weak a position as compared to prison administrations and personnel organizations. In other cases advisory councils have not been formed at all, since the communications between administration, staff and inmates of small open institutions in most cases are excellent and do not need any formalization. . . .

In October 1970 a hunger strike was staged at the Österåker Central Prison. It was caused by certain differences of opinion between the administration and the Advisory Council. These concerned, among other things, visiting conditions, the founding of a special study department, the utilization of exercise facilities, etc. This conflict was extensively reported by mass-media and the inmates were supported in various ways by organizations outside the institution. A large portion of all the country's inmates went on a sympathy strike. Some 2,500 of the country's 5,000 inmates participated in the strike to support the inmates at Österåker.

The National Correctional Administration intervened and took over the negotiations with the Advisory Council at Österåker. The discussions finally resulted in certain promises from the Administration to examine the conditions at Österåker. The Administration also promised that within two months it would arrange consultations with representatives of inmates from all over the country.

One representative of the inmates was to be elected at the central institutions of each region. The inmates were also given the right to add to their delegation two representatives from outside their own collective.

Negotiations with the delegation of the inmates were started on November 30. Representatives of the personnel organizations also participated in the discussions. It proved difficult, however, to reach any agreement within such a relatively large assembly. On December 1 the negotiations broke down, and the next day inmates of institutions all around the country went on a hunger strike. The National Correctional Administration's proposal to resume negotiations within a smaller working committee was rejected by the inmates. The hunger strike was called off in a few days. No more than 1,000 inmates participated.

Informal contacts were re-established, and on December 7 the proposed small working committee was formed. The committee prepared a report which was discussed by the whole group of delegates on January 11 and 12, 1971. The negotiations resulted in certain commitments from the National Correctional Administration. The Administration proposed, among other things, more freedom and better working conditions for the advisory councils, more generous leave of absence regulations, better vising conditions and considerable limitations to the censorship of letters. These reforms are being carried out during the first half of 1971 in the form of new directives from the Correctional Administration.[61]

A different perspective on these events is provided by Norwegian sociologist Thomas Mathiesen, who was active in the formation of the Norwegian Association for Penal Reform (KROM) in 1968 and has served as chairman of that group. Norwegian prison authorities have more traditional views on penology than their neighbors in Sweden and KROM has not received the official recognition given by Swedish authorities to that country's penal reform group, KRUM.

While Mathiesen and KROM have not been invited to participate in negotiations in Norwegian prisons, Mathiesen was invited by his Swedish colleagues to attend their planning meetings, and during the actual discussions with prison officials he was permitted to be present as a member of the inmates' advisory board. Mathiesen characterizes the position occupied by prisoners as essentially powerless. Unlike free-world workers who make a fundamental contribution to the operation of a factory through their labor, inmates make no real contribution to the daily operation of the prison.[62] If prisoners strike, even in Swedish prisons where all prisoners put in a forty-hour week and some work is contracted through private industry, the products of inmate labor are so inconsequential that little impact is felt on the prison system except for the annoyance and inconvenience of the disruption. During the "prison democracy" negotiations, the National Prison and Probation Administration was primarily concerned that the concessions won by the inmates would cause the prison guards and the work supervisors to strike—the withholding of services by these workers was seen as critical in the operation of the prisons. It is also apparent in the language of the account by the director-general that the usual qualifications and caveats found in communiques from prison administrators applied even in the discussion of prison democracy: "Order and security must not be jeopardized." "Regulations [have been] designed to prevent detrimental effects on the inmates. . . ." "The National Correctional Administration *gave instructions* as to how the process of consultation was to be outlined." "The negotiations resulted in certain *commitments* from the National Correctional Administration." The need for the correctional authorities to maintain a dominant power position was clear throughout the meetings with inmate representatives.

While the inmates and their KRUM advisors wanted to negotiate, the officials wanted the meeting to be talks. A look at the list of demands of the Österåker conference group does, however, present a contrast to the lists developed by inmates at Attica, Folsom, and other American prisons:

[1] *Recognition of FFCO—Förenade Fångars Central Organisation* (United Prisoners' Central Organization, established by the eight representatives of the prisoners while KRUM's annual meeting was taking place, with the eight representatives as an interim board);

[2] *clearly specified rights for the inmate councils* (uncensored communication with the mass media, KRUM, other organizations and individuals, as well as between prisons; freedom to act inside the prison; a right to be heard when relevant new laws are introduced; an equalizing of work as inmate representative with participation in the school program, etc., and payment according to a minimum standard—see [7]);

[3] *abolition of censorship* (no censorship of mail; telephone booths in all institutions; free access to the telephone booths);

[4] *more liberal rules concerning visits* (identical visiting regulations for all institutions; a right to at least six hours of individual visiting per week; a right to have visits in the cell; a right to receive visits from anyone, without restriction);

[5] *a considerable expansion of the furlough system* (regular furloughs to be granted after 1/8 of the sentence served; remand of over four weeks included in this; furloughs to be given at intervals of one month; 'visiting furloughs' to be given at least once a month if the prisoner has a right to regular furloughs; inmates without the right to furloughs to be given forty-eight hours of continual visiting time *inside* the walls, once a month);

[6] *immediate review of the system of leaves;*

[7] *increased wages* (a general wage increase, equal for all inmates; a minimum wage of 1.25 Swedish kroner [twenty cents] per hour until negotiations concerning wages could be commenced

between the Prison Department and the Swedish Association for Institutional Labourers—established a while earlier; 1.25 kroner to be paid to all inmates, also to those studying or for other reasons not placed in regular work; 80 per cent of the wage to be paid in cash, the rest to be saved; canteens to be installed in all institutions);

[8] *an equalizing of labour with other activities* (abolition of the duty to work; studies and therapy equalized in economic terms with work; sessions with the treatment staff to take place during working time and without a reduction in wages; all prisoners to be offered a primary school education program, free of charge, *without* being kept in separate educational prisons; later lock-up at night);

[9] *a new library system* (according to the same principle as at Hall security institution);

[10] *improved working conditions for the psychologists* (assumed to be presented by a representative of the Psychological Association);

[11] *increased reliance on probation with an improvement of the economic resources of that system;*

[12] *abolishment of all special restrictions for foreigners in the prisons;*

[13] *similar regulations for female and male prisoners;*

[14] *abolishment of the youth prison system in its present form;*

[15] *a right for all inmates to receive gifts;*

[16] *abolishment of all types of involuntary isolation.*[63]

Mathiesen himself characterized this list as "an impressive list of important demands which, taken together, would mean a shattering of the prison system in its present form."[64]

Corrections officials contended that many of the demands called for legal changes that were beyond their authority. They proposed that a "working committee" composed of three prisoners and three staff representatives redraft the list before actual negotiations took place. A national meeting of prison officials and inmates took up the revised list of demands.[65]

After two days of discussion, the corrections officials prepared a communique summarizing the results of the talks. The inmate representatives disagreed with its contents. After considerable argument and debate, during which the inmates won very few points, the Prison Department proposal was essentially adopted. Inmates and KRUM representatives complained that few actual changes were assured and even those were delayed by the qualification in the agreement that "the carrying out of proposals is to take place to the extent permitted by economic and staff resources."[66] Insistence on this condition came from the representatives of the personnel unions. KRUM leaders were disappointed by the absence of any real commitment by the Prison Department to bring about the improvements that survived the working committee stage (demands 11-16 were dropped before the full committee met). They felt that the exercise emphasized the inability of inmates to negotiate from a position of strength. While the new rights won by the inmates seemed insignificant to KRUM, prison employees were critical of the process. They contended that the Prison Department had been threatened by the inmates (the strikes) and should not have discussed any demands under such circumstances. The director-general took note of staff discontent in a news release entitled "Prison Democracy in Sweden," issued three months after the Österåker meeting. (The statement was released through the Swedish Information Service in the United States and other countries but was not issued in Sweden.)[67]

While prison employees, KRUM leaders, and many inmates were disturbed and distrustful of prison democracy, members of the National Prison and Probation Administration apparently felt that a new method had been pioneered in their country that not only could deal with inmate discontent but also promoted rehabilitation. This optimistic view was contained in the director-general's statement:

In my reasoning I have taken for granted that participation in democratic organizations and cooperation in democratic forms would have an improving effect on the inmates. It can be hoped that the inmate experiences a new identification—as a member or leader of a social movement aiming at the reforming of the prison society—and leaves his old criminal identification behind. This might help him to take a new look at himself at his discharge. If he engages in social and political activities this might keep him from committing new crimes. This idea is perhaps too optimistic and there is the risk that an active member of an advisory council will be identified with his institution. In the institution he is the leader who sits in negotiations with the warden —after his discharge he is the unskilled worker with no education, insufficient experience and low status. This might give rise to severe tensions. . . .

According to those who are learned in law, the negotiations which started November 30, 1970, at Österåker prison are unique in history. They placed on an equal footing the delegates of the country's 5,000 prisoners on one side and representatives of the correctional authorities and the personnel organizations on the other. Naturally, they were met with apprehension by some people, but they will no doubt prove useful in many ways to the National Correctional Administration— not the least in our efforts to prevent criminality.[68]

Mathiesen criticizes Martinsson's statement but notes that the public announcement of the policy might, ironically, benefit the inmates since "the authorities—who also seek an international reputation—will in a somewhat paradoxical way become dependent on the contribution of prisoners—the contribution to the maintenance of pseudo-democracy."[69]

But the kind of prison democracy extolled by the National Correctional Administration in which its representatives and those of the employee unions and the prisoners would sit down to iron out agreements at national negotiating sessions was short-lived. In June 1971 some seven hundred inmates in thirteen prisons went on a hunger strike to protest the confinement in isolation of three fellow prisoners. The strike failed to bring about the release of the three, but new national talks were promised for the fall. Inmate representatives were invited to participate by the National Correctional Administration which also agreed to a television program about the proceedings. According to Mathiesen, the prison department was interested in the talks because they were seen as a method of bringing the central administration prison staff members and inmates together with no middleman to interpret inmate or staff interests. "But in addition, authorities had clearly discovered that talks are entirely unthreatening to the system, and that they are in fact *an important way of supplying the system with new—and badly needed—legitimacy.*"[70]

Prior to the actual meeting, members of KRUM who were advising the inmate representatives expressed their reservations about anything meaningful coming from the talks. They pointed out, as did one of the inmate representatives who had been present at the first national discussion, that many issues from the early sessions were still unresolved. It was agreed that definite commitments to specific demands had to be obtained from the prison department at the meeting. The new list of demands comprised the following:

1. Inmate newspapers should be uncensored and published with no limit on the number of copies.
2. Reports in inmates' prison record files that relate to personal history and characteristics should be abolished.
3. Inmate file information related to parole decisions should be limited to data that do not make the prisoner a "marked man."
4. Inmates should have access to all statements written about them.
5. Parole supervision should be abolished.
6. Telephone booths should be placed on every floor in the prisons.
7. Guards and inmates should wear civilian clothes.
8. Visiting and furlough rights should be extended.
9. Punishment within the prison, such as isolation or transfer of inmates to specific security sections, should be ended.
10. Inmates should be free to move around within the prison.
11. Forced work should be abolished.
12. Every inmate should be given the opportunity and facilities for study.
13. The geographic isolation of the women's prison should be ended.
14. The construction of new prisons should be stopped.[71]

The implications for fundamental reforms in the penal system are clear in the proposals regarding files containing personal information about the inmates and in those to abolish parole supervision and end punishment within the prison system. Had the prison department agreed to take up and resolve these issues at the table, these talks might have assumed historic proportions.

However, these demands were never negotiated because the National Prison and Probation Administration (NPPA) and KRUM could not agree on the ground rules for the talks. Administration officials asserted that resolving some of the items required action by Parliament and that the most they could do was promise that if agreement was reached on an issue, an effort would be made to encourage Parliament to authorize the changes. The inmates countered by arguing that the NPPA had the power to agree to the changes. It appears that both the prison department and KRUM had reasons not to acquiesce with regard to the procedural obstructions that prevented the second national bargaining session. KRUM wanted to demonstrate to the inmates that once negotiations extended beyond issues, the prison department would no longer play "democracy." The prison department was under pressure from the staff unions not to give in to any inmate demands unless they were trivial. The stand by KRUM and the NPPA regarding at-the-table decisions was a useful technique that permitted both parties to justify their refusal to begin the talks. The NPPA, for example, did not issue a summary of the decisions made at the first national meeting until after the demise of the second. The inmates therefore did not know the extent to which the earlier set of demands had resulted in new policies or procedures or why there had been a delay in implementing some demands about which agreement had been reached.

The breakdown in negotiations at Kumla was followed immediately by a wave of food and work strikes in the prisons. The strikes were stopped after the minister of justice announced that representatives of a royal commission were working on a long-range plan that promised substantial changes in the Swedish corrections system. Prison authorities accused KRUM of sabotaging the natural discussions by influencing the inmate representatives to raise "impossible demands." KRUM was characterized as a radical political organization comprising persons outside the prisons who were willing to sacrifice improvements in the living and working conditions of the prisoners in order to try to achieve larger revolutionary goals. KRUM contended that the national negotiations served largely a public relations function and that the National Prison and Probation Administration had provided one more example of seductive liberal rhetoric designed to mask the same old purpose of social control.

The term prison democracy is no longer used in Sweden, but inmates are still working to establish some sort of dialogue with prison officials. The prisoners union (F.F.C.O.) is still alive and permits only prisoners to join—even ex-prisoners cannot be members. The union contends that it has no interest in political issues; its concerns are only the daily living problems of the prisoners.

In 1976 the union received permission from the National Prison and Probation Administration to hold a meeting at Kumla Prison for some twenty-five to thirty inmates representing different prisons. Its purpose was to help the inmates get organized, with the clear understanding that future negotiations between the union and prison officials would be restricted to the everyday problems of inmates. (The NPPA official who authorized this meeting commented to me that the F.F.C.O. had criticized several strikes in Swedish prisons—one over the quality of the vegetables at a prison housing conscientious objectors and another over inmate swimming facilities and difficulties in seeing the doctor at a prison for drunken drivers. The F.F.C.O., according to this official, regarded strikes over such issues as a bad tactic since they undercut public concern for all prisoners.)

Actually the early efforts after KRUM's establishment in 1966 were dedicated more to prison reform efforts than to exposing the power differentials between offenders and the state. KRUM is an acronym for Riksförbundet för Kriminalvårdens Humanisering (the National Association for Penal Reform). Although KRUM began its work by advocating more psychological treatment programs for inmates, its members soon became aware that prison treatment was a well-intentioned, liberal reform that was not improving the inmate's lot substantially. Thomas Mathiesen illustrates the shift in goals of this organization over a relatively short span of time:

In 1967 a KRUM pamphlet said that:

The National Swedish Association for Penal Reform (KRUM) will attend to the interests of those who are punished, and ease their readjustment to society. KRUM works for a radical reform of the correctional system and the treatment of prisoners. Legislation and treatment of criminals ought to be liberated from punitive thinking. The present system of institutions ought to be abolished, and incarceration reduced to a minimum. Offenders who have social handicaps ought to be met by a social policy which is liberated from moralization and authoritarian thinking.

The general meeting in March 1971 adopted the following statement of objectives:

KRUM wishes to analyze and fight the class society, which through its unequal distribution of power and opportunity contributes to the creation of groups which are socially, economically, and culturally expelled. KRUM is working to abolish imprisonment and other types of forced incarceration within the correctional system, child and youth welfare, mental health care, alcohol care, narcotics care, handicap care, etc.

The new formulation differs in several respects from the old one. In the first place, fighting the "class society" has now been added as an important independent goal. Secondly, this goal is placed *ahead of* the goal related more directly to criminal policy. In the third place, the task of changing criminal policy is now only one of several similar tasks within the general area of social policy.[72]

In 1971 I participated in a conference in Spåtind, Norway, at which representatives of Sweden's KRUM, Norway's KROM, and Denmark's KRIM reviewed some of the myths about prison systems—the myth of rehabilitation, the myths about prison labor and education, the myths about general deterrence, and the myth of prison democracy.[73]

The discussions at Spåtind shifted as ex-prisoners sought to direct attention to specific events that distressed them and to specific staff members in the prisons whom they regarded as insensitive or worse. The scholars, journalists, and lawyers present tried to direct their attention toward systemic problems. This conflict between the here-and-now concerns of the prisoners and longer-term changes in economic and political systems in which prison systems are imbedded threatened to divide the reform groups. Thomas Mathiesen was able to prevent this division by reminding the intellectuals that as members of a prison reform organization they needed to understand the problems of prisoners and the prisoners needed to recognize that significant and lasting changes in prisons required more than the removal of specific staff members. (The division between intellectuals and prisoners in Finland's KRIM led the intellectual faction to form its own organization. This more radical group, called the November Movement, could not survive without the prisoners.)

The problem of prison reform organizations that included both reform and revolutionary elements was brought to a head by the Swedish prison democracy experiment. The failure of the second round of discussions seems to have been fixed, rather successfully by the corrections officials, on the radical position taken by KRUM. The decreasing influence of KRUM in Swedish prisons has been paralleled by a drop in its dues-paying membership from seven thousand in 1967 to four hundred in 1975.[74] In her article about the fate of KRUM since 1974, Polly Smith attributes the drop in its support to three factors. First, liberals left the organization because they

> did not agree with the assertion that a class society is a precondition for prisons as they are now and that change efforts should be directed toward eradicating class differences and abolishing imprisonment. Instead, liberals endorsed the reformist position with intentions of servicing inmates and humanizing prisons.[75]

Second, Smith observes that given KRUM's radical position, inmates "perceived themselves as hostages waiting for a better society. Inmate needs are immediate and cannot wait for the eventual dissolution of classes and prisons."[76] The third factor was the shift in public positions toward imprisonment taken by a new minister of justice, Lennart Geijer. Under Geijer's direction the reorganization of the correctional system proceeded, including its efforts to deinstitutionalize. Geijer's views were at least reformist and, from some perspectives, radical counterparts to KRUM's position. This shift, Smith points out, posed a problem for KRUM. As a supporter of deinstitutionalization, it could not disagree with the government, but to support these efforts meant joining forces with the political power structure.[77]

KRUM, for the time being at least, seems to be a force with limited influence on Swedish penal policy. Its short history, however, should be instructive to other political reform groups. Swedish prison reformers and prisoners, like their American counterparts, are in a different social, economic, and political milieu than that which prevailed in the late 1960s and early 1970s. In 1976 a black American, serving time for drug law violations at Hall Prison where the prisoners union was founded, told me that inmate response to all organized inmate interest groups—KRUM, F.F.C.O., and ordinary inmate councils—was apathetic.

An additional feature of the prison democracy experiment merits attention. This experiment provides an example of prison conflict in which inmate resistance involved work stoppages, hunger and thirst strikes, and appeals for political support through the mass media. It did not produce the physical violence that has characterized inmate-staff confrontations in American prisons.[78] The same forces for and against change operate in Sweden and in many American correctional systems; but in Sweden the manner in which all parties have sought to deal with the problem has differed, and the substantive issues of concern to Swedish prison reformers and prisoners are far more sophisticated than those of most of their colleagues in the United States. Movements toward those more advanced issues require that American prisoners first win some basic rights; most important is the right to organize in behalf of their own interests. The failure of prison democracy—an experiment that would not have been given serious consideration in any American prison system—does, however, provide evidence of the difficulty inmates have in bringing about fundamental changes in even the most enlightened systems.

Discussions of prisoners' rights and prison programs in Sweden usually raise the question how all the remarkable features of Swedish penology contribute to achieving one of the traditional goals of prison systems—the reduction of recidivism. This question implies a continuation of the treatment ideology that is being abandoned in some American penal systems—that is, the theory that somehow imprisonment can be a positive experience for inmates.[79] The other justifications for imprisonment—incapacitation, punishment, and general deterrence—now are being advanced. In Sweden other goals have been proposed, the most important being making efforts to reduce the damage imprisonment does to inmates and to provide inmates with training in the basic skills necessary for survival in the free world. But for those who ask only whether Sweden's correctional practices result in lower recidivism rates, evidence is now becoming available.

## Evaluations of Swedish Correctional Programs

The information presented in most official government reports, journalistic accounts, and articles by American scholars has concentrated on innovative features of Swedish penal policy and practice likely to impress American audiences. Only occasionally have writers asked how all these things work when it comes to reducing recidivism. Until very recently the response of Swedish corrections officials and researchers would have been, we don't know. The development of a research capacity within the National Prison and Probation Administration can be identified with the appointment in 1971 of Norman Bishop to a new Research and Development Unit. Bishop has explained the paucity of research as follows:

> In the past it may be that a concern for organising what seemed a progressive and above all a humane system, was considered to be its own guarantee of effectiveness. Under such circumstances research perhaps scarcely seemed necessary. Today we are far less sure but the resources available for research are small and Sweden is only at the very beginning of seeking to provide increased resources. As it is, University-based research is handicapped by an insistence on teaching rather than research and an absence of research assistant posts. A good deal of student research is conducted through psychology and sociology departments and the schools of social work but it too suffers from the absence of adequate technical supervision. A Ministry of Justice Committee on Treatment Research catalogued studies for 1967-1970 and concluded that the majority were methodologically poor, lacked bases or conclusions which were suitable for the development of practice and, in short, demonstrated mainly the absence of informed and co-ordinated research enterprises.[80]

Bishop also notes that the Ministry of Justice survey found only one-sixth of the 190 studies they examined to be "effect studies," and many of these were flawed in terms of adequate methodology. Studies undertaken by the Research and Development Unit itself or authorized or commissioned by the National Prison and Probation Administration have resulted in a series of research reports (most with English summaries) which are helping to correct this deficiency in Swedish penology.

*National Prison and Probation Administration Studies*

One Research and Development Unit project involved a follow-up study of 273 persons admitted to youth prisons during 1968. Eighty-five percent of the group was reported for new offenses during the two-year follow-up period. This study provides detailed information about the number and nature of new offenses, comparisons of original offenses and those committed after release, and recidivism rates for offenders convicted of crimes of violence. The 233 recidivists produced a total of 467 separate legal actions with regard to their criminal activities.[81] The study also provides correlations of background and prison experience factors with recidivism (examined in terms of the time to the first reported crime).

A more recent study by Krantz, Bagge, and Bishop examined recidivism rates and the relationship between recidivism and other variables—such as age, criminal record, prison experience, and time served—for a 25 percent sample of all persons paroled from prison in the first half of 1973.[82] The follow-up extended for thirty months after parole, and recidivism was defined as "commission of an offence which resulted in a penalty more severe than a fine." The key findings of the study are:

> About two-thirds of the sample committed new offences in the course of the 30-month follow-up period.
>
> The recidivism rate is highest, around 71 percent, among persons up to 30 years. Among the remainder it is about 56 percent.
>
> The risk of recidivism is highest in the first five months after parole.
>
> Fifty percent of the recidivist group have recidivated after about 3 months, and 75 percent after about 9 months.
>
> There is a relation between being recorded in the police register at an early age and a higher rate of recidivism following a later prison sentence.
>
> Recidivism is higher (about 75 percent) among the group having earlier prison experience than among the group without earlier prison experience (about 46 percent).
>
> Persons whose principal offence was a crime of violence showed lower recidivism (53 percent) than persons whose principal offence was a crime against property (70 percent).
>
> The length of the term of sentence is not associated with any significant difference in the incidence of recidivism.[83]

Probationer recidivism has also been studied. For 667 persons, a 10 percent sample of all probationers in 1971, data were gathered for a three-year follow-up. Forty percent of those on probation relapsed into crime—half within six months and three-fourths within the first year.[84]

Still another follow-up study compared recidivism rates of men released from Tillberga with a group accepted for Tillberga but transferred for various reasons and those of a second group of men released from other prisons who matched the Tillberga group in terms of numbers of prior commitments to prison (see table 3-2). The group that had been accepted and transferred was found to have "substantially more criminal backgrounds and more difficult social circumstances," which could explain the difference between the study group in terms of percentages of releasees not reported to the police for criminal activity.

Table 3-2
**Recidivism for Prisoners Released and Transferred from Tillberga Prison**

|  | Tillberga Releases | | Tillberga Transfers | | Comparison Group | |
|---|---|---|---|---|---|---|
|  | % | N | % | N | % | N |
| Three months | 87 | 143 | 80 | 50 | 75 | 67 |
| Six months | 80 | 143 | 60 | 50 | 64 | 67 |
| Nine months | 72 | 103 | 53 | 30 | 57 | 67 |
| Twelve months | 62 | 69 | a | | 49 | 67 |

Source: Borje Olsson, *Efter Tillberga*, report no. 14 (Stockholm: National Prison and Probation Administration, Research and Development Unit, September 1975), p. viii.

Note: Inspection shows the Tillberga released group to have a higher proportion of nonregistered persons for each follow-up period. The differences between the Tillberga released group and the comparison group are statistically significant (the differences are significant at the 5 percent, 2 percent, and 5 percent levels for three, six, and nine months respectively; chi-square test) for the three-, six-, and nine-month follow-up periods but not for the twelve-month period. The differences were due entirely to the performance of those who have had previous prison experience; there were virtually no differences in the rates for those who were "first-timers" in prison.

[a]Only seventeen persons were left in this group at the twelve months follow-up, so no percentage is given.

One of Sweden's recent efforts to improve probation was the establishment, in 1972, of the Stockholm Probation Treatment Center. The center is a social-medical organization with special resources for mentally disturbed clients or those with serious alcohol or drug abuse problems. The center's full-time staff of twenty-five includes a psychiatrist, two psychologists, two nurses, three social workers, a placement consultant, and a housemother, along with secretaries, administrative personnel, and house officer-attendants. Services include a hostel with a capacity of twelve; placement of clients in homes, therapeutic communities, "or collectives out in the country"; casework and psychological counseling including individual, group, and family therapy; and leisure activities for hostel guests during evenings and weekends. All staff share evening, overnight, and weekend work assignments and all participate in the treatment enterprise regardless of prison experience, professional training, or expertise.

Bengt Warren studied the experience of 336 clients who were registered with the Probation Treatment Center during its first year. The most notable findings are these.

> Within six months of being registered at the Center 85 persons have had improved housing. Among those with improved housing there has been a parallel improvement with regard to general social functioning, especially manifest as a decrease of drug or alcohol misuse and improved adjustment to work.

> Fifty-four persons who were unemployed on registration with the Center had proper work or began to study within six months. The improved work situation was accompanied by a marked decrease in intensity of drug or alcohol misuse.

> On registration with the Center, more than 75% of the clients misused alcohol and 42% used central nervous stimulants. The use of cannabis and other psychopharmacological drugs was also noted. A large proportion of the investigated population were multiple misusers. . . . Six months later . . . more than one-third of the population [showed] reduced intensity of misuse. . . . *[I]ncreased* intensity of misuse applied to only 2%. . . .

> Within a year after being registered at the Center one-fifth was sentenced to sanctions involving deprivation of liberty. Approximately one-fifth was sentenced to sanctions not involving deprivation of liberty (usually probation). The remainder, nearly three-fifths of the population, was not sentenced at all during the year after registration. Most of those sentenced were guilty of crimes against property.

> It was difficult to distinguish in a meaningful way the effect of the different measures. It seemed rather that a high frequency of contact was a more important factor than the specific treatment measure used.[85]

Other Research and Development Unit reports have dealt with patterns of drug use among prisoners, recidivism and criminality among persons sentenced to prison for drunken driving (25 percent "relapsed into a repetition of drunken driving" and 42 percent "relapsed into some form of crime sufficiently serious to warrant registration in the central criminal register"), a descriptive study of an experimental, modified therapeutic community in the prison at Gävle, an examination of the postrelease experiences and problems of a group of parolees placed under the supervision of a volunteer welfare society, and a study of the number and types of offenses committed by 192 inmates detained by the Stockholm police as escapees, misusers of leave, or crime suspects during a three-month period in 1976.[86]

These studies indicate a new interest by the National Prison and Probation Administration in evaluating both traditional and experimental penal measures.

## The National Council for Crime Prevention

A major development with important implications for penal policy and research in Sweden was the establishment, on July 1, 1973, of the National Council for Crime Prevention. The intent of the council is to coordinate, plan, and establish priorities for changes in criminal policy. Its tasks are

following and analyzing trends in crime and producing forecasts of such trends,

following, supporting and initiating research and development work on the causes and prevention of crime, as well as evaluating and disseminating the results of such work,

working to coordinate research and development projects in the field of criminal policy, assisting in the framing of criminal policy by means of investigatory studies and initiatives.[87]

Policy for the council is set by a board of sixteen persons who are appointed by the government and include representatives of all political parties represented in Parliament. Other members are the undersecretaries-of-state to the Ministries of Justice, Health and Social Affairs, and Education, members of the association of county councils and local authorities, the leaders of the two major labor confederations, a representative of the Swedish Employees Confederation, representatives of insurance companies, and criminological researchers.

The heads of five central administration agencies—the chief of Public Prosecution and the directors of the National Police Board, the National Prison and Probation Administration, the National Board of Health and Welfare, and the National Board of Education—constitute a special consultative group to the council.

Another group—the "Scientific Reference Group"—is composed of researchers from the fields of criminology, sociology, psychology, psychiatry, and law. The council has a Research and Development Division, whose responsibilities include the dissemination of research results to decision makers and politicians, improving the quality of crime statistics and crime indications (thereby enhancing the accuracy of crime trends), and the funding of research. Research and Development Division priorities are described as follows:

The NCCP functions partially as a research council, lending support, financially and otherwise, to criminological research. The Council may decide to provide special support to projects in areas it deems important by offering grants either to individual researchers or to official agencies within the judicial field. In the introductory phase, the Council's aim was to encourage research on general deterrence. Research on juvenile delinquency has always been a major focus. Recently, the Council decided to provide special assistance to research on economic crime.[88]

This division has already issued several research reports in English that will be of interest to American criminologists. One report contains abstracts of eleven Swedish studies covering statistical, sociological, psychological, and psychiatric aspects of juvenile delinquency. Summaries of the discussions and the papers presented at a council-sponsored International Conference on General Deterrence comprise a second 386-page volume.[89]

Another report by the council's Research and Development Division has been cited already—Eckart Kuhlhorn's preliminary evaluation of the noninstitutional treatment experiment at Sundsvall. Because the preliminary results indicate that the addition of substantial increments in the resources available to probationers and parolees seems to have little positive effect on their ability to deal with problems, Kuhlhorn goes on to consider the larger question of institutional versus noninstitutional treatment. In the course of that discussion he presents findings from a 1974 National Central Bureau of Statistics report on redicivism which included rates for imprisoned offenders and for offenders referred for noninstitutional treatment. These rates are broken down for first offenders and repeat offenders in table 3-3. Kuhlhorn cites a special council report by Gösta Carlsson and Orvar Olsson indicating that these recivivism rates remain the same for first offenders given probation and first offenders sentenced to one to four months of imprisonment even when the age of the offenders is taken into account and sentences for drunken driving are removed.[90] These data provide support for Kuhlhorn's argument that more offenders should be kept in the community under his "intensive supervision" plan.

The high rates reported in these studies will perhaps surprise and even dismay American penologists, for they imply that short-term confinement in Sweden's model prisons seem to have no more positive impact on recidivism than confinement in more traditional American prisons. We shall consider this matter further, but at this point additional research on the impact of institutional versus noninstitutional treatment of offenders should be described.

## Bondeson's Survey of Correctional Treatment Studies

What Douglas Lipton, Robert Martinson, and Judith Wilks have accomplished with their exhaustive review of evaluations of correctional treatment in the

Table 3-3
Recidivism during a Three-Year Period for Persons Sentenced to Serious Penalties

| Sentenced in 1968 to | First-time Offenders | | With Previous Convictions | | All Sentenced | |
|---|---|---|---|---|---|---|
| | N | Percentage Recid-ivists | N | Percentage Recid-ivists | N | Percentage Recid-ivists |
| Conditional sentence | 2,703 | 9 | 579 | 13 | 3,282 | 10 |
| Probation | 2,883 | 32 | 3,949 | 49 | 6,832 | 42 |
| Imprisonment 1–4 months | 2,499 | 13 | 3,463 | 46 | 5,962 | 32 |
| Imprisonment ≥5 months | 210 | 24 | 2,316 | 69 | 2,526 | 65 |
| Youth imprisonment | 12 | 50 | 295 | 83 | 307 | 82 |
| Internment imprisonment | – | – | 614 | 79 | 614 | 69 |
| Care in accordance with the Child Welfare Act | 478 | 47 | 316 | 72 | 794 | 57 |
| Other serious sentences | 156 | 13 | 554 | 40 | 710 | 34 |
| All serious sentences | 8,941 | 20 | 12,086 | 53 | 21,027 | 39 |

Source: Eckart Kulhorn, *Non-Institutional Treatment: A Preliminary Evaluation of the Sundsvall Experiment*, report no. 1 (Stockholm: National Swedish Council for Crime Prevention, April 1975), p. 53.

United States, Swedish sociologist Ulla Bondeson has done for the Scandinavian countries. Her report, "A Critical Survey of Correctional Treatment Studies in Scandinavia 1945-74," was prepared for the Criminal Deterrence and Offender Career Project directed by Ernest van den Haag and Robert Martinson.[91] Bondeson applied the same selection criteria utilized by Lipton, Martinson, and Wilks.[92] Eleven studies survived this screening for methodological adequacy, five undertaken in Denmark,[93] five in Sweden and one in Finland.[94] Three of the five Swedish studies were conducted by Bondeson, and they are significant in several respects. Bondeson is concerned less with measuring the impact of a particular treatment technique on an experimental group contrasted to a control or comparison group than with trying to measure the overall impact of imprisonment (or probation or other penal sanctions). In one study at a girls' training school, she related inmates' knowledge of criminal argot to the degree to which they endorsed criminal norms; she found that the length of time served in the training school was related positively to criminal socialization and that those with high scores on these measures were most likely to be recidivists. Bondeson concludes that confinement, even in a training school with good therapeutic resources, had detrimental effects on the inmates' postrelease adjustments.[95]

In a second study, released in 1974, Bondeson expanded her study of the impact of the socializing experience in institutional settings. She was able to obtain data from 96 percent of the inmates in training schools, youth prisons, prisons, and preventive detention facilities on a variety of measures related to criminal ideology, criminal identification, inmate solidarity, and the use of criminal argot. Her results indicate that confinement in all the institutional settings produced harmful results for inmates. Some began a dependence on drugs, and almost all experienced a sense of social isolation, monotony, defeatism, loss of autonomy, and stigmatization.[96] Few inmates felt that they were helped by psychological or medical treatment or by educational and vocational training programs. Bondeson concludes:

> the negative effects of confinement far outweigh the positive effects, and this is true for all types of institutions and for both sexes. All forms of negative influence increase with length of stay irrespective of type of institution.[97]

Bondeson's review of treatment evaluation studies includes a description of Börjeson's 1966 study that pointed up the negative consequences of institutional treatment when the experiences of matched samples were compared to non-imprisonment measures. A preliminary report from Bondeson's more recent study—a two-year follow-up of 450 persons sentenced to conditional sentences, probation, and probation preceded by one or two months of penal confinement—provides recidivism figures of 12 percent, 30 percent, and 61 percent respectively, findings consistent with those of Börjeson. These results indicate that the more dramatic interventions in offenders' lives do not produce better results in terms of reduced recidivism.[98] While several of the Danish studies covered in Bondeson's review of Scandinavian research suggest that certain treatment efforts may have a positive impact, there are no such results for Swedish correctional programs, and Ulla Bondeson thus comes to the conclusion that

> it thus seems that not only do the benign Swedish correctional institutions produce as few positive effects and almost as many negative effects as the more repressive American institutions, but that the treatment-oriented institutions (like the training schools) create as

much of a criminal subculture as the more custodially oriented prisons. This is true for both men and women; in fact the women seem to be more criminalized [within both] the training schools and prisons than the men.

One interpretation of these unexpected findings is that it is not the absolute level of deprivation that determines the emergence of inmate subcultures but the degree of *relative deprivation*. Because the pupils of the training schools are told they will be sent to a place where they will be given treatment and training, and then experience the fact that they get little help, they more easily perceive institutionalization as imprisonment, and their feelings of deception and bitterness grow the more stronger. Also, since the institutions are more open, and the contacts with the society more close, the contrasts between the institution and the society grow more blatant.

Another possible interpretation is that in a welfare state where the standard of living is high and dependable people are assisted by the state in the community, the sanction of depriving people of the good things of an affluent society and forcefully putting them aside may seem specially brutal both to those affected by the measure and to the public. Hence, the *labelling* effect would be expected to be especially strong.

Irrespective of the interpretations given, the results seem clear enough. Despite shorter terms of confinement, more open institutions, and more treatment resources given both during and after institutionalization, the Swedish correctional institutions seem to produce recidivism rates as high as the American.[99]

Bondeson's evaluations and those of other independent researchers along with the National Prison and Probation Administration's Research and Development Unit and Sweden's Crime Prevention Council studies all lead to the conclusion that even in the penologists' Valhalla, successful means have not been found to reduce crime by those who are brought into the so-called corrections system. These findings may lead Americans to ask whether Swedish penal policies and practices really have much to offer after all. The answer to that question, however, depends on agreement about the goals of prison systems. Reducing recidivism is only one goal, but before considering other goals the extent to which these negative findings are influencing penal policy in Sweden should be reviewed.

## Trends in Swedish Penal Policy: Deinstitutionalization and Decentralization

The Commission on Correctional Care, established in 1971, met with inmate representatives as promised by the minister of justice after the collapse of the prison democracy experiment. It presented its report to Parliament in 1972, and consideration of its recommendations began. During the spring of 1974 the Correctional Care in Institutions Act was approved with the new provisions going into effect July 1, 1974. This legislation represents some shifts in Swedish penal policy, and several provisions should be of interest to penologists in the United States. For example, the principle of interfering as little as possible with an offender was given strong endorsement. Stated another way, the commission acknowledged the failure of confinement in maximum-security prisons to bring about reduced criminal conduct. It also recognized the expense of maintaining prisoners in maximum security compared with the greater use of probation and local prisons for short-term confinement. The practical implications of this position are that as few offenders as possible should be imprisoned, and for those who are incarcerated, remedial efforts in the prison should be coordinated with the needs of the offender when he or she returns to the community. It was also agreed that efforts to help offenders and to modify their behavior should take place in small, local prisons close to the offender's home rather than in large, national prisons, and that the usual social services available to all citizens should also be available to offenders. The major changes in policy toward a greater emphasis on community treatment are as follows.

*Changes in Probation and Parole*

A 90 percent increase in the number of professional staff positions (from 400 to 760) was authorized to enhance probation and parole services. The additional personnel were intended to reduce the case loads of probation officers from about 100 to 30, enhance the quality of prehearing investigations, and "provide better assurances that the defendant's own views will be properly taken into account in the case studies."[100] Defendants awaiting court decisions on their cases were also to be offered treatment and social services if they were desired. The reduction of the probation supervision period to one year, in most cases, was intended to allow a greater concentration of services for offenders with drug or alcohol problems and more frequent contact, for control purposes, of probationers and parolees.

*Changes in Local Prisons*

The commission was of the opinion that it is unrealistic to expect offenders not to want to return to their homes and neighborhoods after their release from prison. It called for a new focus on positive aspects of the offender's home and community situation and giving assistance to offenders in dealing with problems in their families or home communities. By placing as many offenders as possible in the fifty-odd local prisons (equivalent to county jails and workhouses in the

United States), contacts with family and friends could be maintained, job placement may be facilitated, and probation and parole may be able to help the offender prepare for release and continue to assist when he or she arrives in the community. Since most local prisons are small, housing between twenty and sixty inmates, the commission hoped that inmates would receive more personal attention than they would likely get in the large national prisons which have capacities of several hundred inmates.

A building program to double the capacity of the local prisons was approved but is being reconsidered in the light of an overall decrease in the inmate population. Local prisons, then, are intended to house both prisoners sentenced to terms of less than one year and prisoners transferred from national prisons in the final stages of their sentences in order to prepare them for release into the local community.

An interesting feature of confinement in the local prisons involves the proposal to use local services for prisoners rather than employing special staff in the prisons.

> An important principle of the reform is that persons serving sentences should have the same right to society's arrangements for social support and care as do other members of society. The fact that the clients of the correctional system have committed crimes and have special difficulties in adjusting to society must not mean that the community's other organs for support and care disclaim responsibility for them. The logical consequence of this is that society's normal service organs should be utilized to the greatest extent possible to help the clientele of the correctional system. The local institutions should therefore not be self-sufficient in their treatment resources. Clients must as far as possible be enabled to participate in the same training, teaching, medical care, labor market, club activities, cultural activities, etc., as other citizens of society. During the prisoner's term in the institution this is made possible chiefly by the grant of town-pass, furlough, or other temporary absence from the institution.[101]

## Local Prisons: A Regional System

Under the Penal Care Act, by 1978 Sweden is to be divided into fourteen regions—a region corresponds to one or two counties—with each region having a remand prison or jail, a number of local prisons, and associated probation and parole offices.

## Changes in National Prisons

The National Prison and Probation Administration will continue to operate fifteen closed or maximum-security prisons and some half dozen open or minimum-security facilities. The closed prisons will receive offenders with sentences of more than one year, those who are considered to be dangerous and likely to attempt to escape, those who are said to need psychiatric treatment, and repeat offenders who are sentenced to indeterminate sentences as internment prisoners. The primary consideration in the national prisons is the protection of society "and the right of personnel to personal safety."[102] Local services for inmates in national prisons will be limited, and these facilities will, therefore, have to employ their own psychiatrists, psychologists, teachers, and other professionally trained personnel.[103] The national prisons classified as open are intended to house short-term offenders for whom space may not be available in local prisons. It is assumed that inmates in open prisons will require no special treatment resources.[104]

The new legislation provides greater opportunities for so-called town passes which permit inmates to work, go to school or job training, or participate in other activities outside the prison. This provision is intended primarily for inmates in local prisons, but the privileges may be granted for special reasons to inmates of national prisons.[105] Another feature of the legislation permits some prisoners to live outside the prison:

> As a preparation for release, prisoners can be given the opportunity of living outside the institution even before the earliest possible date for release. In special cases, for example, a prisoner can be placed for rehabilitation purposes in a school with a boarding establishment, a treatment home for drug addicts, a particularly suitable private home, or in military service.[106]

Other features of the act restrict examination of inmate correspondence or monitoring of inmate telephone calls to cases in which security reasons warrant them. Access to coin-operated telephones for inmates in both open and closed prisons was authorized.[107] The opportunity for inmates to negotiate with the administrations of the prisons in which they are confined was reaffirmed, provided that suitable forms of negotiation are employed. Changes related to prison discipline include the following:

> Solitary confinement is retained in the new law as a disciplinary measure, but the maximum duration of this punishment is reduced from thirty days to seven. Under the new law it is also possible to direct as a punishment that a certain specified time, at the most ten days, be not counted towards the working-out of the sentence the inmate is serving. More than one such direction may be given during an inmate's time in the institution, but the total time added in this way may not exceed 45 days, or 15 days in the case of persons serving prison sentences of at most four months or undergoing institutional care in combination with probation. When considering an inmate's release on parole or transfer to non-institutional care, misconduct which has

already resulted in disciplinary action shall not be specially considered, in contrast to earlier practice.[108]

In addition:

> Disciplinary measures will no longer include the removal of certain privileges such as access to reading material and the right to buy goods at the prison; instead a new measure, that of the disciplinary warning, will be introduced. It is envisaged that in many cases it will be sufficient to remind the recalcitrant prisoner of the advantages in the form of furloughs, visits, etc., which he can benefit from by a cooperative attitude. Furthermore it is stressed that the threat of transfer to a closed institution should be used with extreme caution, since this measure could easily be a way for the prisoner, and indeed the prison staff, of avoiding coming to terms with his problems through "flight."[109]

The use of isolation as punishment can be further restricted if Parliament enacts proposals advanced by former Minister of Justice Lennart Geijer:

> [S]egregation for purposes of investigation shall be abolished forthwith. Segregation requested by the inmate is to be left unchanged. Nor is any change proposed for segregation occasioned by consideration of national security or danger to life and limb or serious damage of prison property or detrimental influence over other inmates. Nor is any change of immediate character proposed, i.e., escape plans from a closed institution. [Another rule pertaining to discipline] should be modified so that it permits the temporary segregation of intoxicated persons, for example, on return from furlough. It would cease as soon as the inmate was no longer under the influence of alcohol or drug. [Rules pertaining to segregation], it is proposed, should be reworded so that it becomes more restrictive—that is, it shall not be used unless very good reasons can be given for supposing that an investigation would be impossible without it. The period would be reduced from the present 7 days to 4 days. The present terminology ("kept confined to a room ...") should be changed to read "segregated from other inmates" and, to emphasize still further that the segregation is to be no stricter than is required for the purposes of the investigation, a sub-para should be added to say that as far as conveniently possible easement of conditions shall be arranged.... The changes proposed would not permit the segregation of an inmate, for example, merely because he refuses to work; this is the case at present. ...
>
> [I]solation as a punishment is no longer necessary as a way of dealing with disciplinary problems in the prisons.[110]

Finally, to insure that prison and probation and parole staff understand the changes mandated by the act, a special course involving twenty hours of instruction was offered to all employees with additional in-service training to follow.

The Swedish Institute has issued several reports on the correctional care act and should be credited with issuing a review by William Borden that contains a number of caveats. Unfortunately the publication does not identify Borden in terms of his nationality, his position, or his qualifications. Borden's comments, it seems safe to assume, come from a respectable person in the eyes of the Swedish Institute, and thus his qualifications of various provisions of the act are worth noting.

In Borden's view, the act includes some "catch-all" sections that permit provisions to be restricted temporarily in order to "maintain order and security within the institution"; on the other hand, provisions may be relaxed in order to avoid harm to the inmate. The inmate's right to confer with prison officials does not mean that the officials are bound to do what the inmates ask and discussions may not be held if they violate "security regulations." Furthermore, use throughout the legislation of language such as "may," "ought," "to the extent suitable," "if there are not extraordinary reasons," and "if security requires" still allows the prison department substantial discretion in applying provisions of the act.[111]

Citing criticism of the correctional care act by KRUM and a number of inmate councils, Borden reminds his readers that implementation of liberal forms, as embodied in this legislation, depends on the inclinations of prison officials.

[T]he Act can be interpreted differently. First, it does not require cooperation with probation officers or with state organs—it only suggests that there ought to be such cooperation. Nor does the Act require that the inmates have a say in their treatment. Even if officials do decide to confer with inmates individually or collectively, they are under no obligation to take their views into consideration. The prisoners' councils have been mislabeled prisoners' democracies; prison officials make the decisions.

The Act provides no legal criteria to determine if a prisoner shall be warned or isolated for disciplinary infringements. Warning or isolation? Will the warden be too quick to isolate? While the seven day isolation rule applies to disciplinary punishment, it does not apply— for example—if an official determines that one inmate has a detrimental effect on another. And what constitutes a detrimental effect? Again, it's a matter of interpretation. A guard may also isolate an inmate in order to subdue his violent conduct. Will the warden isolate the man if he merely suspects that such conduct may take place? And what really is violent conduct? Does actual violence have to be threatened or attempted? . . . .

Should an inmate get an additional leave? Should he be eligible for a work-release program? Officials can also use their discretion in determining if the prisoner's benefits under the proposal are to be temporarily restricted for maintaining order and security. But then, how much order is necessary to maintain order? How temporary is temporary? How restrictive is restrictive? And what is absolutely necessary for prison security?

The real test of the Act will come after it has been put into practice.[112]

The proposed changes in Swedish penal policy could bring about a substantial increase in local community input, influence, and control over the corrections system. The number of persons to be housed in local prisons is estimated to be two thousand or approximately half of all the prisoners in the correctional system. Whether Swedish citizens and local community services will take on new responsibilities for helping offenders and whether efforts to reduce the isolation of the local prisons from the community will reduce the stigma of imprisonment are provocative questions about which there is still no empirical evidence.

A related development that bears watching will be the effort to bring lay citizens into the decision-making processes of various government bureaucracies from the national boards to the regional and local levels. It is proposed, for example, that the National Prison and Probation Administration, local prison superintendents, and regional prison directors make no major policy decisions without the concurrence of new boards which include lay citizens. Whether this citizen involvement will produce a conservative influence on penal policy remains to be seen.

To some extent these Swedish penal policy discussions involve the same issues being debated in the more enlightened state legislatures in America. Imprisonment in the United States has proved to be costly and ineffective in reducing recidivism; Minnesota and California have implemented probation or community corrections subsidy programs that provide incentives for counties to keep offenders in local facilities or on probation rather than send them to the state prisons. The deterrent effects of imprisonment may be effective for only certain categories of offenders, notably white-collar criminals and some property offenders, most of whom hardly need to be held in prisons like Attica or San Quentin. Given these conditions, long-term, maximum-custody imprisonment would be a last resort for only violent, persistent or mentally disabled offenders. But in Sweden, as in the United States, there is concern over rising crime rates, and vocal segments of populations in both countries complain about what they see as the trend towards "coddling" criminals. The directions that penal policy will take in the next decade in each of the fifty state systems and that of the federal government in the United States will surely not be the same. As for Sweden, the defeat in 1976 of the Social Democrats, after forty-four years as the ruling political force, led to the replacement of Minister of Justice Lennart Geijer who was so much involved in efforts to bring about fundamental shifts in penal policy. The direction of the new Swedish government, according to most analysts, will be along the same lines

developed by the Social Democrats. If such is the case, for the great majority
of Swedish offenders the penal sanctions will consist of fines, conditional sentences, and probation, including intensive probation supervision. These developments will be in line with Geijer's contention that the only justification for
imprisoning someone is the protection of other persons. Geijer's views are set
forth at some length here because they should be seriously considered by those
who may be under the impression that if prison conditions in the United States
can be elevated to the levels achieved in Sweden, the damaging effects of imprisonment can be negated:

DEPRIVATION OF LIBERTY (imprisonment) was once seen as an
alternative to physical punishment for serious violations of the law.
During the middle of the 19th Century, physical isolation (the cell
system) came to be regarded as one answer to the problem.

It was believed that the offender would be purged in his cell: by simply
being there and mulling over his situation he would see the error of his
ways and leave prison as a better person.

We have now officially abandoned the idea of revenge. And yet, despite
every reform, and no matter what is written in the penal code, revenge
is what we practise. However much we talk about and work with
criminal care, imprisonment is revenge. . . .

My firm opinion—and it becomes all the more unshakable the longer I
study this problem—is that protection of others is the only argument
that can be offered in defense of incarcerating a person in any kind of
prison. One can define "protection" in different ways. But the estimated number of persons from whom the public might need to be protected does not exceed 10-15 percent of those in prisons today.

Some people must be taken care of for our own safety: habitual criminals or participants in organized crime, drug-pushers, perpetrators of
heinous crimes of violence, etc.

During this century the prison system has been increasingly criticized
by lawyers, sociologists, social workers, doctors and laymen with
experience of the prison system. The damaging effects have been
brought to light. By 'damaging' is meant not merely the harm done to
the persons being sanctioned—but also to their families. Wives and
children of prisoners often find themselves in a difficult social and
psychological situation. And not only that: society as a whole is
harmed in the sense that imprisonment lays the groundwork for recidivism and antisocial attitudes. Furthermore, prisons are "bad business" for society. Prisons cost a lot and give a "negative dividend". . . .

There is a tendency in developed societies to put people who do not fit
into the highly effective environment out of sight. The aged, the mentally ill and the handicapped are dumped into institutions. Those of us
who are healthy, industrious and efficient do not want to see them in
our midst. We deal in the same manner with violators of the law; they

are sent to prison. They too are often recruited from those groups of individuals who cannot cope with the competitive society's tough terms. So it is, even though we know today that such isolation is injurious and that we *all* need human contact with other groups. If we allow ourselves to think that everything is fine when we push unpleasant persons out of our sight and into institutions, we are making things easy for ourselves.

"But surely they must atone for their crimes," an old man said, who stopped me on the street to talk about crime in society. This opinion is widespread, crossing the boundaries of political conviction. . . . Flogging is still recommended in some of the anonymous letters I get.

I think that very few people hold this opinion. The very fact that people make these suggestions anonymously indicates that they know full well that such thoughts are not respected by people in general. A significantly larger number believe that prison punishment is too "soft." Prisoners, they think, are "spoiled." They have free food and lodging, television, furloughs; "love rooms" have even been arranged in prisons. Here is a criticism that must be taken more seriously. Since deprival of freedom—imprisonment—is punishment, a way of "getting even," it seems inconsistent to them that the punishment is sweetened by the addition of all kinds of good things, to the point where the difference between life inside and outside prison becomes minimal.

Let's look at what has occurred. The reform work within the prison system during this century has been carried forward by liberal thinking about humaneness and the idea that prisoners can be "treated"—as sick persons are treated in hospitals—and get "well," in the sense that afterwards they will not return to crime. The Swedish prisons of today differ appreciably from those of the 1800s. . . . Today it costs on the average 250 Swedish crowns ($56) a day to keep a person in prison. The prisoner is often in better physicial condition when he leaves prison. During the 1800s many prisoners died of different illnesses. Many took their own lives.

In spite of all the reforms, the results have not been impressive. There are too many recidivists. In Sweden 50 percent of the people in prison have been imprisoned at least once before. Twenty percent have served two or more sentences. . . .

The fact is that the psychological effects of imprisonment still remain. Some people adapt thoroughly to prison life and can't manage when they get out. Contact with other offenders strengthens their antisocial attitudes and nurtures their hatred of society.

I do not mean that it is wrong to "humanize" the stay in prison—but a cage is still a cage, even if gold-plated. In the long run we are not behaving responsibly toward our fellow citizens, either, by having a system that yields such poor returns on the investment. If a private company were run in this manner, it would soon be forced into bankruptcy. . . .

All reforms in dealing with prisoners contain a built-in contradiction. First, a person is deprived of his freedom, as *punishment* for having broken the law. Afterwards, one tries to do the utmost to make his punishment as bearable as possible. In this way the "punishment" is hollowed out to such an extent that the prison society does not differ from the rest of society except in the context of the deprival of freedom. We have blundered into a dead-end street.

In the administration of justice we have failed to find methods that truly come to grips with criminality. We plod along in old, well-worn paths and often base our procedures on antiquated patterns of thought. In any event, criminality has not been affected by the use of prison punishment.[113]

The studies by Ulla Bondeson have raised doubts about the ability of any prison system, no matter how humane, to reduce significantly the negative aspects of imprisonment. The studies by Eckart Kuhlhorn and several of those undertaken under the direction of Norman Bishop have raised doubts about the possibility that even greatly enhanced programs and services for probation can significantly reduce recidivism rates for that group. While recent Swedish experience indicates that improved prison and probation services have not produced markedly better results, there is no evidence that either the crime rate or the recidivism rate has been made worse by these efforts.[114]

Before directly addressing the question what Sweden's efforts have to do with the development of penal policy in the United States, one other complicating factor must be noted. This development will test Swedish ingenuity, not only in the area of correctional treatment, but more important, in the areas of deterrence and incapacitation.

### International Criminality and Swedish Penal Policy

Swedish citizens in the 1970s have experienced several political assassinations: the murder of the Yugoslavian ambassador by Yugoslavian dissidents and the murder of two West German diplomats in their embassy by persons alleged to be members of the Bader-Meinhof group. In 1974 another group of Yugoslavians hijacked an SAS plane in Sweden, demanded (and received) $125,000, and forced the release from prison of their comrades who had been convicted of killing the ambassador. On another occasion a revolutionary group outside Sweden was reputed to be prepared to take as hostage one or more members of Parliament in order to force the release from prison of a member of their group, leading to heavy police protection for government officials. In 1977 Swedish police arrested seventeen persons, identified as members of the June 2nd Movement, who planned to abduct former immigration minister Anna-Greta Leijon because she had ordered the extradition of the five terrorists who had occupied the West German embassy. Other events included an attempted prison break with armed prisoners holding guards as hostages and a bank robbery committed by professionals who flew in from another country. Along with the Swedes, people in other Western European countries watched on television in 1973 as several bank robbers were caught up in a six-day siege in a Stockholm bank. The women bank employees held hostage by the robbers spoke fondly of their captors, and one of them later visited in prison the leading figure in the drama, a young man named Clark Olofsson.

Olofsson's exploits have made him a kind of folk hero in Sweden. After spending his teenage years in and out of youth prisons (he ran away six times), Olofsson was sentenced to adult prison for his involvement in a holdup during which a policeman was killed. He has since broken out of prison five times. When he was in prison, he wrote for the prison newspaper and became a national television personality as a result of his participation in panel discussions on prison reform. During one period when he was in prison, he met a social worker who fell in love with him. This young woman then wrote a series of articles admitting that Olofsson had committed robberies but arguing that society was to blame for his actions. After being returned to prison following the bank siege, Olofsson received numerous marriage proposals. He selected one young woman and married her in the prison chapel with the judge who sentenced him performing the ceremony and the chief detective who prosecuted him serving as best man. (This action prompted one citizen to bring to the ombudsman a complaint of improper conduct against the judge and the detective. The ombusman ruled that the two had not acted illegally but had used poor judgment.) An Associated Press release about Sweden's "Flamboyant Badman" contends that Olofsson has become a media hero because there is "a deep yearning for a little disorder in affluent and law-abiding Sweden."[115]

But Clark Olofsson is not the only professional criminal and escape artist in Swedish prisons. The closed prison at Kumla is Sweden's most secure institution. In 1975, in a special unit in Kumla, six inmates under the supervision of five guards succeeded in overpowering three of the guards when the other two left to get a food cart. The inmates destroyed the unit and then, holding knives against the guards, made their way to the prison gate and ordered it open. The gate was opened, but guards standing nearby moved quickly and subdued the inmates. Four of the inmates were then transferred to Hall Prison, the maximum-security institution for internment (repeat) offenders. These same inmates then succeeded in having a gun smuggled into that prison. Once again they took several guards hostage, and this time successfully escaped over the prison wall.

The growth of international criminality in Sweden, particularly that related to increased drug traffic and alcohol and cigarette smuggling, has been attributed by one police official to "specific Swedish circumstances." These include milder penal sanctions than offenders are likely to receive in other countries, according to Esbjörn Esbjörnsson:

> International gangs have realized that for many reasons Sweden is a profitable market for organized crime. It is, of course, impossible to make a quantitative assessment, but without a doubt one would venture to suggest that Sweden today is the object of an extensive "new" international criminality, particularly in relation to the size of the country. (In truth, it must be admitted that our own professional criminals can possibly be held responsible for a certain reciprocal activity in foreign countries.)
>
> There are a number of different reasons for this development in Sweden during the last few years. It is due, on the one hand, to the generally improved travel facilities throughout the world. On the other, the development depends on specific Swedish circumstances. Here, the growth and extent of narcotic abuse, together with the prices paid, which are high even by international standards, are the major incentives. The escalation in price for central nervous stimulants on the road from Italy to Sweden is a striking example. The price of cannabis in Sweden has been high compared with other countries for a considerable period. At present, the price in Stockholm is double that in Copenhagen, London, and Paris. In addition, the illegal traffic in narcotics leads to other types of organized criminality. The profits from narcotics dealings are often invested in other profitable criminal operations. The suggestion that Swedes are naturally trusting, whether true or not, may have played its part, as well as the knowledge that Sweden has not previously been involved in the more subtle forms of international criminality. The standard of living in Sweden is probably another contributory factor. Yet others include the absence of passport control within the Nordic countries and the slight protective measures employed by banks and other establishments handling money, hitherto. Finally, it is common knowledge among more sophisticated criminals abroad that the Swedish practice of punishment is often less severe than on the Continent. It is also known that the penal system provides a good chance of being released on probation. Additionally, it is well known that if an unqualified sentence involving loss of freedom is imposed, there is a good chance of finding ways to serve only a limited part of the sentence. It is clearly established, for instance, that German criminals are well informed of the system of leave used in Swedish prisons, as well as of the possibilities of being placed in open custody in Sweden. It is thought that in criminal circles the circumstances described above are deliberately put on the scales when judging the risk of planning crimes to be committed in Sweden.[116]

The increase in the number of international criminals who use a variety of deadly weapons, special automobiles, and jet planes to rob banks, transport drugs, and secure the release of comrades who have been captured, has raised serious security and management problems for the National Prison and Probation Administration. Concurrently Swedish prison guards have been complaining about what they regard as an increase in violence or at least threat of violence. This problem is exacerbated in the guards' view by the new limits placed on the use of segregation and isolation as punishment within the prisons.

The guards' union has proposed that the current staff complement be doubled, and a new national commission has been appointed to study the problems of the guards and disciplinary problems in general. The Swedish press, according to prison officials, criticizes guards for searching visitors and examining the mail of certain prisoners to detect for drugs, while at the same time the department is censured for the increased use of drugs, including heroin, in the prisons. A serious problem that has come with more open visiting policies in Swedish prisons is that some inmates have begun drug use in prison, and others traffic in drugs from within prisons. Prison terms for selling hard narcotics have been increased, and the inmates who took hostages were given additional three-year sentences. New special security units for high-escape-risk inmates have been constructed at the prisons at Kumla and Norrköping. At Norrköping, where Clark Olofsson has been confined, the security unit holds six inmates who are permitted no contact with other prisoners, and three guards must be present when any inmate in this unit leaves his cell.

Another issue related to housing prisoners from foreign countries is the communications problem that is posed for inmates and staff. At Kumla Prison, with a population of under two hundred inmates, many of whom are serving time for drug trafficking, there were, in the fall of 1976, inmates representing thirty-two nationalities not including the Danish, Finnish, Norwegian, and Swedish prisoners. Of the 9,901 persons admitted to correctional institutions in 1976, 1,939 were foreigners.[117] The largest contingent of foreign prisoners came from Finland, followed by Denmark and Yugoslavia.

To some extent the response of the National Prison and Probation Administration to these problems has been what would be expected in the American penal system—special maximum-custody units for foreign drug dealers, terrorists, and Clark Olofsson. But even in this difficult management area, Sweden's inclination to try something different has not been completely suppressed. For example, the half-dozen inmates in Norrköping Prison's special section for escape risks are not permitted to leave the prison on home furloughs. But as a compensation they may have frequent, even daily, private visits from family members or girl friends. The prisoner's visitors are searched for drugs, but once they are within the special unit they may have their meals with the inmate and may spend the day with him. The prison administrator's position is that having "tough" units can make it easier for other prisoners, and those kept securely within the tough units should not be punished further but rather should have some compensatory privileges.

While new directions in penal practice such as these may seem impossible to American prison administrators, Sweden's prisons house a growing number of offenders who, in some respects, pose more sophisticated security and control problems than inmates in American prisons. But whether the penal policy issue involves the use of volunteer parole officers, special intensive probation supervision, shorter prison sentences, private visiting facilities, home furloughs, the establishment of a justice ombudsman, a prisoners' union, or daily private visiting for escape artists in maximum-custody units, the question for this essay is the extent to which Sweden's prison and parole practices are likely to serve as realistic examples for American corrections officials.

### Can Sweden Point a "Middle Way" to Penal Reform in America?

Some features of Swedish correctional policy and practice described in the preceding pages would be adopted quickly if American prison administrators were permitted to implement them. There is little disagreement that prison management problems would be eased if prisons housed no more than two or three hundred inmates, if prison administrators had as many staff as there are prisoners, if disparities in sentences were greatly reduced, and if many different types of prison facilities were available to house different types of inmates. Some prison administrators in this country would also applaud the establishment of a unified prison, jail, and community corrections department for each state. A few might even agree that seeking a more even distribution of persons from all social classes in our jails and prisons (through mandatory confinement of all drunken drivers and more extensive use of prisons for white-collar criminals) would help to arouse and sustain the interest of the media, the politicians, and the general public in prison conditions. The involvement of thousands of citizens as volunteer parole supervisors and intensive supervision as a new means of controlling the conduct of probationers might also be well received by corrections officials (although probation officers would perhaps oppose the latter proposal).

A much smaller number of American corrections administrators would approve of in-prison private visiting quarters for inmates, home furloughs, full-market wages, a justice ombudsman, a prisoners' union, or restrictions on the use of segregation and isolation as punishment in prison. Almost all those who might be willing to consider these changes can be expected to argue that even trial efforts in these areas cannot be made because the public, the legislature, the governor, the press, and the guards' union would never agree to them. In describing the Swedish penal system as a possible model for American correctional departments, one must recognize that it makes a difference whether the proposal is to have small prisons with large staffs, or holiday prisons or conjugal visiting. On the other hand, this distinction may not be very important because even the basic organizational features of the Swedish prison system which pertain to the size of prisons and number of staff are not likely to be

adopted in the United States. Focusing on the features of Swedish penal practice that seem frivolous or politically impossible, however, permits American
corrections officials to reject all the elements of Swedish corrections as unrealistic. In fact, most corrections commissioners in this country have no more
chance of convincing their state legislatures to appropriate enough money to
increase staff-inmate ratios in their prisons substantially than of gaining approval
for a conjugal visiting program. The most significant change in the past decade
in American penal practice is the development of the movement toward community corrections. The basis for this development, which includes diversion
programs, probation subsidies, and so-called deinstitutionalization efforts,
however, is not justice, humane treatment, or rehabilitation, but economics.
Legislators have been convinced that keeping offenders in community facilities
and programs is cheaper than putting them in state prisons. In America the
primary concern has not been how to spend more money in the corrections
field but how to spend less. Changes in penal practices in American prisons and
jails reflect our ranking of economic, social, and political priorities, and prisons
and jails always rank near the bottom.[118]

## Prison Systems as Part of Larger Social, Economic, and Political Systems

American penologists who visit more than two or three prisons in Sweden
know that the prison system of the country does not stand out as any more
innovative or progressive than other human service delivery systems. Sweden's
health, education, social welfare, housing, and transportation systems could
stand as models for this country as clearly as the prison system does. All Swedish citizens receive "cradle-to-grave" health care services, public education from
nursery to university, inexpensive, fast, efficient, comfortable mass transportation, a minimum of four weeks vacation, and some additional services, most
of which have yet to be proposed in the United States:

> Children in nursery school are given free breakfasts and lunches; old
> people and students enjoy 50 percent discounts on state railways;
> parents get tax-free payments of about $6 a day for six months when a
> child is born in addition to a tax-free "child allowance," of about $30
> a month. Writers get royalties each time someone takes their books out
> of libraries. Medical care is free, and some funerals are subsidized.[119]

The same article describes the Swedish government's plan for a new, national pension plan to make retirement more comfortable. The plan would lower
the pension age from sixty-seven to sixty-five but provides for flexibility that
allows workers to postpone retirement until age seventy if they wish or to

advance their pensions to begin at age sixty. In addition, part-time employment may be combined with partial pensions until workers themselves decide to retire. The attitude of the government was expressed by Kenneth Grathall, legal advisor of the Ministry of Social Affairs:

> A sudden switch from working life to full retirement can be detrimental to many workers—it can harm them mentally. We want to give people the chance to adjust. . . .

> It was unions, supported by doctors and psychologists, who said it would be better if people went into retirement slowly. We found that people who worked many years and then retired didn't know what to do with their lives. They missed the social contacts, the friends, at work.

> They found themselves unproductive after years of productivity. It was the government's obligation to change policy and help these people.[120]

Another new government program called parental insurance is intended to encourage fathers to participate on a more equal basis with mothers in the business of raising and caring for children. Swedish women's rights advocates had argued that sharing the burden of raising children was an integral part of sexual equality. Others had argued, from a more traditional perspective, that more direct participation in child rearing would help strengthen the family and make the world of children a world less dominated by women. The essential features of this interesting social experiment have been described as follows:

> The program . . . is essentially an extension of the scheme under which working mothers are given generous maternity-leave allowances to remain with their infants during the period immediately after birth. As the innovation now operates, mothers stay with their babies for the first four months, and then the father can take over for an additional three months while his wife goes back to her job. During this time, mother and father receive 90 percent of their regular salaries, which is what they would get if there were out sick.

> The parents are allowed to divide up the total seven-month span as they wish, and there is no requirement that either or both must use the entire period. However, the two may not be absent from work simultaneously and draw allowances.

> The scheme, which is known as "parental insurance," also permits either mother or father to take turns caring for ill children under the age of 10. In this case, too, the parent is guaranteed 90 percent of his or her regular income.

> During its first year, official statistics show, about 1,000 fathers took advantage of the program. By last year the number had risen to nearly 5,000—roughly 10 percent of those who were eligible. Eligibility is automatic, of course, with the birth of a child.[121]

The price Swedish citizens pay for all the services provided by their government is, of course, reflected in the taxes they pay. While per capita income is higher in Sweden ($8,308) than in America ($7,013),[122] taxes in Sweden can range up to 85 percent of income, and even those in the $20,000 per year range can expect to give up half that amount to taxes. An article in the *National Observer,* which contends that Swedish socialism has made its citizens "the world's richest people," reports that

> the typical Swedish worker is expected to earn about $12,500 this year [1976]; close to $5,000 of that will go to taxes . . . on top of that, he pays a hidden sales tax—called a value-added tax—of 17.65 per cent on everything he buys.[123]

By exercising controls over private business and industry, Sweden has largely succeeded in eliminating the kind of poverty found in many parts of the United States. This fundamental step, along with considerable success in maintaining close to full employment, has come from the efforts by the Social Democrats and other political parties to raise the wages of workers while heavily taxing middle- and upper-income groups. With the reduction of poverty and subsistence living and the provision of education opportunities, health care services and low-cost housing for the entire population, the slums that characterize American cities have disappeared throughout Sweden. A final accomplishment of the Social Democratic Party before its narrow defeat in the 1976 elections was the approval by the Parliament of legislation giving workers a veto on corporate decisions on all levels. This law also requires employers to secure workers' agreements to important changes such as the sale of a business, staff transfers, and changes in production and organization.

All this is not to say that Swedish citizens, like Swedish prisoners compared with their counterparts in American prisons, are happy or satisfied. For example, despite continued rapid economic growth and increased affluence, Swedish workers have advanced a plan calling for the annual transfer to workers' funds of 20 percent of the profits of all Swedish companies with fifty or more employees. These funds would in turn be used to purchase newly issued stocks "and thus Swedish labor, according to some estimates, would gain control of industry within ten to fifteen years."[124] From the perspective of Swedish and American corporate interests, this proposal would appear impossible, in contrast to other plans such as easing retirement and helping fathers participate more actively in raising children.

American newspapers and news magazines, perhaps reflecting interests made uneasy by aspects of Swedish life such as socialized medicine, governmental operation of mass transportation, and providing workers with the right to participate in corporate decision making, not to mention worker control of industry, periodically present articles built around the trouble-in-paradise theme. The standard argument as presented in a *Forbes* magazine article, for example, is that "Sweden has a fine industrial system, almost full employment, no slums, no poverty—but the middle classes are getting tired of paying the price."[125] As American businessmen seem to take relief in the complaints they hear from the middle class, visiting American corrections officials, and some academic criminologists seem at first surprised and then relieved to hear Swedish prison reformers complain about their oppressive prison system. These complaints help the businessmen, the legislators, and the corrections administrators reject the Swedish models for health care, welfare, or prison systems. Furthermore, the features of Swedish social programs considered by Americans are not seen as part of larger efforts to reduce income differentials between socioeconomic groups and to raise the level of opportunities, the quality of human services systems, and physical living conditions to levels enjoyed by middle-class citizens. Experiments in American corrections departments—such as ombudsman offices, increased family visiting, furloughs, higher wages for prison labor, and prisoners' unions—are not implemented as part of a more fundamental effort to change the social, economic, and political forces that produce from the poor and the disadvantaged America's prison population.

A country that cannot guarantee adequate health care, even for its law-abiding citizens, or achieve tax reforms, despite the widely publicized gross inequities of the tax laws that plague middle-class citizens, is hardly likely to undertake fundamental reforms of its prison systems. An important point, a political point, is that the basic needs of all Swedish citizens for a minimum income, job security, satisfactory health care, educational opportunities, adequate housing, good public transportation, and other social services have been met. In their examination of European social services Alfred Kahn and Sheila Kamerman describe day-care centers for young children, assistance for people at home, and housing for the elderly in Sweden—services that are available to all citizens, not just the poor. They point out that the American government provides many benefits for the rich (mortgage guarantees, real estate loans, interest deductions, business-expense deductions, agricultural subsidies, tax shelters, and a myriad of loopholes in the tax laws) and some benefits for the poor (unemployment compensation, aid to dependent children, welfare payments, social security benefits) but fails to recognize the need for social services and benefits by average people under ordinary circumstances:

> Our cultural and political traditions say—or are believed by some people to say—that governmental activity in this sphere is probably counterproductive: government interferes, creates dependency, distorts preferences, perhaps inhibits freedom. We Americans are willing to let government act in specific ways for those already "deviant," "dependent," or "failures." Under these latter circumstances, programs are meant to use controls and serve as instruments of desirable change. To create programs for other people, for people not in trouble, is to ensure dependence.

In some European countries people respond to social developments on another premise. At least they seem to want government to do more for individuals in some categories and for families—and apparently have fewer cultural and ideological inhibitions. Some of them say that communal "solidarity" requires some programs, that individuals have a right to expect responsible citizenship and tax payment. The result seems to be less-inhibited social innovation or experimentation in program forms in the social services. Since programs are designed for the typical citizen, for any citizen, not just for the dependent and the cast-offs, programs can be of good quality and need not be demeaning.[126]

Meeting the basic needs of average citizens seems to be a necessary prerequisite in order to reduce the resentment and opposition that come from providing special supportive services to the poor, the disadvantaged, and, particularly, those whose actions are defined as criminal and delinquent.[127]

Another major difference between the United States and Sweden that must be taken into account in comparisons of the social institutions of the two countries is the size and makeup of their populations. Some 8 million Swedish citizens reside in an area the size of the state of California. They are all white, and they share a common cultural heritage. The size and historical development of the United States is different, and American social, economic, and political problems are more complicated. Many social problems in America reflect the mix and clash of diverse racial and ethnic groups—a conflict that has a history of several hundred years. In discussions of crime problems in Sweden, however, allegations are heard that the Finns and the "Southern Europeans" contribute a disproportionate share to the crime problem. We have already noted that many inmates of Swedish prisons are foreign nationals.

Open conflicts between young Swedish "roughs" and Assyrian immigrants living in Stockholm occurred several times in 1977, and gypsy families from Russia and Czechoslovakia were threatened in Malmö. An increase in unemployment has been given as one reason for this development; another reason is that Sweden's 750,000 immigrants have resisted efforts to spread them throughout the population and are beginning to form ghettos. But another reason advanced by a white foreigner living in Sweden is that Swedes are uncomfortable with anyone who is not one of them:

It's a kind of xenophobia. The Finns are just as blonde as the Swedes, but the Finnish immigrants here are treated with considerable contempt. Skin color enters into it when you're talking about blacks and Turks, but the truth is if you're not Swedish you just don't quite fit, blue eyes or not.[128]

Racism is a new problem for a country that has emphasized, as the United States has, equality among all its citizens. Sweden's opportunities for experience in this area of human relations have been limited in the past, so limited that

there is no agency to hear civil rights complaints. But the nuances of ethno-
centrism in Sweden and the new problematic relationship between Swedes and
outsiders do not rest on the history of violence, oppression, and discrimination
that characterizes relations between blacks, Indians, Chicanos, and whites in the
United States. Certainly most American prison officials, guards, and inmates
would contend that their problems would be reduced dramatically if everyone in
their prisons, including all the staff, were from the same racial or ethnic group.
Racial conflict underlies so much of the crime problem in the United States and,
consequently, so many of the problems in the prisons that comparisons between
Sweden and the United States as a whole are not very meaningful. When we add,
in addition to differences between size and heterogeniety of populations, the
distinction between Sweden's welfare capitalism and America's relatively uncon-
trolled corporate capitalism, comparisons between the two counties are even
more strained.

More meaningful comparisons can be made between Sweden and a handful
of states, notably Wisconsin and Minnesota. The populations of these states
are almost entirely white (Minnesota is 98.2 percent white; Wisconsin 96.6
percent).[129] The Minnesota and Wisconsin legislatures allocate larger proportions
of resources to social services than do most other states.[130] Their unemployment
rates are lower compared with most states, educational levels are higher, illit-
eracy rates are lower, the percentage of persons below the poverty line is lower,
and Minnesota and Wisconsin have reputations for clean governments and
enlightened public officials. And, of course, large segments of the populations
of these two states are of Scandinavian origin. Both states are noted for their
highly professional departments of corrections and their innovations in correctional practice. In Minnesota, for example, a program to provide subsidies has
been implemented to encourage counties to keep their offenders in local communities and out of the state prison. Minnesota is forty-ninth among the fifty
states in the number of persons sentenced to prison per 100,000 population.
(The number of prisoners per 100,000 is 35.1 in Minnesota and 56.4 in Wisconsin, as compared to California's rate of 105.6, Georgia's 191.4, New York's
78.5, and the U.S. average of 103.6). Jail figures are similarly low—27.6 per
100,000 in Minnesota and 39.0 in Wisconsin, compared with 124.2 in California,
131.9 in Georgia, and the U.S. average of 68 per 100,000.[131] Minnesota is about
to tear down its old maximum-security prison, which houses some one thousand
inmates, and replace it with two smaller facilities with staff-inmate ratios of
1.5 to 1.

Criminal justice officials in Minnesota have shown considerable interest in
Swedish correctional policies and practices, and some changes along lines developed in Sweden have been attempted. Private visiting has begun for minimum-
custody inmates at the state prison; telephones have been installed in the cell
houses from which inmates may make unmonitored calls; and 7 percent of the
state's inmates are in new work programs paying wages of up to $4.62 per hour,

with the inmates responsible for paying room and board charges and state and federal taxes. Inmates in this program also earn sick leave, vacation time, and bonuses when the shop meets production goals. An example of American adaption of a Swedish innovation is Minnesota's corrections ombudsman. A justice ombudsman for all citizens would not be tolerated by the state's law enforcement agencies who do not wish to allow civilian review of their actions. Establishment of the corrections ombudsman is a step in the direction of dealing with inmate complaints of injustice, but the office has been kept sufficiently weak that a direct confrontation with the authority of corrections officials is avoided. The corrections ombudsman does not have subpoena power and does not have the authority to bring charges against prison staff or department of corrections officials who do not correct actions by their staff found to be improper. The ombudsman's investigative jurisdiction includes only the state prisons, not local or county jails, workhouses, or detection facilities. Nevertheless the principle of outside investigation of inmate complaints has been established. It is possible, therefore, in a state such as Minnesota to try out selected Swedish correctional innovations. But Minnesota and, to some extent, Wisconsin are seen by most of the other states as being as dissimilar to them as Sweden is. In addition, Minnesota and Wisconsin, compared to other states, have relatively little crime. (The rate of reported violent crimes per 100,000 population is 207 in Minnesota and 151.8 in Wisconsin, compared with rates of 665.4 in California, 459 in Georgia, 856.4 in New York, 549.7 in Illinois, and 481.5 in the United States as a whole. The rate of reported property crimes per 100,000 population is approximately 4,100 in Minnesota, 3,800 in Wisconsin, 6,500 in California, 4,800 in New York, and 4,800 in the United States as a whole.[132]) When citizen fear and concern about crime are not as great as they are in most major American cities, proposals can be advanced that more be done for, rather than to, offenders. It is easier to talk about prison reforms in relatively crime-free Minnesota and Wisconsin than it is in New York City, Atlanta, or Detroit.

States such as New York, Ohio, Illinois, Michigan, and California with large racially diverse populations, high unemployment, and severe economic problems are so far from achieving the economic, social, and political reforms that produced all of the Swedish human service delivery systems, including the corrections system, that consideration of the Swedish model of anything is fantasy. These states have too much work to do to meet the basic needs of their law-abiding citizens before they are likely to turn to efforts to bring about any significant improvements for their citizens who are in jail and prison. For one or two all-white, affluent states in the upper midwestern United States with a strong Scandinavian heritage, Sweden has provided examples of innovations in penal policy and practice which have been and may be adapted, not adopted, in those states. No more than these token changes should be expected. As long as prison reform in the United States is seen as an order of business separate from social, economic, and political reforms, the Swedish model of a corrections system will be unrealistic. For the great majority of American states, Sweden's middle way to prison reform is too radical to be permitted in the near future.

**Notes**

1. Hero Buss, "In for Repairs," *Sweden Now,* Swedish Information Service, March 1970, pp. 35, 38. (translated by Donald Henry).

2. Ibid.

3. Ruth Link, "Where Prisoners Are People," *Sweden Now,* Swedish Information Service, 1973, p. 36.

4. Link states "the Swedish authorities are in some respects more radical than KRUM which has shown a disappointing lack of interest in what happens to prisoners *after* (or instead of) imprisonment, and concentrating on criticizing conditions and pressing for great personal integrity and freedom *inside* various prisons" (p. 41).

5. Svante Nycander, ed., "Criminal Welfare," *The Swedish Dialogue* (Stockholm: Swedish Institute, 1973), p. 14.

6. "Sweet Revolutionary," *Svenska Dagbladet,* August 27, 1972, in *The Swedish Dialogue,* pp. 15-16.

7. "A Prison in Sweden Is More Like a Hotel," *New York Times,* October 15, 1971. Copyright © 1971 by the New York Times Company. Reprinted by permission.

8. Paul Britten Austin, *The Swedes* (New York: Praeger, 1970), p. 49.

9. Michael Durham, "For the Swedes a Prison Sentence Can Be Fun Time," *Smithsonian* 4 (September 1973):46.

10. "Swedish Prisons," *Outlaw,* November, 1973.

11. Ibid.

12. Ibid.

13. George E. Berkley, Michael W. Giles, Jerry F. Hackett, and Norman C. Kasoff, *Introduction to Criminal Justice* (Boston: Holbrook Press, 1976), p. 501.

14. Peter E. Burke, "Prison Reform in Sweden," in Walter C. Reckless, ed., *The Crime Problem,* 5th ed. (Pacific Palisades, Ca.: Goodyear Publishing Co., 1973), p. 532.

15. John Conrad, *Crime and Its Correction: An International Survey of Attitudes and Practices* (Berkeley and Los Angeles: University of California Press, 1965), pp. 120-136, 249-256.

16. Louis Bultena, *Deviant Behavior in Sweden* (New York: Exposition Press, 1971), p. 59. Reprinted with persmission.

17. Ibid., p. 71.

18. Ibid., p. 69.

19. Harvey H. Siegel, "Criminal Justice—Swedish Style: A Humane Search for Answers," *Offender Rehabilitation* 1 (Spring 1977): 293.

20. Ibid., p. 294.

21. Norval Morris, "Lessons from the Adult Correctional System of Sweden," in *Corrections: Problems and Prospects,* ed. David M. Peterson and Charles W. Thomas. (Englewood Cliffs, N.J.: Prentice-Hall, 1975), pp. 279-298.

22. Ibid., p. 280.

23. Richard A. Salomon, "Lessons from the Swedish Criminal Justice System: A Reappraisal," *Federal Probation* 40 (September 1976):47.

24. Paul C. Friday, "Sanctioning Sweden: An Overview," *Federal Probation* 40 (September 1976):48.

25. See Erland Aspelin, "Some Developments in Swedish Criminal Policy," in *Some Developments in Nordic Criminal Policy and Criminology* (Stockholm: Scandinavian Research Council for Criminology, September 1975), pp. 4-18, for a more detailed review of the following: (1) decriminalization (for example, efforts to decriminalize pornography, offenses against religious beliefs, desecration of the flag, carnal abuse of a sibling, abortion, homosexual activity with a minor), (2) depenalization dealing with problematic conduct by making it no longer punishable under the law and therefore no longer the responsibility of the police and criminal courts and providing instead sanctions through administrative agencies (for example, tax offenses calling for the addition of an extra or penalty tax, fining minor smuggling offenses, failure to insure a motor vehicle, shoplifting, defrauding hotels, taxis, restaurants, trains, and buses, health insurance fraud), and (3) efforts to extend the coverage of criminal sanctions to include illegal possession of weapons, deportation "for the prevention of certain violent offences with an international background," aircraft hijacking, aircraft sabotage, "agitation against particular groups . . . those who openly threaten or express contempt for groups of a particular race, national or ethnic origin of faith," "arranging pornographic performances without authority permitting such performances to include crude sexual or sadistic behavior or permit persons under the age of eighteen years to take part in such performances," tax fraud, offenses against the environment (pollution of water, poisonous substances in weed killers or using substances dangerous to health or the environment). Interested readers should also see an excellent article by Alvar Nelson, "The Politics of Criminal Law Reform: Sweden," *American Journal of Comparative Law* 21 (Spring 1973):269-286.

26. Michael S. Serrill, "Profile: Sweden," *Corrections Magazine* 3 (June 1977):11-36.

27. Other straightforward descriptive accounts of various aspects of Swedish corrections: John R. Snortum, "Sweden's 'Special' Prisons," *Criminal Justice and Behavior* 3 (June 1976):151-167. Snortum, in addition, provides some comparative data between the state of California and Sweden. *Justice in*

*Modern Sweden,* by Harold H. Becker and Einar O. Jhellemo (Springfield, Ill.: Charles C. Thomas, 1976), presents some basic facts about Swedish democracy, social life and the organization of police services, the judiciary and the corrections department, all in the style of a government bulletin. The level of analysis is superficial, but the book has several useful appendixes, including a statement of the objectives, history, actions, and organization of KRUM, "The National Swedish Association for Penal Reform," and "The Regulations for the Experiment on Paying Work Earnings Adjusted to Open Market Rates to Inmates at Tillberga Prison."

28. Gunnar Marnell, "Comparative Correctional Systems: United States and Sweden." Reprinted by permission from *Criminal Law Bulletin* 8 (1973): 754-755. Copyright © 1973 Warren, Gorham & Lamont, Inc., 210 South Street, Boston, Mass. All rights reserved.

29. Ibid.

30. Hans Thornstedt, "The Day-Fine System in Sweden," in *Developments in Nordic Criminal Policy*, pp. 28–35.

31. Ibid., p. 29.

32. Bultena, *Deviant Behavior in Sweden*, p. 42.

33. Thornstedt, "Day-Fine System," p. 32.

34. Hanns V. Hofer, "Swedish Prisons: Basic Data," Stockholm University, June 1976, p. 13. The 75 percent estimate is from Thornstedt, "Day-Fine System," p. 28.

35. *Rattsstatistisk Arsbok (Yearbook of Legal Statistics)* 1975 (Stockholm: National Central Bureau of Statistics, 1977).

36. "Facts on Swedish Corrections," National Swedish Correctional Administration, 1975, p. 5.

37. Ibid.

38. *Kriminalvården 1976 (Official Statistics of Sweden)* (Norrköping, Sweden: National Prison and Probation Administration, 1977), p. 10.

39. Richard Sundeen, "Swedish Juvenile Justice and Welfare," *Journal of Criminal Justice* 4 (Summer 1976):109-121. This study describes the major features of the Child Welfare System, the assumptions about delinquency that underlie the system and its actions, and the relationship between the Swedish police and the youth prisons of the corrections department and the Child Welfare System. Considerable statistical data are also provided as well as some interesting descriptions of child welfare programs.

A slightly dated but very valuable detailed comparison of the Swedish Child Welfare System with the California Juvenile Court System may be found in Ola Nyquist, *Juvenile Justice* (Westport, Conn.: Greenwood Press, 1960).

40. Other conditions which may be applied to youthful offenders between fifteen and seventeen include the following from "Facts on Swedish Corrections":

Under a special provision of the Penal Code, a person who has committed an offense before attaining 18 years may be sentenced to a fine even if the minimum punishment for the offense is imprisonment. A person under 18 years may only in exceptional cases be sentenced to imprisonment for a specified term, and life imprisonment may never be imposed for an offense committed before the offender attained 18 years. No age conditions were laid down for the imposition of conditional sentences. However, a person under 18 years may not be sentenced to probation unless this sanction is more suitable than care under the Child Welfare Act. Probation in combination with institutional care may only be ordered if the offender has attained the age of 18 years at the time of the offense.

41. *Kriminalvården 1976*, p. 10.

42. Thomas Ekbom, "About the New Sanction 'Supervision Order' in Sweden," Stockholm, July 1977.

43. *Kriminalvården 1976*, p. 9.

44. "Facts on Swedish Corrections," pp. 7-8.

45. *Kriminalvården 1976*, p. 10.

46. "Facts on Swedish Corrections," p. 8.

47. *Kriminalvården 1976*, p. 44.

48. *Kriminalvården 1971* and *Kriminalvården 1976*, pp. 9-10.

Hofer presents data indicating that admissions to penal institutions during the period 1950-75 increased to a high of 184 per 100,000 population in 1968 and 1969, but dropped to 153 per 100,000 in 1974 (Hofer, "Swedish Prisons," p. 14).

49. *Kriminalvården 1971* and *Kriminalvården 1976*, p. 9.

50. The general social background of Swedish prisoners does not appear to be very different from their American counterparts. According to Hofer ("Swedish Prisons," p. 19), most Swedish prisoners have had prior contact with the correctional system, had high rates of divorce and came from "bad childhood conditions," and had lower levels of education; half of them were unemployed when sentenced, half of them were "difficult to place on the labour market when released from prison," their health was often poor, and a majority of them had alcohol or drug problems.

51. David A. Ward, "Inmates Rights and Prison Reform in Sweden and Denmark," *Journal of Criminal Law and Criminology* 63 (June 1972):240-255.

52. Hofer, "Swedish Prisons," p. 21.

53. Sources of information on the Swedish J.O. are Alfred Bexelius, "The Swedish Institution of the Justice Ombudsman," *Sweden Today* (Stockholm: Swedish Institute, 1966); Stanley V. Anderson, "Prisons and Ombudsman: The Pattern in Scandinavia and New Zealand," Paper presented at the Center for the Study of Democratic Institutions, August 22, 1975, and "The Swedish Ombudsman," *Sweden Today* (Stockholm: Swedish Institute, 1971). A comprehensive discussion of the need for an ombudsman for American prisoners can be found in Timothy L. Fitzharris's report, "The Desirability of a

Correctional Ombudsman" (Berkeley, Ca.: Institute of Governmental Studies, Ombudsman Activities Project, University of California, 1973). This report indicates that "5 to 10 percent of the activities of the Swedish, Danish, and Norwegian Ombudsmen have to do with prisoners" (p. 58). See also Adam Raphael, "Ombudsmen and Prisons: The European Experience," *Corrections Magazine*, January-February 1975.

54. For a description of in-prison visiting facilities and the problems related to these visits, see Ward, "Inmates Rights," p. 246.

55. See "Education in Institutions" (National Swedish Correctional Administration, 1975) for a description of educational and vocational training programs.

56. Buss, "In for Repairs," p. 39.

57. Carl-Henrik Ericsson, "Labor-Market Wages for Prisoners." Swedish Information Service, *Viewpoint* January 1973, p. 2; Durham, "Prison Can Be Fun," pp. 50-51.

58. Eckart Kuhlhorn, *Non-Institutional Treatment: A Preliminary Evaluation of the Sundsvall Experiment*, report no. 1 (Stockholm: National Swedish Council for Crime Prevention, April 1975).

59. Ibid., p. 6.

60. Ibid., p. 55.

61. Bo Martinsson, "Prison Democracy in Sweden," Swedish Information Service, *Viewpoint*, April 16, 1971, pp. 1-3.

62. Thomas Mathiesen, *The Politics of Abolition* (London: Martin Robertson, 1974; New York: Halsted Press, 1974), pp. 128-129.

63. Ibid., pp. 137-138; Information om Österåker-Overlaggningarna 11-13 January 1971, Kriminalvårdsstyrelsen (National Correctional Administration), February 8, 1971.

64. Mathiesen, *Politics of Abolition*, p. 138.

65. Ibid., p. 154.

66. Ibid., p. 164.

67. Martinsson, "Prison Democracy in Sweden," p. 4.

68. Ibid., pp. 3-5.

69. Mathiesen, *Politics of Abolition*, p. 174.

70. Ibid., p. 213.

71. This list was compiled from the following sources: a letter from inmate Harri Miekkalinna to Clas Amilon, National Correctional Administration (F.F.C.O. Informationscentralen, Fängelset); National Correctional Administration, Forslag Till Dagordning, November 19, 1971 (press release); and National Correctional Administration, November 23, 1971 (untitled communique).

72. Mathiesen, *Politics of Abolition*, p. 43.

73. Aslak Syse, ed., *Kan Fengsel Forsvares* (Oslo: Pax Forlag A/S, 1972).

74. Polly D. Smith, "An Update: Developments of KRUM Since 1971," March 25, 1977, p. 1.

75. Ibid., p. 2.

76. Ulla Bondeson, *Fången i Fångsamhället* (Malmö: P.A. Norstedt and Soners Forlag, 1974), p. 599. In her study of inmates in thirteen penal institutions in Sweden (youth and adult prisons), Bondeson found that inmates, irrespective of type of prison, were not concerned with issues "connected with openness or permeability of the institution . . . more furloughs, open institutions, conditional release after half the time and work outside the institution. Items associated with work and education also ranked very high . . . abolition of restrictions like censorship and isolation ranked almost as high . . . . Better facilities like room for conjugal visiting, hobby room and gymnastics halls were considered quite important . . . . Having an inmate council was judged more crucial than having better contact with KRUM."

77. Ibid.

78. The contrast between the demands of inmates in American and Swedish prisons has been described in Ward, "Inmates Rights."

79. See, for example, Norman Bishop, "Beware of Treatment," in *Developments in Nordic Criminal Policy*, pp. 19-27. An excellent review of knowledge about the "positive" and "negative" effects of imprisonment based on Swedish and American literature may be found in Bondeson, *Fången i Fångsamhallet*, pp. 589-598.

80. Norman Bishop, "Prison Research in Sweden," Paper presented to the American Association for the Advancement of Science, Section on Science and Social Institutions, December 30, 1972, p. 4.

81. Ove Sterflet, Lars Bagge, and Norman Bishop, *Återfall Efter Ungdomsfängelse*, report no. 13 (Stockholm: National Prison and Probation Administration, Research and Development Unit, June 1975), pp. vi, ix.

82. Lars Krantz, Lars Bagge, and Norman Bishop, *Recidivism among Those Conditionally Released from Prison during 1973 (Villkorlight Frigivna 1973: En Uppföljning Med Avseende På Återfall)*, report no. 24 (Norrköping: National Prison and Probation Administration, Research and Development Unit, August 1977).

83. Ibid., p. 3.

Offenders sentenced to prison in Sweden are eligible for parole after serving two-thirds of their sentences if the sentence is longer than six months (after half of the sentence in exceptional cases), and release from prison at that time is taken for granted. That is, the uncertainty of the parole systems in the United States—whether the sentencing system calls for determinate or indeterminate sentences—is not a concern voiced by Swedish inmates, and it has not been raised as an issue by the prison reform groups. KRUM has called for the abolition of parole, but this refers to ending the termination of required activities associated with parole and the end of any form of supervision after release.

84. Börje Olsson Lars Bagge, and Norman Bishop, *Skyddstellsynsdömba 1971: En Återfallsstudie*, report no. 19 (Norrköping: National Prison and

Probation Administration, Research and Development Unit, November 1976).

85. Bengt Warren, *Frivardens Behandlingscentral*, report no. 20 (Norrköping: National Prison and Probation Administration, Research and Development Unit, December 1976).

86. Börje Olsson, *Narkotik Amissbruk Och Sociala Förhållanden Hos Nyintagna Vid Fem Centralanstalter 1973*, report no. 9 (Stockholm: National Prison and Probation Administration, Research and Development Unit, September 1974); Eskil Berglund and Kenneth Johansson, *Rattfyllerister*, report no. 8 (Stockholm: National Prison and Probation Administration, Research and Development Unit, Uppsala University, August 1974), p. 2; Ann-Charlotte Landerholm -ek, *Forsoksverksamhet Vid Gävle Fangvårdsanstalt Med Modifierat Terapeutiski Samhälle-Initialskedet*, report no. 1 (Stockholm: National Prison and Probation Administration, Research and Development Unit, December 1972); Nils Gustafsson and Yvonne Treiberg, *Nyligen Frigivan Och Skyddsvärnet*, report no. 6 (Stockholm: National Prison and Probation Administration, Research and Development Unit, January 1974), p. 69; Rolf Åström, Lars Bagge, and Norman Bishop, *Gripna i Stockholm* (Norrköping: National Prison and Probation Administration, Research and Development Unit, 1977).

87. "The National Council for Crime Prevention," Stockholm, 1979.

88. Ibid.

89. *Swedish Studies on Juvenile Delinquency* (Stockholm: National Council for Crime Prevention, 1976); *International Conference on General Deterrence*, report no. 2 (Stockholm: National Swedish Council for Crime Prevention, Research and Development Division, 1975).

90. Kuhlhorn, *Non-Institutional Treatment*, p. 53.

91. Douglas Lipton, Robert Martinson, and Judith Wilks, *The Effectiveness of Correctional Treatment: A Survey of Treatment Evaluation Studies* (New York: Praeger, 1975); Ulla Bondeson, "A Critical Survey of Correctional Treatment Studies in Scandinavia, 1945-1974," in "Crime Deterrence and Offender Career Project," ed. Ernest van den Haag and Robert Martinson, report prepared under a grant from the U.S. Office of Economic Opportunity, New York, 1975.

92. These criteria were

1. The study must represent an evaluation of a treatment method applied to criminal offenders.
2. The study must have been completed 1945 through 1974.
3. The study must include empirical data resulting from a comparison of an experimental group with control group(s) or from a comparison of a treatment group with some comparison group(s), that is, the treatment group may be compared with the general inmate population, matched control subjects, base expectancy rates, or itself (a before-after comparison).
4. These data must be measures of improvement in performance on some dependent variables which include recidivism, parole or probation per-

formance, institutional adjustment, educational achievement, vocational adjustment, personality and attitude change, drug and alcohol readdictions, or cost benefits.

5. Specifically excluded are after-only studies without comparison groups, prediction studies, descriptive studies of treatment programs, and clinical speculations about feasible treatment methods [van den Haag and Martinson, *Crime Deterrence*, p. 257].

93. Two of the Danish studies are of interest because they report that the treatment efforts seemed to have some positive impact on the clients. See Karen Berntsen, "Treatment for Drug Addicts," and Karen Bernstsen and Karl O. Christiansen, "A Resocialization Experiment with Short-Term Offenders," in van den Haag and Martinson, *Crime Deterrence*.

94. Uusitalo's study of comparable groups of offenders in closed prisons and open prisons (labor colonies) in Finland reported no difference in recidivism rates between the two groups. Uusitalo concludes that the advantages of using labor colonies in lieu of traditional prisons are that they are far less costly to build and run, that inmates in open prisons can work more productively and do jobs for which they are paid, which in turn permits a reduction in the welfare cost of maintaining their families (van den Haag and Martinson, *Crime Deterrence*).

95. *Crime Deterrence*, pp. 226-268, 299-300.

96. Ibid., pp. 269-274, 301-305.

97. Ibid., p. 274.

98. Ibid., pp. 277-279, 275-276, 306-307.

99. Ibid., p. 328.

100. "The 1973 Correctional Care Reform," Stockholm, Swedish Institute, *Current Sweden*, no. 87, August 1975, p. 2. The official "Act on Correctional Treatment in Institutes" was published in English by the Office of Public Information, National Correctional Administration, Stockholm, May 1974. In addition, see "Swedish Code of Statutes: Decree of the King in Council Containing Certain Regulations Regarding Its Supplementation of the Act on Correctional Treatment in Institutes," also published in English by the National Correctional Administration in May 1974.

101. "The 1973 Correctional Care Reform," p. 4.

102. Ibid., p. 5.

103. According to Smith, the housing capacity of the national prisons has been determined to be "excessive" for the needs of the system under the new act.

The National Correctional Board has just suggested closing down three blocks of Kumla prison, Sweden's largest maximum security (i.e., closed) institution. This prison has in fact been a thorn in the correctional board's flesh since its opening in the early sixties. It had been built in response to "the pressure of public opinion" after a series of escapes from closed prisons in the fifties. Demands for "greater security" called forth plans for a total of six large closed prisons, of which Kumla was to be the first. The scale was to be large by Swedish standards—Kumla has a total capacity of 435 places. This was justified as an economy since it was argued that by having prisoners under one roof the ratio of staff to prisoners could be lowered.

By the time Kumla had been built, opinion had swung the other way, for it was already beginning to be understood that, in fact, large prisons were not an economy in the long term. Even though the cost per bed may be higher in smaller prisons, seen in terms of rehabilitation they are far more effective—not only are they more humane, in that closer human contacts can be made, facilitating a more positive form of supervision, but, even seen in purely financial terms, by helping to reduce recidivism they are ultimately less a burden on the taxpayer. Thus it was that the second prison to be built on the "Kumla patterns," Osteraker, was only completed to fifty percent of the original plans, and after Osteraker no more large prisons have been built in Sweden. As of September 1st, 1974, there were 139 prisoners at Kumla, which means that very close to 300 places were "vacant." Clearly the suggestion to close down three blocks comprising 60 places is to be welcomed: the number of staff can be reduced by 26 at the same time.

Desmond Smith, "Opening up the Prisons," Swedish Institute, *Current Sweden*, no. 53, Stockholm, November 1974, p. 7.

104. A summary of the Criminal Care Act by Alan Wilson, "Proposals for Reform of Swedish Criminal Care," Royal Ministry for Foreign Affairs, September, 1972, lists the categories into which offenders were divided:

1. Offenders whose criminal handicap and personal disposition are difficult to treat. Such offenders may be dangerous and liable to attempt escape if not guarded.
2. Offenders who are, for general preventive reasons, sentenced to short periods (one to three months) in institutions. These offenders—drunken drivers, especially—do not normally require guarding, nor do they require the services of non-institutional care.
3. So-called "normal" offenders, those who present only a small security problem and can probably be helped to adjust to society through rehabilitation measures taken in institutional or noninstitutional care.

It is proposed that, if institutionalized, groups one and two should be dealt with in national institutions, and group three in small, local institutions.

105. Smith states:

Whereas short furloughs are previously granted primarily only for the visiting of close relatives who were seriously ill, for funerals, or for "strong reasons . . . with regard to the length of prison sentence," permission may now be granted under the general heading "to facilitate readjustment to society"; long furloughs, which were previously granted for only up to fourteen days, and that only after two-thirds of the sentence had been served, can now be acceded to after half the sentence and with no statutory limit on the length of the furlough.

Because it is planned that Group A prisoners at least will be serving their sentences in their home areas, it is expected that visits from relatives and friends will be quite frequent, especially at the beginning of the sentence before the prisoner has opportunity for furloughs. According to the "Work Manual for Local Prisons" issued in connection with the new regulations those visits will be in accordance with the "general open attitudes towards contact with the outside world" and only in "very exceptional cases . . . will they require supervision." Where the local community institution lacks a suitable visitors' room "permission for the inmates to receive visits in their living quarters should be considered" (ibid., p. 3).

106. "The 1973 Correctional Care Reform," p. 9.

107. Smith reports that the act authorizes inmates to have "keys to their rooms which are even to be equipped with wardrobes for the inmates' civilian clothes so as to be readily accessible for their visits outside the institution" ("Opening Up the Prisons," p. 4).

108. Ibid., p. 10.

109. Smith, "Opening Up the Prisons."

110. Translation by Norman Bishop of an article, "The Minister of Justice Proposes—Away with Isolation as Punishment," by Lars Bolin, Acting Head of the Treatment and Security Division. The article appeared in the National Prison and Probation Administration staff journal, *Kriminalvården*, June 1976. Personal communication with the author.

111. William Borden, "Penal Currents," Swedish Institute, *Current Sweden*, no. 30, April 1974, pp. 7, 9.

112. Ibid., p. 10. Smith also issues a word of caution:

Isn't it a case of putting new wine in old bottles? The criticism has been made that it will be impossible to meet the demands both of access to local communities and of job variety within the older prisons, many of them in geographically isolated parts of the country and with staff who are mainly drawn from locally unemployed farmers, timberworkers, etc. Is it being too blue-eyed to suggest that these prisons can ever offer more than the most basic of requirements? Again it should be emphasized that the proposed changes cannot be made overnight. Many of the proposals will take five years, some up to fifteen, to carry through, and as has already been seen in the case of estimates of places in institutions, original plans may have to be drastically revised. . . .

The final test of the new provisions may well prove to lay with the probation service, however. The new open attitudes must stand or fall, ultimately, on the ability of the probation service to cope with its vastly increased duties and responsibilities. . . .

113. Lennart Geijer, "Probation—Not Prison," *Sweden Now* 10 (1976): 39-40. Reprinted with permission.

114. Bishop, "The Minister of Justice Proposes," p. 10, has made this point in his comment that while there may be some methodological problems with some of the follow-up studies, "no one in the Nordic countries has yet been able to demonstrate a contrary proposition in that imprisonment is more effective in securing the resocialization of offenders than measures applied under conditions of freedom."

115. "Flamboyant Badman Is Media Folk Hero of Sorts in Sweden," *Minneapolis Tribune*, September 7, 1976.

116. Esbjörn Esbjörnsson, "International Criminality in Sweden" in *Scandinavian Studies in Criminology* 5, ed. Nils Christie, (London: Martin Robertson and Co., 1974), pp. 12-13.

117. *Kriminalvarden 1976*, p. 24.

118. For a detailed treatment of the state's ever-present desire to cut costs when it comes to "the mad and the bad," see Andrew T. Scull, *Decarceration: Community Treatment and the Deviant, A Radical View* (Englewood Cliffs, N.J.: Prentice-Hall, 1977). In her historical study, "Prisons in Sweden: an Historical Analysis of Penal Practice" (September 1974), Annika Snare argues that the main function of the prison has come to be segregation of nonproductive persons from the rest of society.

119. "Sweden Plans to Ease Retirement with Part-Time Work, Small Pensions," *Minneapolis Tribune*, October 27, 1975, p. 8.

120. Ibid.

121. Goran Albinsson, "Helping Bring Up Baby in Sweden," *Minneapolis Tribune*, August 16, 1977, p. 8.

122. "Dutch, Swedes, Norse Pay Highest Tax," *Minneapolis Tribune*, June 13, 1976, p. 19.

123. "This Is Socialism," *National Observer*, March 20, 1976, p. 4. Reprinted by permission of the *National Observer*, ©Dow Jones & Company, Inc. (1972). All rights reserved.

124. Leonard Silk, "Sweden Takes Role as Social Laboratory," *Minneapolis Tribune*, June 27, 1976, p. 11.

125. "Trouble in Paradise," *Forbes*, April 1, 1972, p. 22. Reprinted by permission. Other articles in this category include "Something Souring in Utopia," *Time*, July 19, 1976; Goran Albinsson, "The Oppression of Taxes in Sweden," *Minneapolis Tribune*, July 4, 1976; "Swedes Uneasy about Wealth as Rest of World Suffers," *Minneapolis Tribune*, December 29, 1974; "Swedes' Troubled Mood," *Newsweek*, March 23, 1970; Bernard K. Johnpoll, "Socialists Hear Rumbling of Discontent in Sweden," *Nation*, 1973; "Sweden Shows Scars of

Prosperity," *Minneapolis Tribune*, April 18, 1971; and "Sweden: Paradise Lost," *Newsweek*, March 15, 1971.

126. Alfred J. Kahn and Sheila B. Kamerman, *Not for the Poor Alone: European Social Services* (Philadelphia: Temple University Press, 1975).

127. Odin W. Anderson, in his comparative study of health care in the United States, England, and Sweden, *Health Care: Can There be Equity?* (New York: Wiley, 1972), p. 210, observes that the quality of Sweden's hospital and medical system, characterized as "the most generously distributed in the world," says something about that country's concept of "distributive justice" which are the services citizens have a right to expect from their government.

128. "Sweden Confronted with Racial Problems in its Own Backyard," *Minneapolis Tribune*, July 18, 1977, p. 8. See also "Sweden: Racial Time Bomb," *Time*, August 8, 1977, p. 41.

129. *Statistical Abstracts of the United States, 1976* (Washington, D.C.: U.S. Government Printing Office, 1977), table 37.

130. Per capita expenditure for public schools amounts to $421 in Minnesota, $340 in Wisconsin; the average figure for the United States in $314. Per capita public welfare expenditure is $134 in Minnesota, $125 in Wisconsin; the United States average is $117. *Statistical Abstracts of the United States, 1976*, tables 229 and 6; *The Book of the States, 1976-77* (Washington, D.C.: U.S. Government Printing Office 1977), p. xxi.

131. U.S. Department of Justice, *National Prisoners Statistics Bulletin* (Washington, D.C.: U.S. Government Printing Office, 1976), p. 10, and *The Nation's Jails* (Washington, D.C.: U.S. Government Printing Office, 1972), table 2.

132. U.S. Department of Justice, *Crimes in the United States, 1975* (Washington, D.C.: U.S. Government Printing Office, 1976), table 4. Violent crimes include murder, forcible rape, robbery, and aggravated assault. Property crimes are Part I offenses, including burglary, larceny-theft, and motor vehicle theft.

# 4

# Imprisonment as an Allocation Process

*Alfred Blumstein* and
*Daniel Nagin*

The debate over the use of imprisonment typically finds conservatives, who argue for longer and more punitive sentences, vigorously engaged with liberals, who argue for more lenient and shorter sentences. These debates are frequently characterized more by rhetorical intensity than by any conscious attempt to assess the social costs and benefits associated with alternative sentencing policies.

Prison is potentially useful in controlling crime through some combination of (1) reducing the individual's subsequent criminality after release either through *rehabilitation* or *special deterrence*, which are conceptually quite similar; (2) imposing punishment on the convicted in order to communicate a symbolic message to other potential criminals, thereby deterring them from committing future crimes (generally described as *general deterrence*); and (3) simply isolating the identified criminal from the larger society, thereby reducing crime through an *incapacitative effect*. Much of the debate on imprisonment policy, at least in principle, is over the magnitude of these three crime-control benefits, the social costs of achieving them, and the question whether the benefits are worth the cost.

In this chapter we explore these various crime-control strategies and draw them together into a common framework that derives from some recent observations reflecting considerable stability in the amount of imprisonment a society imposes on its members. When the amount is stable, then the central question of imprisonment policy is transformed from one of "more versus less" into one of how to allocate that limited resource. Thus we examine some aspects of the debate over sentencing policy and explore the issue from the perspective of an allocation process.

## Functional Perspective on Imprisonment

We begin our exploration of allocating the imprisonment resource by characterizing the functions of imprisonment and then focusing on the key variables that affect the achievement of those functions. Aside from the clearly utilitarian functions to be emphasized here, imprisonment serves a further retributive objective. Even if imprisonment had no crime-control effects, it would be used as a punishment device, partly for expressing society's outrage at certain kinds of crime, partly for making clear the disapproval of certain kinds of behavior, and

169

partly as a means of reinforcement for those who do operate within the confines of the law.

## Utilitarian Functions of Imprisonment

Imprisonment is the final stage of the elaborate criminal justice process that filters out only those few who should be given this penultimate social sanction. In 1975, for instance, the FBI estimated that there were 9.3 million arrests—2.3 million for the FBI's index crimes of which 450,000 were for the violent crimes: criminal homicide, forcible rape, robbery, and aggravated assault.[1] Yet, fewer than 100,000 persons were sent to state or federal prisons in 1975. Any judge who imposes this extreme punishment for utilitarian reasons can have three principal utilitarian objectives: rehabilitation, deterrence, and incapacitation.

Much of the claim that prison is ineffective in crime control typically focuses on one of these, finds it less than adequate, and uses that finding as a basis for a more general rejection of imprisonment. For example, it has been argued (and perhaps shown) that prison is ineffective at rehabilitation, and many argue further that prison may even be counterproductive in rehabilitation. These positions have provided a basis for arguing against the use of imprisonment. It is entirely conceivable, however, that prison could be quite criminogenic—that is, people leaving prison are more crime-prone than those coming in—but if its deterrent and incapacitative effects are sufficiently large, then prison would still be defensible. In this examination of imprisonment we try to deal with these three effects together.

**Rehabilitation**. Rehabilitation reflects the dominant theme that has dictated imprisonment policy, or at least its articulation, over the past century. Beginning with the introduction of the concept of the penitent in a penitentiary to the various formulations of the medical model, imprisonment has long been viewed primarily as providing an opportunity for reforming the identified evil-doer in society. He has been the target of much attention, and considerable efforts have been expended to reform his criminal behavior. The targets of the reform may have been at various times his soul, his psyche, his social environment, or his lack of opportunities for legitimate functioning in the larger society. These strategies have principally been reform and rehabilitation, and they have been attractive because of their positive commitments for social good not only for society but for the offender himself. If rehabilitation were effective, then many positive values would be served. Crime would be controlled, the lives of the offenders would be enhanced, and all this would be accomplished without resorting to the punitive acts that many find offensive.

The rehabilitation strategy has suffered a number of serious attacks in recent years. These attacks have followed from the discouraging findings of numerous evaluations of rehabilitation programs. With few exceptions the evaluations have failed to show that any particular rehabilitation program is better at reducing recidivism rates than any other, or even better than none at all. These arguments were first presented by Robinson and Smith in 1971 and received much more public attention with an article by Robert Martinson in *Public Interest* in 1974, which summarized the more extensive review of the evaluation of Lipton, Martinson, and Wilks.[2]

There may well be reasonable bases for skepticism about the definitiveness of the conclusions promulgated by Martinson and the others. For example, most of the evaluative experiments were not characterized by a definitive finding of no effect, but rather by either (1) a reported finding of a positive rehabilitative effect, which was shown to be fallacious because of important flaws in the design or analysis of the experiment or (2) a failure to find an effect, which could have resulted from insufficient sensitivity of the experimental design to the effect (inadequate statistical "power") which might have existed.

The prevalence of failure to reject the null hypothesis may also have been a result of the rigorous demands of experimental design. A rigorous evaluation is possible only with a well-defined technology. A technology is typically a prescribed set of procedures that are defined well enough to be transferred across different practitioners and so are independent of them. It is possible that such narrowly defined technologies are inherently doomed to failure and that treatments and programs that are much more individualistic are required to achieve an effect. Such programs would have to be adapted specifically to the individuals under treatment and would inherently involve a significant amount of judgment by the rehabilitative professionals. If this is indeed the case, then it becomes extremely likely that the well-designed evaluations that make up the bulk of the null-effect findings are precisely the ones that were preordained to failure.

Whether or not the conclusions regarding rehabilitative null effects are valid, they appear to have had a major impact on contemporary thinking about imprisonment policies. They have implanted in the managers and practitioners of rehabilitation a sense of frustration and futility. The advocates of the medical mode of rehabilitative treatment have been subject to attack from various sides. The findings of null effect have been used to argue for less intervention by the criminal justice system. Indeed, the position presented by Robinson and Smith was implicitly for less intervention. They stated:

> Since the more unpleasant or punishing alternatives tend also to be the more expensive, the choice of appropriate disposition for offenders should be determined by the amount of punishment we want to impose and the amount of money we are prepared to spend in imposing it; it should not be obscured by illusions of differential rehabilitative

efficacy. If the choice is, in fact, merely between greater and lesser punishments, then the rational justification for choosing the greater must, for now, be sought in concepts other than rehabilitation and be tested against criteria other than recidivism.[3]

More recently the results have fueled an attack on rehabilitative strategies by advocates of explicitly punitive strategies. One advocate for deterrence is Gordon Tullock who, in an article in *Public Interest*, declared, "We have an unpleasant method—deterrence—and a pleasant method—rehabilitation—that . . . never has worked. . . . We have to opt either for the deterrence method or for a higher crime rate."[4]

Similar arguments were made in favor of strategies focusing on incapacitation, which is also achieved through the act of imprisonment. Advocates of this view have ranged from former Attorney General William Saxbe to former President Gerald Ford to Professor James Q. Wilson, who argued for incapacitation in a *New York Times Magazine* article entitled "Lock 'Em up and Other Thoughts on Crime."[5]

**Incapacitation.** Incapacitation refers to the crimes averted that would have been committed by the imprisoned offenders had they been out on the street. If an individual serving a prison term of $S$ years would have committed crimes at a rate $\lambda$ during his period of incarceration, then $\lambda S$ crimes are averted. If, in fact, his criminal career would have ended during the prison term, then the number of crimes averted is decreased correspondingly. The incapacitative effect is thus strongly influenced by the rate at which the incarcerated individuals would have committed crimes, since imprisoning a high-crime-rate person clearly averts more crimes than locking up a low-crime-rate person. The more persons imprisoned, the more crimes are averted; and the longer the duration of imprisonment, the greater the volume of averted crimes. In addition, any rehabilitative or criminogenic effects that imprisonment may have should also be considered in computing the long-term crime-control efficacy of incapacitation.

The profile of an individual criminal career is characterized in figure 4-1. During the criminal career the individual's crime rate is $\lambda$ and remains fairly steady until imprisonment, when his crime rate drops to zero because of incapacitation. After his release from prison, if rehabilitation were effective, there would be a decrease in $\lambda$ or a shortening of $\tau$, the duration of the criminal career, or both, as shown in the hatched profile on figure 4-1. On the other hand, if prison were criminogenic—that is, individuals came out of prison with greater crime propensity than they entered with or come out with a lengthened criminal career—then the longer-term effects of incapacitation would be reduced by an amount reflected by the dotted portion of the postimprisonment career in figure 4-1. The null-effect finding in the evaluations of prison-based rehabilitation programs suggests that both these effects are small or that they at least cancel each other.

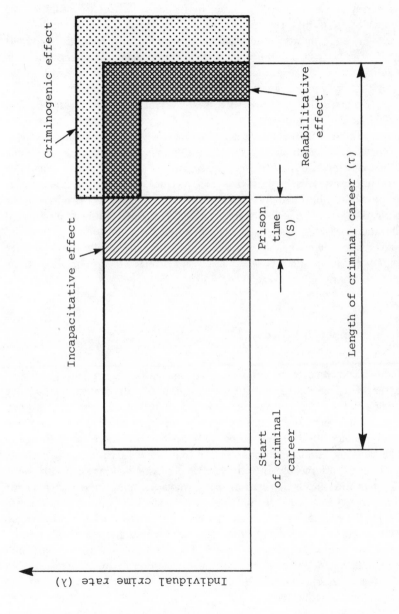

**Figure 4-1.** Profile of a Criminal Career

**Deterrence**. Deterrence, often referred to more specifically as general deterrence, refers to the effect on others achieved by imprisoning identified offenders. Thus any time a convicted person is locked away, two crime-reducing effects are achieved. One is the direct incapacitative effect of insulating the larger society from that person and his further depravations. The other, the deterrent effect, is more indirect and results principally from the symbolic import of the convict's imprisonment; the general deterrent effect works on other potential criminals rather than on him and so depends strongly on the nature of the symbolic message communicated by the act of imprisonment. Most analysts attempting to measure the deterrent effect have assumed that this effect is somehow proportional to the objectively measured punishment largely because the other, perceptual aspects are so difficult to measure.

In view of its symbolic character, the symbolic message can be communicated in many diverse ways. The "transmitter" —society in general and the criminal justice system in particular—can enhance the symbolic message by increasing either the "signal"—the amount of punishment delivered—or its "amplification" of the signal—the factors affecting the perception of the amount of punishment other than through changes in the sanction itself. Thus principal determinants of the signal of the deterrent effect of imprisonment are the intensity with which the prison sanction is delivered, the probability of imprisonment, and the expected sentence.

## The Imprisonment Policy Trade-offs

The component aspects of rehabilitation, incapacitation, and deterrence all relate to the crime-control effectiveness associated with imprisonment. Aside from the possibility of a criminogenic effect of prison on prisoners, the presumption is that increases in the use of imprisonment, whether in certainty or in severity, should result in less crime. This can be made more specific by plotting the expected number of man-years of imprisonment per crime (a measure of the intensity of the use of imprisonment) against a measure of the crime rate. That relationship is depicted as the downward-sloping curve (labeled costs of crime) in figure 4-2, where the rate of decrease in the crime rate depends on the combined incapacitative and deterrent effects associated with an increase in sanctions. The level of crime associated with a given level of intensity of prison use represents the social costs of crime associated with a particular sanction policy and decreases as the rate of sanction delivery increases. This curve is the focus of attention of those who are most concerned with implementing actions to reduce crime.

Any crime-control policy, however, inherently involves a trade-off between the crime-control effectiveness and the social costs associated with implementing it. Thus the crime-control effects must be weighed carefully against the other

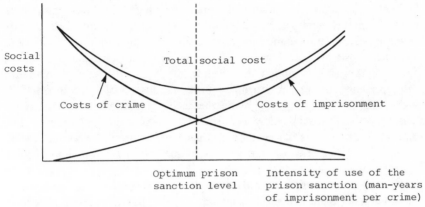

**Figure 4-2.** Social Costs versus Intensity of Use of the Prison Sanction

social costs associated with increasing the use of imprisonment. One must also be concerned with other aspects of the costs associated with imprisonment, and these tend to increase as sanction levels increase. These social costs include as a minimum the budgetary cost of building, maintaining, and managing prisons (the food, the guards, treatment programs, correctional managers), the welfare costs associated with supporting prisoners' families, the lost economic capacity resulting from the removal of workers from the labor force, and the dehumanizing effects of imprisonment on the prisoners, guards, and prison officials, as well as on the society at large. Perhaps of even more fundamental concern is that increasing imprisonment may require relaxation of various due-process constraints. For example, hearsay evidence might be admitted, confessions might be coerced, or the requirement "beyond a reasonable doubt" required for conviction might be replaced by the "weight of the evidence" or something in between. (In terms of subjective probabilities, one might view "beyond a reasonable doubt" as reflecting a 95 percent certainty, whereas the "weight of evidence" might require only slightly more than a 50 percent certainty.) As the use of imprisonment expands, more true criminals will be imprisoned, but more innocent people will also be imprisoned.

Since social policy must be concerned with the social costs of both crime and imprisonment, it must be concerned with the sum of these costs. Thus we also show in figure 4-2 the total social costs, which are represented by the U-shaped curve, representing the combined social costs inherent in crime and crime control. It is this total cost that should be of concern to any public body.

The striking feature of this total-social-cost curve is its U shape. The social cost of too little use of imprisonment is high, because there would be too much crime; and the social cost of too much imprisonment would also be too high, because we might come too close to a police state, and the fear of criminals might be replaced by a comparable fear of the police.

These considerations lead to the notion that there is an optimum level of imprisonment that any society must choose, representing its own balancing of the social costs of crime and crime control. (In the context of this model of the total social costs associated with an imprisonment policy, programs to "eliminate crime" are entirely undesirable, even if they were feasible.) This optimum level represents an implicit weighing of the various social costs involved. A society that places a great weight on the cost of crime would tolerate more punishment. One that is more concerned about governmental excesses and wants rigorous controls placed on the crime-control authorities would have to tolerate more crime. This optimum level of imprisonment—the minimum point of the U-shaped curve—which provides a minimum total social cost represents the level of imprisonment that the society should choose at any given time, and the costs-of-crime curve at that point reflects the crime rate that society will then have to tolerate.

Since the exact costs of crime control are often difficult to articulate and deal with in making decisions about imprisonment, various constraints are imposed that inhibit incurring such costs. Most common are the statutory maximum sentences for particular types of crime. These statutory limits inhibit the amount of imprisonment that could be imposed by any judge or sentencing authority. The constitutional due-process prohibitions against involuntary self-incrimination, illegal searches and seizures, uninformed consent and confessions, and the protection of the right to counsel all provide constraints on the imposition of the sanction and are reflected ultimately in constraints on the probability of conviction or the probability of imprisonment after conviction.[6] Thus in many cases explicit weighing of the costs of crime against those of crime control is not necessary, since the latter are reflected in the constraints imposed on the criminal process and the sentencing decision.

### Homeostatic Imprisonment Rate

One may view the prison population as the outcome of a social calculus that weighs these conflicting social costs. The consequence of these social decisions, the time series of imprisonment rates, has an exceedingly interesting characteristic. In at least three countries that have been examined—the United States since 1929, Norway since 1880, and Canada since 1880 (see figure 4-3) —the imprisonment rate, in terms of the number of prisoners per general population, has fluctuated within an extremely narrow range. In the United States the average rate has been 110.2 per 100,000 population with a standard deviation of 8.6; in Norway it has been 52.5 per 100,000 with a standard deviation of 8.2; and in Canada it has been 42.5 per 100,000, sixteen years of age or older, with a standard deviation of 6.1.

These observations of a stable imprisonment rate can be interpreted as

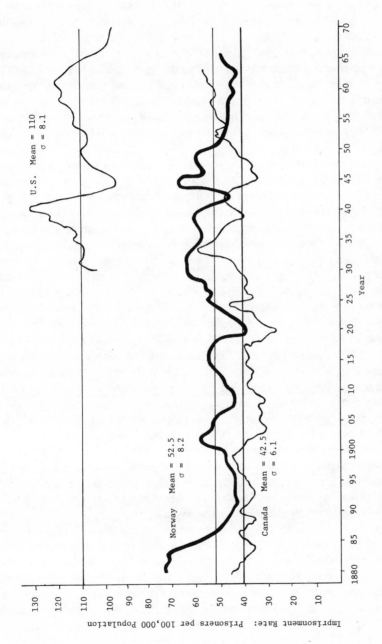

**Figure 4-3.** Annual Imprisonment Rates in United States, Norway, and Canada

reflecting the balancing of the competing pressures that influence the imprisonment rate. The factors pressing for increased use of imprisonment include the
pressures by the powerful establishment for increased crime control, pressures
by moralistic forces for enforcement of their moral principles, and pressures by
the police, prosecutors, and prison officials for expansion of their functions
in the operation of the society. In continuing opposition to these pressures are
the libertarians who argue for the rights of individuals to choose their own
modes of behavior, civil libertarians who seek to inhibit the imposition of government control over individual behavior, and the ordinary citizens who identify
with those who are imprisoned (the number of such people grows as the number
of prisoners grows).

If this limited number of observations of a roughly constant imprisonment
rate is indeed found to be indicative of a more general phenomenon, then
one must begin to characterize the various mechanisms used by a society to
adapt its crime-control actions to the changing crime rate. As crime rates increase, some of the acts formerly handled become decriminalized. Thus homosexuality is now largely removed from the province of criminal law. For many
acts that remain within the criminal law—such as minor shoplifting—prosecutors
and judges become more lenient in their punishment, especially when these acts
are committed by first-time offenders, and parole boards let prisoners out at
earlier stages in their sentences.

Adaptation also can occur in other ways. Greater restrictions can be applied
to some aspects of the crime-control process (such as assuring that all defendants are fully advised by counsel and are not enticed into offering confessions
that are less than fully voluntary). Such revisions in the applicable criminal
procecures achieved by the United States Supreme Court under Chief Justice
Earl Warren could be interpreted as an implicit reflection of this process of
seeking other values (increasing certain aspects of due-process liberty), since
a diminution of crime-control intensity was necessary in any event.

As these adaptive changes in crime-control policy come about, the mix of
imprisoned populations will shift. A greater portion of the prison population
will be there for the more serious crimes; people will serve less time for particular prison sentences; and prisons will become populated more by the habitual offender than by the occasional wrongdoer.

All these mechanisms of adaptation to maintain the constant imprisonment rate can indeed be noticed in changes in the prison populations in the
United States from 1960 to 1974.[8] In 1960 there were 185,227 persons in
state prisons, and 3,384,200 index crimes were reported to the police. Murder
and robbery, two of the most serious crimes, accounted for 27.2 percent of the
total prison population. In contrast, by 1974 the number of index crimes had
tripled to 10,253,400, yet the state prison population remained nearly un-
changed at 187,500. Moreover, the proportion of inmates serving time for
murder or robbery had increased from 27.2 percent to 40.7 percent; in

exchange, the proportion committed for less serious offenses decreased. In 1960 incarcerations for auto theft, embezzlement, fraud, and forgery accounted for 14.1 percent of the state prison population. By 1974 that proportion had declined to 6.0 percent.

The prisoners' average time served (as measured by the total population divided by the rate of input of new prisoners per year) remained constant; it was 2.4 years in 1960 and 2.2 years in 1970. This is a further indication of the process of accommodation to the growth in seriousness of crime. People convicted of the less serious crimes are less likely to be in prison, and thus those who are in prison serve a shorter time than did their counterparts convicted of the same offenses in an earlier period when there was less serious crime.

The constant U.S. imprisonment rate has been maintained in the face of the tripling of reported index crimes and a comparable but somewhat lower increase of about 150 percent in the number of reported arrests for these crimes. The reported crime rate represents a steadily growing statistic attributable to many factors, including growth in the proportion of incidents reported to the police (partly because of the increased visibility of police and news about crime), increasing use of the formal criminal justice system for resolution of conflicts and disputes that formerly might have been settled privately, demographic shifts that have increased the proportion of the more crime-prone subgroups of the population, and perhaps an increased willingness to engage in criminal activity by persons who feel anonymous in the impersonal urban environments where the traditional social controls of family, community, and church have significantly diminished.

Some of these trends may be reversed. The most likely opportunity for this is the aging of the extended postwar baby boom, bringing that group out of the high-crime ages. Most of these conditions, however, are likely to persist or even worsen, and thus the future environment can reasonably be predicted to be one of high and perhaps increasing rates of crimes coming to the attention of the police. Similarly arrest rates for the index crimes have been increasing with the rising crime rate, although at a somewhat slower pace. Arrests for the more common offenses such as drunkeness (which still represents the largest single category of arrests) and disorderly conduct (which involves considerable exercise of police discretion) have been declining, perhaps as an adaptation to the growth in the more serious index category.

The growth in arrest rates has already largely cheapened the threat of arrest as a deterrent sanction in itself. The high prevalence of arrest records among certain groups has undoubtedly had the effect of reducing markedly the stigma associated with having an arrest record. This has happened at least because of the growing prevalence of the use of arrest. In Wolfgang's Philadelphia cohort[9] 34 percent of the cohort had already experienced an arrest by age eighteen; in another study, it was projected that 60 percent of young males in the United States will be arrested for a nontraffic offense at some time in their lives.[10] A kind of inflationary effect has simply cheapened the sanction. One consequence of this cheapening has been the imposition  of restrictions that now prevent the use of arrest records, without confirmation of a conviction, for employment considerations or for other labeling or stigmatizing functions.

Similarly the act of conviction, which had been viewed traditionally as a major stigmatizing sanction, is now also largely diminished in its import.[11] Effective stigmatization calls for strong ties to a reference community, and that community must be one that honors the formal pronouncement of the stigma. Most offenders are not tied strongly to a mainstream community, and whatever community they do identify with probably has no great respect for the judicial system which tries to impose the stigma. Furthermore, even if a first conviction had a large stigma component, a second or subsequent one would have much less. With recidivism rates to conviction in the range of 50 percent to 75 percent, only a minority of active offenders are vulnerable to the stigma of an initial conviction. Thus as the "front-end input" to the criminal justice system grows, and in the face of the much more rigidly constrained imprisonment rate, the dominant remaining sanction of the criminal justice system that might have a significant impact on crime rates is imprisonment itself. However, the problem of allocating imprisonment becomes more demanding. It is now even more important that the allocation be rationalized carefully to make its use most effective, as well as just and equitable, since ultimately it must carry the major portion of the crime-control effect of the criminal justice system. As the incidence of arrest and conviction increases, the impact of these sanctions will further diminish, and the burden of carrying the criminal justice system's crime-control function will fall still more heavily on imprisonment.

To rationalize the allocation of the imprisonment sanction, it is useful to have a model relating the effects of alternative imprisonment policies on the crime rate and the imprisonment rate. Development of such a model is explored in the next section.

### A Model of the Crime Rate and Prison Population

To be concise in presentation and meaning in this discussion of imprisonment policy and its effects, a number of variables will be used consistently:

$\lambda_i$ = the individual crime rate of offender $i$ during the period of his criminal activity. (The unsubscripted variable $\lambda$ represents the average individual crime rate of a group of offenders.)

$\tau_i$ = the duration of the criminal career of offender $i$. (The unsubscripted variable $\tau$ represents the average criminal career of a group of offenders.

$q_a$ = probability of arrest for a crime

$q_{c/a}$ = probability of conviction after arrest

$q$ = probability of conviction for a crime; $q = q_a q_{c/a}$

$Q$ = probability of being sentenced to prison once convicted

$S$ = imprisonment time served for those incarcerated

$QS$ = expected time served per conviction, an aggregate measure of sanction intensity reflecting the combined effects of $Q$ and $S$. The product $QS$ represents the average penalty a convicted person might expect. (If the probability of imprisonment is 0.25 and the average time served by those imprisoned is 2.5 years, then $QS = [0.25] \, [2.5] = 6.25$ years.)

$C$ = the crime rate in a community measured in crime per capita

$\eta$ = fraction of time an offender is free in the community (unincarcerated) to commit crimes. (Then $1 - \eta$ is the fraction of potential crimes averted through incapacitation.)

$P$ = proportion of the population who engage in criminal acts. (This proportion should be influenced by the magnitude of the deterrent effect, which in turn depends on the magnitude of sanctions delievered.)

Describing the incapacitative and deterrent effects of imprisonment in rich detail would involve an analysis of the complex dynamics of crime commission, the evolution of crime-committing behavior over the course of a criminal career, and a variation in crime-committing and career patterns across the criminal population. Some offenders commit only a single offense and so have only a minimal criminal career. For the large majority who commit more than one offense, the rate at which crimes are committed ($\lambda_i$), the length of the career ($\tau_i$), and the types of crimes committed can vary appreciably among individuals and over the course of their careers. Even for a given offender, there is evidence suggesting that individual $\lambda$'s vary with age and that the types of offenses committed change over the course of the career.

The path to achieving these richer representations requires starting from a much more simplified base and letting a model evolve to address this richer set of complexities. The simplified model, in addition to being a stepping-stone to a more complex model, highlights the dominant effects of imprisonment on the crime rate and yields some significant insights into the relationship of the prison population to the crime rate. Even the simplified model provides some first estimates of impact, and these add an illuminating quantitative perspective to an overall assessment of the crime-control potential of imprisonment.

In developing a model relating crime rate $C$ to the sanction variables $Q$ and $S$, the different crime types are not distinguished but are treated as a single aggregate crime rate, which in turn can be treated most naturally as the total index crime rate.[12] In 1974, for example, nearly 80 percent of the prison population had been sentenced for one of the index crimes.

Ignoring individual differences in crime-commission rates also provides an important simplification. In this case the aggregate crime rate $C$ (the total number of crimes committed per year per capita) can be represented as the product of the proportion of the population that is criminal and their individual effective crime rate, namely:

$$C = (\lambda\eta) \cdot (P) \qquad\qquad (4.1)$$

where

$\lambda\eta$ = the effective crime rate per criminal and equals the product of (a) the individual crime rate while free and (b) the proportion of the criminal career that a criminal is free ($\eta$)

$P$ = the proportion of the population that is criminal, reflecting the deterrent effectiveness of the criminal justice system as well as other socialization and criminogenic conditions in the society

We can now develop estimates for $\eta$ and $P$ as a function of $Q$ and $S$, and then relate those to the imprisonment rate $I$.

*Proportion of a Criminal's Time Free ($\eta$)*

A criminal's vulnerability to incarceration is directly related to the frequency $\lambda$ with which he commits crimes. As $\lambda$ increases, the criminal more frequently risks capture and the consequent risk of incarceration. Thus $\eta$ is inversely related to $\lambda$. Other variables affecting $\eta$ are the risk of conviction given commission of a crime $q$, the risk of imprisonment given conviction $Q$, and the time served in prison when incarcerated $S$. Increases in either $q$ or $Q$ increase the likelihood of a prison term for each crime committed while free and so decrease the proportion of time the offender will be free. Similarly increasing the length of incarceration $S$ also reduces the proportion of time free.

In pioneering analytical work, Benjamin Avi-Itzhak and Reuel Shinnar and Shlomo Shinnar[13] derive the following functional relationship between and the parameters $\lambda$, $q$, $Q$ and $S$:

$$\eta = \frac{1}{1 + \lambda qQS} \qquad\qquad (4.2)$$

The product $qQS$ in the denominator is the expected sentence for committing a crime. In figure 4-4 $\eta$ is plotted as a function of $qQS$ for three values of $\lambda$ (2.5, 5, and 10 crimes per year). The parameters $q$, $Q$, and $S$ can easily be measured empirically. The value of $\lambda$ is much more difficult to measure because individual crimes (as opposed to arrests) are not observed, and self-reports are of dubious validity. For each value of $\lambda$ the value of $\eta$ declines as $qQS$ increases. For example, for $\lambda = 5$ the proportion of time free is·0.67 when $qQS = 0.1$ and and declines to 0.50 for $qQS = 0.2$. Moreover, for any given value of $qQS$, $\eta$ is smaller (offenders are free for a lesser proportion of the time) as $\lambda$ increases. For $qQS = 0.1$, $\eta = 0.8$ for $\lambda = 2.5$; $\eta$ declines to 0.67 for $\lambda = 5$ and is further reduced to 0.5 for $\lambda = 10$.

These graphs confirm the intuitive hypothesis that incapacitation effects can be substantial if prison terms are made sufficiently certain and lengthy. To put the intuitive sense into a practical perspective, consider an estimate of $qQS$ for 1970. In 1970 the probability $q$ of conviction for an index offense was about 0.048 and the probability of imprisonment given conviction $Q$ was about 0.25.[14] The average time served was about 2.6 years. Their product $qQS$ is 0.0312; that is, the expected time served per crime was about 0.0312 years, or eleven days. If index offenders committed an average of 2.5 crimes per year when free ($\lambda = 2.5$), then they would be incarcerated only 7 percent of the time. For $\lambda = 5$ that proportion nearly doubles to 13 percent but still remains small in absolute terms. Put in a different perspective, these figures suggest that if $\lambda = 2.5$, the incapacitative effect of the 1970 sanction variables reduced potential crime by 7 percent, and if $\lambda = 5$ that reduction was 13 percent. (These figures all report on the incapacitative effect alone and ignore the potential deterrent effects of imprisonment.) Only if $\lambda = 10$ do the incapacitative effects begin to appear to be substantial; in this case, $1 - \eta = 0.24$.

## The Criminal Proportion in the Population (P)

In the model the deterrent effects of the sanctions $Q$ and $S$ are reflected in $P$, the proportion of the population engaging in crime. Their deterrent effects derive from two factors: (1) the threat, with probability $Q$, of having to serve a sentence $S$ if convicted and (2) the stigma of having been imprisoned regardless of sentence length. The threat of stigmatization therefore depends only on $Q$ and not on $S$.

The probability $q$ of conviction after committing a crime may also act as a deterrent. However, this variable is not incorporated explicitly into the model specification of $P$ because, unlike $Q$ and $S$, it is less freely available as a policy variable.

The assumption that the deterrent effects of $Q$ and $S$ are reflected in $P$, the proportion of the population that is criminal, implies that the deterrent

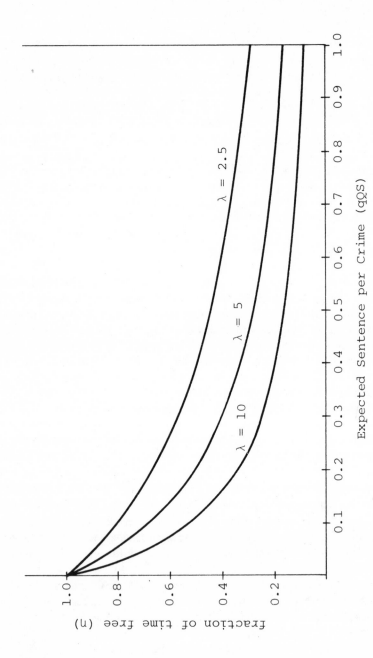

**Figure 4-4.** Fraction of Time Free ($\eta$) versus Expected Sentence Per Crime ($qQS$)

effects act on the net entry rate into the criminal population, or the recruitment rate minus the dropout rate. Thus from a behavioral perspective the two imprisonment sanctions $Q$ and $S$ are presumed to affect the entry decisions of potential criminals and the dropout decisions of active criminals. Any additional effect that $Q$ and $S$ may have on the $\lambda$ of active criminals will cause the model to understate the potential crime-reducing benefit.

Following the successful use of the logistic function in modeling individual-choice behavior in such areas as choice of a transportation mode and college choice,[15] we assume here that the choice to engage in criminal activities also follows a logistic function, with $P$ defined as

$$P(Q,S) = e^{u(Q,S)}/(1 + e^{u(Q,S)}) \qquad (4.3)$$

where $u(Q,S)$ is the expected disutility of imprisonment for crimes and is assumed to take the following form:[16]

$$u(Q,S) = \gamma_1 + \gamma_1 Q + \gamma_2 QS \qquad (4.4)$$

The parameter $\gamma_1$ measures the stigma effect of imprisonment. The deterrent effect on conviction of an expected sentence of length $QS$ is reflected by $\gamma_2$. If both these effects exist, then $\gamma_1$ and $\gamma_2$ are both negative.

The intercept $\gamma_0$ is included in $u(Q,S)$ so that the size of the potential criminal population, the proportion that would commit crimes in the presence of even trivially small imprisonment sanctions $[P(0,0)]$ can be adjusted. If $\gamma_0$ were not included in the model, then from equations 4.3 and 4.4, $P(0,0) = 1/2$, thus limiting the size of the potential criminal population in the absence of imprisonment to exactly half the total population.

The parameter $\gamma_0$ can be viewed as incorporating all factors other than $Q$ and $S$ that affect the size of the criminal population. Included among these are socialization effects and the host of socioeconomic and demographic factors that have a substantial effect on the size of the criminal population. Also included are the effects of the nonimprisonment sanctions such as apprehension, conviction, and probation. Since the parameter $\gamma_0$ is a function of these excluded factors, its assigned value could be determined in principle by the prevailing values of these excluded variables. Viewed from this perspective, $\gamma_0$ is not merely an innocuous intercept but a key parameter of the model.

The function $P(Q,S)$ decreases as either $Q$ or $S$ increases and the other is held constant. This, of course, is consistent with the deterrence hypothesis— the higher the sanctions, the lower the entry rate into criminal activity.

We can now substitute equation 4.2 for $\eta$ and equation 4.3 for $P$ into the general crime model, equation 4.1, to provide a formula for the crime rate as a function of prison sanctions $Q$ and $S$:

$$C(Q,S) = \left(\frac{\lambda}{1 + qQS\lambda}\right) \left(\frac{e^{u(Q,S)}}{1 + e^{u(Q,S)}}\right) \tag{4.5}$$

Because both the incapacitative and deterrent effects grow as $Q$ and $S$ increase, $C$ will decline with increases in either of these variables. Indeed, even if there are no deterrent effects—$u(Q,S) = \gamma_0$, leaving $P(Q,S)$ a constant—the incapacitation effects alone will cause $C$ to decline as either of the variables $Q$ or $S$ increases. For any given value of $QS$, the crime rate with deterrent effects included is lower than when they are ignored or absent.

### The Imprisonment Rate

When the aggregate crime rate is $C$, then the equilibrium imprisonment rate per capita $I$ is the product of $qQS$ (the expected man-years of imprisonment per crime) and $C$ (the crime rate per capita). Then the product $(qQS)C$ is the number of man-years of imprisonment imposed per capita per year.

Even without a deterrent effect, the crime rate declines with increases in $Q$ and $S$ because of their incapacitative effects. The introduction of deterrent effects simply increases the rate of decline. When there are deterrence effects, however, the imprisonment-rate relationship behaves in a way very different from the way it behaves when they are absent. If there are no deterrent effects, then the criminal proportion in the population $P$ is some constant value for all values of $Q$ and $S$. Since $\eta$, the proportion of time an offender is free, is inversely related to $QS$, then $\eta$ approaches zero as $QS$ increases—offenders spend most of their time locked up. Since in the absence of deterrent effects $P$ does not decline as $QS$ increases, the number of this fixed criminal population in prison will increase steadily as $QS$ becomes large.

When deterrent effects are considered in the model (allowing for the possibility that $P$ will decline as $Q$ or $S$ increases), a larger prison population is not necessarily a consequence of an increase in sanction levels. If the deterrent effects of the increases in sanctions promote a sufficiently large decline in the criminal population, then increases in prison penalties per crime, $qQS$, may be more than offset by the reduction in the crime rate resulting from the decline in the criminal population. Specifically if a 1 percent increase in $QS$ results in more than a 1 percent decline in the crime rate $C$, through the combined increase in incapacitation and deterrent effects, then the imprisonment rate [the product $(qQS)C$] will also decline. Stated in an extreme form, if sufficiently large penalties are threatened, then those threats may have to be invoked only occasionally if deterrence is sufficiently pervasive.

Figure 4-5 shows a typical plot of the imprisonment rate as a function of $QS$ for selected values of the parameters. Initially the imprisonment rate

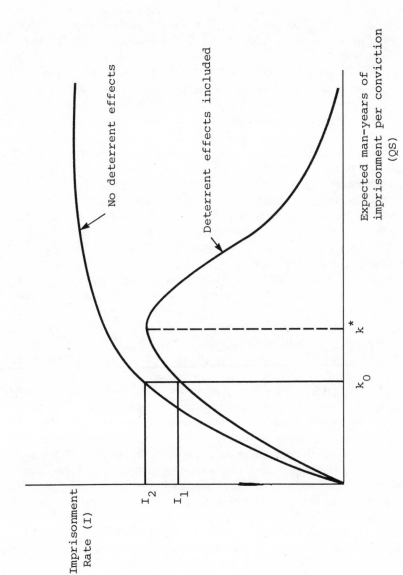

**Figure 4-5.** The Imprisonment Rate as a Function of Prison Sanction Level

increases until $QS$ reaches some value $k^*$, and the imprisonment rate decreases for $QS > k^*$. Figure 4-5 also shows the prison population for the same parameter values but with no deterrent effects. For any given value of $QS$, say $k_o$, the prison population without deterrence $I_2$ is always greater than that predicted when deterrent effects are present $I_1$. Thus even when the deterrent effect is insufficient to reduce the prison population, the presence of an effect moderates the magnitude of the increase.

Figure 4-5 suggests that the benefits of reduced crime accruing from higher sanctions need not require a substantial increase in the prison population and might even result in a reduction. The degree to which this is the case depends on the magnitude of the deterrent effect.

There are now no reliable estimates of the magnitude of the deterrent effect of prison sanctions (either $Q$ or $S$) on index crimes. In the absence of such evidence we present a parametric analysis of the operation of this model to illustrate the issues involved.

In this illustrative sample we use data from 1970 on index crime rates and sanctions. In 1970 the probability $Q$ of imprisonment given conviction (the frequently quoted certainty of punishment) for an index crime was about 0.25. The implications of a drastic increase in that probability to 0.75 could reflect the response to the many calls being heard for increases in the certainty of punishment and would reflect the intent of mandatory-minimum legislation. It is possible that this increase in $Q$ would overcrowd the prisons and so might require an adjustment in $S$, the time served in prison. The amount of that adjustment would be related to the magnitude of deterrent and incapacitative effects resulting from the threefold increase in $Q$.

The deterrent effect is measured by the parameters $\gamma_1$ (reflecting the stigma component of deterrence) and $\gamma_2$ (reflecting the expected-sentence component). Since there are no good estimates of the magnitude of either of these (or even of their sum), some critical judgments are required.

In developing this illustrative application of the model we represent the estimate of the magnitude of the deterrent effect by the elasticity of crime with respect to sanctions (the percentage reduction in crime associated with a 1 percent increase in the sanction $QS$). We assume an elasticity of 0.2, reflecting a presumption that in 1970 a 1 percent increase in the imposition of sanctions would have led to a 0.2 percent reduction in the criminal population. This assumption implies that the size of the criminal population at $QS = 0$ is actually 20 percent greater than the criminal population estimated for 1970.

We must also estimate the way in which the deterrent effect is partitioned between the stigma component, associated simply with the fact that a person has been sent to prison, and the component due to the expected sentence $QS$. For example, we attribute 25 percent of the deterrent effect to stigma and 75 percent to expected sentence. Finally we must select a value of the individual crime rate $\lambda$, which we assume to be five crimes per person per year.

For this illustrative example figures 4-6 and 4-7 show the estimated number of index crimes and the prison population in 1970 for two values of $Q$ (0.25, the actual 1970 values, and 0.75, a major increase associated with a presumed mandatory minimum-sentencing policy). Under the 1970 sentence policy of $S = 2.6$, the number of crimes under the mandatory-minimum policy would have been 3 million, or 55 percent of the 5.5 million that occurred under the same sentence but with $Q = 0.25$. The mandatory-minimum policy would have resulted in 280,000 prisoners for index crimes, an increase of 60 percent over the 175,000 calculated for 1970.[17]

For the case $Q = 0.25$ we see that increases in $S$ increase the prison population. For $S = 10$ the prison population would have exceeded 325,000. The prison population reaches a maximum value of 360,000 at $S = 12.5$ years and declines for larger values of $S$. If $Q = 0.75$, the crime rate declines much faster as $S$ increases, and the maximum prison population of 300,000 occurs at the relatively low value $S = 3.7$ years. Thus at least under the condition of this example, increasing sanctions does not necessarily increase the prison population. The crime rate under the mandatory-minimum policy ($Q = 0.75$) is lower than in the case where $Q = 0.25$ for any given value of $S$. In addition, however, for all $S > 5.5$ years, the mandatory-minimum policy would also have fewer people in prison than for $Q = 0.25$. For $S < 5.5$, the mandatory-minimum policy would have a higher prison population.

For all values of the same total sanction $QS$, the society has less crime if $Q = 0.75$. This occurs because an increase in the certainty of punishment accomplishes more than an increase in severity. This is reflected in the stigma term $\gamma_1 Q$ in equation 4.4.

Figures 4-6 and 4-7 have a horizontal line drawn at the prison population of 176,000, which is 80 percent (the index-crime proportion in prison) of 0.11 percent (the average imprisonment rate) multiplied by the 1970 U.S. population. If this population became a meaningful constraint, then $QS$ would be limited to about 1.5 if $Q = 0.75$, whereas $QS$ could become as large as 4 if $Q = 0.25$. In both cases the crime rates at the constraint would be comparable and close to the actual 1970 crime rate. Some means for penetrating that constraint, at least for some short time, would be required for the mandatory-minimum policy to be feasible.

## Exploration of Some Policy Issues

A major focus of this chapter has been revising the thinking about imprisonment policy. The primary focus of most policy debate is the absolute level of imprisonment. However, there appears to be far less flexibility in that absolute level than the intensity of the debate would suggest. The historical evidence supporting the relative stability of imprisonment rates shows that it is more

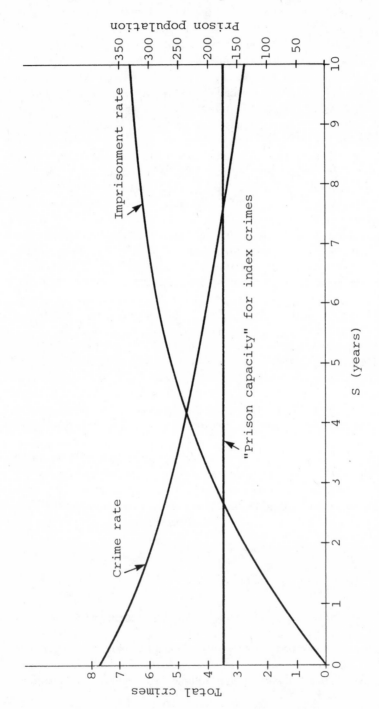

**Figure 4-6.** Estimated Number of 1970 Index Crimes and Prisoners versus Average Sentence under the 1970 Imprisonment-Risk Policy ($Q = 0.25$)

Note: $\lambda = 5$ index crimes per year; deterrence elasticity $= -0.2$; stigma $= 25$ percent of deterrence.

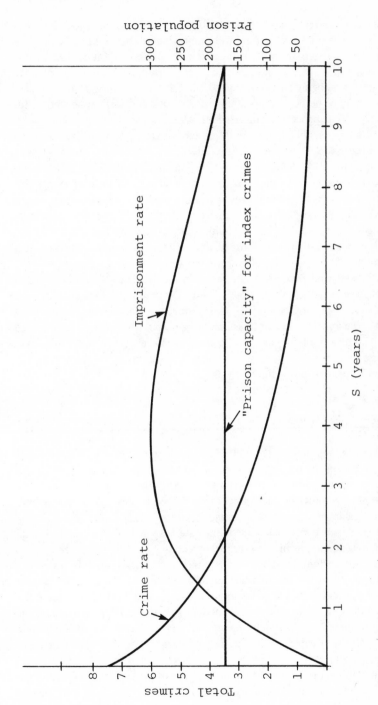

Note: λ = 5 index crimes per year; deterrence elasticity = −0.2; stigma = 25 percent of deterrence.

**Figure 4-7.** Estimated Number of 1970 Index Crimes and Prisoners versus Average Sentence under a Mandatory Minimum Policy ($Q$ = 0.75)

appropriate to consider imprisonment policy in terms of the allocation of a fairly fixed resource rather than in terms of adjusting its absolute level.

Changes are needed in both substance and process to rationalize setting imprisonment policy in the context of these observations. The substantive changes invoke a recognition that some of the factors influencing the imprisonment decisions may be counterproductive for equity and justice, as well as for crime control. The process changes emphasize that sentencing policy is an allocation process and that there should be more explicit considerations of the nature of those allocations. Because the allocation process is a dynamic one, with changing values and changing crime environments, there should be a process that continually revises the allocation procedures in light of those changes. This would be a marked change from current practice, in which the allocation process is totally decentralized and implicitly achieved only through a variety of decision makers distributed throughout the criminal justice system. The ultimate decisions are thus made by the last actor in the sequence rather than by the most appropriate one.

The rationalization process should focus on the issue how the limited prison capacity can best be allocated to those offenders who represent the most serious threat to the society, both currently and potentially. These are the offenders who commit the most serious crimes at the highest rate, and the allocation to those who commit the least serious crimes at the lowest rate should be diminished correspondingly. This must be done, of course, while preserving the appropriate due-process procedures.

*Records Maintenance Policy*

The process by which individuals are selected for imprisonment depends to a significant degree on the nature of the criminal records they have compiled. This practice makes sense under both retributive and utilitarian perspectives. From the retributive viewpoint the punishment is enhanced for offenders who demonstrate the most chronic repetitive criminality. In utilitarian terms repeated convictions are evidence of both a high crime rate (particularly if these follow in rapid succession) and a continuing criminal career.

Thus it is important for the records policy to properly reflect crime-commission patterns so that the most serious offenders are identified. The current policy in most jurisdictions is to maintain adult criminal records for the duration of the individual's life and even longer. In part this is a consequence of the manual-record technology, which makes revising such records difficult and tedious. It is also motivated by the desire of police to know all they can about potential suspects in a crime or by the desire of probation investigators to learn about the individuals' previous criminality as part of presentence investigations. Record information is demanded by these investigators because it is free to them; to do otherwise would represent a significant operational cost in manual files. Thus the policy of maintaining adult records indefinitely is generally followed.

Modern information-processing technology provides the opportunity for reconsidering this policy. It is easy to program computers with algorithms for erasing certain information after a specified time has passed or for relocating the storage of certain information so that it cannot be retrieved unless certain conditions (for example, indictment for a serious felony) are met. This technology provides an opportunity for easy implementation of elaborate and detailed sealing and purging rules for individual criminal records. Thus an offense can be eliminated from a criminal record after a specified time has elapsed, and that period could be longer for the more serious offenses.

Rules can also be developed for sealing an entire criminal record if the individual has been free of criminal convictions for a specified time, and the period could be longer for some kinds of records (say those with violent crimes) than others. Such sealed records could not be retrieved unless the individual were accused of some serious offense, at which time the record might then become accessible for sentence determination. After some longer period of time the records could be totally erased, so that the individual would no longer be in jeopardy of any later official review of that recorded information. One of the privileges inherent in an erased record might be the right of the individual to deny any prior criminal record, if he were asked officially.

Such a record-decay process can have beneficial consequences, not only because it could enhance the redemption of an individual after a reasonable period of time but also because it could enhance crime control. To the extent that the imprisonment decision uses criminal records, allocation of prison space should be focused on individuals whose rate of conviction is relatively high; they would not have the opportunity for record decay until long after their criminal careers were completed.

To the extent that the stigma associated with a criminal record represents a significant component of the deterrent effect (and this has been shown to be significant at least for the offense of draft evasion,[18] which is particularly relevant to individuals without a prior felony record), the decay of the record provides an additional incentive for keeping a clean record to those who have been able to go straight for the prescribed period of time. Even during the period before the record is sealed, the prospect that it will eventually be sealed increases the individual's stake in avoiding subsequent conviction. Reducing the number of people carrying such stigmatizing information enhances the impact of that stigma.

The irrationality of retaining adult records indefinitely is matched in reverse by the policy regarding juvenile records. The argument for decaying adult records over a finite time has its counterpart in urging that a juvenile's records should also decay over a finite time rather than instantaneously on his eighteenth birthday. In most jurisdictions records of juvenile arrests and punishment are maintained separately from adult records. This permits judges to operate under the fiction than an arrested and convicted eighteen-year-old is a first-time offender even though he may have a lengthy record. Perhaps even more serious, a juvenile who is wise to the workings of this system faces only a minimal deterrent threat to encourage him to function in a law-abiding way during his juvenile years. He knows that his punishment as a juvenile will be minor and that his crimes as a juvenile may not affect his sentence if and when he is tried and sentenced as an adult. The motivation for avoiding the execessively long stigmatization of a juvenile is appropriate. On the other hand, there should be some recognition that such policies diminish the deterrent effect on him as a juvenile and reduce his vulnerability to receiving a stiff sentence as an adult. When juvenile records are not taken into account in sentencing convicted offenders who have just reached the age of majority, then all convicted offenders are treated similarly, regardless of their prior juvenile criminal activity.

Concepts similar to the finite decay of records proposed for adults should also be incorporated into the operation of juvenile records. It is reasonable, for example, that the rate of decay (the duration over which records are retained) be faster for juveniles in order to enhance their opportunity for redemption and cleaning the slate, but an instantaneous erasure at a known time provides too much opportunity for gaming the system. Therefore a policy of record decay similar to that described for adults (including purging of events, sealing of records, erasure of records, but with different decay) should be formulated for juvenile offenders. In this system times until decay would be formulated as a function of the individual crime types (the more serious offenses are kept for longer periods) and the length of prior record (longer records would be kept for longer periods of time than records with single convictions).

Such a system would assure that imprisonment is allocated to the persons who commit the more serious acts at a higher rate and thereby away from those with the relatively less serious prior records as juveniles. It would also target the use of imprisonment on the more serious offenders as they reach adulthood, the time of highest crime rates.

*Population Sent to Prison*

It can be reasonably anticipated that trends of urbanization, the loosening of the traditional controls exercised by family, community and church, the anonymity of the urban environment, and the more frequent resort to the formal criminal system for settling disputes will all result in an increasing volume of events to be handled by the criminal justice system. The one countertrend is the demographic aging of the population.

If the society is to avoid expanding its prison population significantly—and we have every reason to believe that it would like to do so—then it would appear desirable to be more explicit about the way in which the increasingly strained resource of imprisonment is allocated. This requires that there be much more careful thinking about those who should not be sent to prison and that more formal social policies be declared to affect those judgments. There is little disagreement with the use of imprisonment for persons who commit the more serious crimes, for those who commit crimes at the highest rates, and for those who are most persistent in the crime-committing activities. The more difficult problem is establishing a means of allocation at the margin. A number of steps can be identified to help provide policy guidance to that reallocation process.

For some offenses decriminalization becomes the more appropriate policy, especially when the difficulty of enforcing certain behaviors through criminal sanctions is recognized. To a large degree this has already happened with mari-juana use, where a very small portion of the prison population consists of marijuana users. It is still true that approximately 10 percent of the prison population is made up of drug offenders. To the extent that persons convicted of drug offenses are those who have engaged in other, much more serious crimes, then they could and should have been convicted of the other crimes. To the extent that they were major dealers in drugs, then appropriate controls and regulations of the distribution networks for drugs would appear to be the more effective mechanisms. If a significant portion of the prison spaces for drug offenders are consumed by those whose only crime is the possession or use of drugs (and they appear to make up about 6 percent of the prison population), especially the less serious drugs, then it becomes important for society to decide whether the spaces should be allocated to drug users or to the marginal burglars or robbers who are now frequently set free on probation.

In view of the growing strain on the imprisonment capacity, it becomes important to search for other means of delivering the sanctions available to criminal law. Imprisonment should be viewed as a last resort, where the other methods cannot work. Options here would include various forms of restitution by the convicted offender to the victim. This would involve an appropriate payment where the offender is able. In other cases the offender may be assigned to perform supervised public service work, with part of his income being as-signed to his victim. This would be particularly appropriate for the relatively minor offenses of larceny and for certain burglars with minimal records.

For those individuals who can be identified clinically as having the most potential for rehabilitation and successful functioning in the community, such community-based programs are clearly to be preferred. They represent the most humane form of treatment and perhaps the best hope for improving the be-havior of the individual. They also represent the least drain not only on the dollar cost of imprisonment but also on the available prison space. For some such community-based treatment programs, it may become necessary to provide much more intensive supervision of the identified offender than is now the case, thereby enhancing his deterrence (by increasing the likelihood that he will have to suffer the sanction if he violates the law and by providing a minor degree of punishment associated with the restriction on movement associated with the supervision).

## Use of State Sentencing Policy Commissions to Regulate Sentencing Policy

There has been a recent movement toward adopting the concept of presumptive, or flat-time, sentences. This movement has been generated partly in reaction to the flaws in the indeterminate-sentence process. Under an indeterminate-sentencing procedure the time an individual serves in prison is determined principally by a bureau of corrections or a parole board. Their decision is based presumably on their professional judgment of the prisoner's rehabilitation. But inevitably many forms of negotiation and manipulation enter the process, largely because of the difficulty in reaching an objective and definitive professional judgment on the prisoner's progress toward rehabilitation.

Major opposition to the indeterminate sentence has developed from the perspectives of both the inequities involved in the use of parole discretion and its poor crime-control effectiveness. From a civil-libertarian point of view the indeterminate sentence provides too much opportunity for disparate sentences among different individuals who have committed similar crimes and have accumulated similar records. The time a prisoner serves is determined much more by his ability to display the appropriate rehabilitation posture than the appropriateness of the sentence for his deed. A prisoner who has become wise to the system could size up this process and thus count on a lesser sentence; he is therefore less deterred from committing crimes than if he had to face the average sentence for that crime.

The movement for presumptive sentences has seen its realization in the enactment of a number of determinate-sentence laws. California was among the first states to enact such legislation. In the California legislation offenses are categorized into four classes and sentence ranges are prescribed for each class (1.3, 2 or 3 years; 3, 4, or 5 years; 5, 6, or 7 years; and life with or without parole). When a person is convicted of an offense in one of the classes, the judge is expected to give him the middle sentence in the range, but he can choose one of the outer ranges if there are aggravating or mitigating circumstances involved. However, the option to sentence the individual to probation remains for most offenses. In addition, extra time can be added to the sentence if the individual is charged with having used a firearm in the crime (2 years), caused "great bodily injury" (3 years), or has served a prior prison term (1 year for each prior term, or 3 years if an earlier offense was a "violent" crime).

There are some difficult questions regarding the anticipated impact of such a sentencing law on the operation of the prison system. In California there appears to have been no explicit estimate of the anticipated prison population that would result from the new law. It is conceivable, for example, that if all persons convicted in California were sentenced in accordance with the new law, the imprisonment rate would increase by a factor of two to four.

To the extent that there are indeed pressures for maintaining a homeostatic imprisonment rate in California, it is likely that relief valves will be found. The traditional relief valve has been the parole decision, but the determinate-sentencing law appears to have reduced significantly the capacity of the parole function to regulate prison populations. If overpopulation becomes a problem in California, pressures may then build on judges to use probation more frequently and on prosecutors to adjust the nature of the charges (for example, deciding not to charge an armed robber with the use of the weapon).

The final issue, then, will not be whether an allocation is made, but who gets to make it and on what basis. The California law appears to have reduced substantially the discretionary parole powers of the adult authority. The net effect of the legislation on the discretionary powers of the judge is uncertain, although the judge's power has probably been increased. The major recipient of the discretionary authority appears to be the prosecutor. The criteria used by each would inevitably be different, and it will be important to observe the unfolding of this process as the law becomes implemented.

There are two basic modes by which presumptive sentences can be determined. The legislature can specify the penalties directly; or alternatively, the legislature can empower a sentencing commission with the responsibility. California has chosen the former mode.

We recommend that the legislature leave this responsibility with a sentencing commission for two reasons. First, a commission would have greater flexibility to adjust penalties when conditions like prison overcrowding indicate the advisability of at least selective changes in penalty specifications. Second, it could assemble a staff of analysts to monitor trends in sentencing practices and project the implications of these trends on such issues as sentence disparity and prison populations. Such a commission would be charged with making an annual review of the operations of the sentencing policies within its state. The commission would be responsible for collecting data from each of the courts and prisons within the state to estimate the impact of alternative sentencing policies on the current and projected prison populations. The commission would necessarily have a technical staff responsible for specifying the data to be reported by the courts and prisons and for organizing the data into appropriate estimates of the impact of the alternative sentencing policies on the corrections system. It would also be charged with estimating the impact of the current policies on crime through analysis that would build on the models presented here. This information would be provided by the technical staff to members of the commission for their consideration in arriving at proposed sentencing schedules. As predictions of impact were tested and sources of error identified, the process of estimation should improve over time through the development of experience, data, and corrective methods. With these analyses the commission should be able to estimate the impact of alternative sentencing schedules and guidelines on crime, prison populations, and budgets. With such information the commission could then exercise its judgment on appropriate sentencing schedules.

The commission should be empowered by its legislature to establish appropriate sentencing schedules. The schedules would take account of the prison capacity of the state and community judgments of the relative seriousness of the various types of crime, all within policy guidelines established by the legislature. The proposed sentence schedules would thus reflect the combination of the retributive and the utilitarian issues which should be considered in developing criminal sanctions.

The state sentencing policy commission would revise the sentencing schedules on the basis of an annual review, and the schedules so formulated would be submitted to the legislature for approval, revision, or veto. When a sentencing schedule is submitted, its implications for the prison population and budget (for operations and for construction if current capacity is to be exceeded) would be provided to the legislature. This would force the legislature to consider not only the appropriate degree of "toughness" but also the impact of sanction levels on prison populations and state budgets.

Such a commission should include representatives from the judiciary, prosecutors, legislators, the defense bar, public citizens, and appropriate research experts. The interaction between the different perspectives, skills, and values of these representatives is necessary in formulating appropriate sentencing policies.

With a process of this sort we anticipate that the allocation process would indeed become more rational, would more closely reflect the appropriate community standards, and would still leave within the judiciary and the prosecution the appropriate discretion for handling individual cases. Moreover, explicit considerations of the most appropriate applications of imprisonment sanctions should be expected to moderate the rate of crime because sanctions would be applied to those offenses and against those offenders where they would do the most good, consistent with appropriate constraints on maximum use.

## Notes

1. United States, Department of Justice, Federal Bureau of Investigation, *Uniform Crime Reports, 1975* (Washington, D.C.: U.S. Government Printing Office, 1976), p. 179.

2. James Robison and Gerald Smith, "The Effectiveness of Correctional Programs," *Crime and Delinquency* 17 (1971):67-80; Robert Martinson, "What Works?–Questions and Answers about Prison Reform," *The Public Interest* 35 (Spring 1974):22-54; Douglas Lipton, Robert Martinson, and Judith Wilks, *The Effectiveness of Correctional Treatment: a Survey of Treatment Evaluation* (New York: Praeger, 1975).

3. Robison and Smith, "Effectiveness of Correctional Programs," p. 4.

4. Gordon Tullock, "Does Punishment Deter Crime?" *The Public Interest* 36 (Summer 1974):103-111.

5. James Q. Wilson, "Lock 'Em up and Other Thoughts on Crime," *New York Times Magazine*, March 9, 1975, pp. 11, 44-48.

6. See Herbert L. Packer, "Two Models of the Criminal Justice Process," *The Limits of Criminal Sanction* (Stanford, Ca.: Stanford University Press, 1968), for an excellent treatment of these issues.

7. Since 1974, the imprisonment rate in the United States has increased markedly. By the end of 1976 the rate was 129 per 100,000, or more than two standard deviations above the long-term average. Whether the increases since 1974 represent a short-term displacement around a stable longer-term average or a permanent departure to a higher long-term level remains to be seen. We anticipate that the former will prove to be the case.

In all three countries the behavior of each of these time series is characterized by a second-order autoregressive process, which suggests an underlying process associated with a second-order differential equation. Such a process can be interpreted as reflecting shifts in the threshold of crimes deemed punishable by imprisonment in light of changes in criminality in the population, with the threshold shifting in order to maintain the constant imprisonment rate. See Alfred Blumstein and Jacqueline Cohen, "A Theory of the Stability of Punishment," *Journal of Criminal Law and Criminology* 64 (1973):198-207; and Alfred Blumstein, Jacqueline Cohen, and Daniel Nagin, "The Dynamics of a Homeostatic Punishment Process," *Journal of Criminal Law and Criminology* 67 (1977):317-334.

8. U.S. Department of Justice, *Uniform Crime Reports, 1975*; James Q. Wilson, "Who Is in Prison?" *Commentary* 62 (November 1976):57.

9. Marvin E. Wolfgang, Robert M. Figlio, and Thorsten Sellin, *Delinquency in a Birth Cohort* (Chicago: University of Chicago Press, 1972).

10. Jacob Belkin, Alfred Blumstein, and William Glass, "Recidivism as a Feedback Response: An Analytical Model and Empirical Validation," *Journal of Criminal Justice* 1 (1973):7-26.

11. Stigma may still be important for some offenses or at least for some groups of people. Blumstein and Nagin examine the effect of conviction and imprisonment sanctions on the rate of draft evasion (which involves only people with no prior felony record) and find that the stigma component of convictions (as opposed to the expected-sentence component) represents the major deterring

factor. See Alfred Blumstein and Daniel Nagin, "The Deterrent Effects of Criminal Sanctions on Draft Evasion," *Stanford Law Review* 28 (1977):241-270.

12. If there is enough switching among these crime types by the offenders, then aggregation is a very reasonable treatment. Wolfgang, Figlio, and Sellin (*Delinquency in a Birth Cohort*) found that such switching was very common among the juveniles in their birth cohort. Alfred Blumstein and Michael Greene (in "Analysis of the Crime-Switching Process in Recidivism," Working Paper, Urban Systems Institute, Carnegie-Mellon University, 1976) found that switching decreased with offenders' ages.

13. Benjamin Avi-Itzhak and Reuel Shinnar, "Quantitative Models in Crime Control," *Journal of Criminal Justice* 1 (1973):185-217; Reuel Shinnar and Shlomo Shinnar, "The Effects of the Criminal Justice System on the Control of Crime: A Quantitative Approach," *Law and Society Review* 9 (1975): 581-611.

14. These values of $q$, $Q$, and $S$ are estimated in Blumstein and Nagin, "Deterrent Effects."

15. S. Warner, *Stochastic Choice of Mode in Urban Travel: a Study in Binary Choice* (Evanston, Ill.: Northwestern University Press, 1962); M. Ben-Akiva and S. Hause, "Estimation of a Work Mode Split Model Which Includes the Carpool Mode," Working Paper no. WP-1, U.S. Department of Transportation, 1974; and M. Kohn, C.F. Manski, and D. Mundell, "An Empirical Investigation of Factors Which Influence College-Going Behavior," *Annals of Economics and Social Measurement* 5 (1976):421-446.

16. Blumstein and Nagin, in "Deterrent Effects," explore the implications of allowing $u(Q,S)$ to have a more general form where $S^n$ ($n \geqslant 0$) is substituted for $S$ in equation 4.4. To make the exposition less elaborate here, we restrict ourselves to the case where $n = 1$.

17. The actual number of prisoners in state and federal prisons in 1970 sentenced for index crimes was 180,000 according to the U.S. Department of Justice, *National Prisoners Statistics, 1970* (Washington, D.C.: U.S. Government Printing Office, 1971).

18. Blumstein and Nagin, "Deterrent Effects."

# 5

# Epilogue:
# On Imprisonment

*Gilbert Geis*

That certain persons must be removed from the free society and placed in captivity or imprisonment is a generally accepted axiom of contemporary social life. Taking this matter for granted is a poignant commentary on the perceived need of political groups to protect themselves from persons in their midst who have violated what are seen to be fundamental rules of human relationships and social order.

The writers in this volume have addressed different aspects of the condition of crime and imprisonment. David Ward discussed the nature and accomplishment of the much-heralded Swedish prison regime, a regime often proclaimed to be marked by exceptional compassion and common sense. Tom Murton, a former (and highly controversial) prison director himself, argued that autocratic management tactics in penal institutions undercut any prospects for inmate improvement. Murton wants prisons to be run in the manner of participatory democracies. He hopes that such benign and constructive arrangements will instill a sense of decency and dignity in prison inmates and that these qualities may inhibit any consequent turn to criminal behavior.

For his part, Robert Martinson considered the actual impact of incapacitation on crime rates. Martinson toyed at some length with an aspect of economic market theory, considering whether the removal of a certain number of offenders from the free society might not merely open up a market for other persons who now want to engage in crime, much as such forces play on the supply of college professors and professional tennis players. Martinson engaged in a good deal of rabbinical speculation about the nature and effects of policies of restraint and incapacitation on criminal offenders. But there is a tough programmatic sinew within his approach. He wants us to look clearly at the key issue whether anybody ought to be incarcerated or whether there might not be other, more acceptable ways to accomplish legitimate goals of social protection. Martinson's penultimate declaration is strongly worded:

> To advocate "locking 'em up" in our present state of knowledge is to acquiesce to the barbarism of confinement and to treat the overkill inherent in restraint as a fact of nature and not an invention of man. In other words, we choose evil instead of having it forced upon us. A democratic and prosperous society will seek ways to reduce this evil and crime as well, for caging a human being to protect society seems to be a confession of impotence in the face of crime.

The impetus for this volume arose from an intense concern in the United States about both criminals and their treatment. A growing body of literature sets forth the nature of this malaise. One illustration comes from the observations of Gary Wills, who asks: "What on earth do we think we are accomplishing with our prison system? That question is hard to answer, because people who think as little as they can about prisons are bound to think confusedly. Analysis is abortive and disjointed."[1] Wills, like so many other commentators, is bitter in his condemnation of the present state of prisons in this country:

> Solitude, deprivation, the breaking up of families, the loss of meaningful work, the denial of heterosexual congress—all the staples of our prison system—do not "reform" human beings, but destroy them. We no longer have any excuse for not knowing that. The record is too clear. We have been far too successful at breaking down dignity and hope. The harder we work along these prior lines of effort, the more we must harm and cripple ourselves.[2]

The writers in this volume agree that something needs to be done about prisons in the United States—something drastic. To adopt a phrase once offered by Kenneth Lamott, they suggest that the American prison system is "like a blindfolded elephant lumbering along at the edge of a precipice."[3] The writers also echo Curtis Bok, who said "someday we will look back upon our criminal and penal process with the same horrified wonder as we now look back upon the Spanish Inquisition."[4] No voice in this volume, however, advances an idea that is taking firm root in the United States today: The trouble with our penal policy is that it is too lenient and not enough offenders who commit crimes are dispatched with speed to prisons and kept there for much longer periods of time than they now are. Many Americans appear to be moving toward such a viewpoint. Witness, for instance, a letter that appeared recently in the *New York Times:*

> Crime in this country could be reduced drastically if we had two kinds of prisons.
>
> The first kind should be made as miserable for the inmates as is consistent with maintaining their good health. First or second offenders would be sentenced to these prisons for as little as a month but no longer than a year. These prisons would be designed to punish and thereby to discourage criminal behavior.
>
> However, certain criminals are not deterred by punishment and must simply be put away for a number of years. Their prisons should be as pleasant as is consistent with security and economy. For it is simply cruel to punish people for a long time . . . when it is clear that they will not respond.[5]

## The Condition of Imprisonment

The scholars who have presented their views here, being social scientists, have understandably refrained from attending to the more personal, uglier aspects of the condition of imprisonment, though their sentiments in this regard are not difficult to discern. Such descriptive matters, the social science ethos maintains, are better left for popular commentators and novelists.[6] However, it may be worth spending a moment in this chapter, where the dictates of social science etiquette do not lie so heavily, to comment on imprisonment as it affects the inmate.

Life in prison often is marked by pathos, indignity, and a sense of the grotesque impermeability of the condition of captivity. Given the delimited span of human life, it seems heartbreaking that some persons are condemned by others (or, if you will, by themselves) to spend parts—sometimes very large parts—of their lives imprisoned. Gresham Sykes, in a telling portrayal of prison existence, has noted that the worst part of imprisonment is the loss of autonomy and the concomitant deprivation of so many things that allow a human being to esteem himself. In an important observation Sykes notes that for men the loss in prison of the opportunity for heterosexual contacts does not produce sexual frustration in any important sense; rather it is especially painful because it removes from the prisoners' world a token of worth and self-value.[7] A woman who tells a man, I love you, tells him that he is, in another human being's sight, appealing and attractive—worthwhile. Presumably, he will attempt to behave in ways that will elicit further approval, and presumably such ways will generally (though far from necessarily) be law-abiding. It is in this manner—by depriving inmates of a positive impetus toward goodness—that imprisonment is believed to fail most.

Prisons throw the human condition into dramatic relief: the trivial becomes tragic; the absurd becomes profound; weakness becomes strength; and unreasoned faith gives life its only logic. Indeed, a former chaplain at San Quentin has maintained that no prison ought to be built if it denies an inmate some wild hope of escape.

> Not that a convict might necessarily bring himself to try an escape. But he has a right to his harmless dreams, the exercise of all his ingenuity in his dream; it keeps his mind alive; and the remote possibility offers a last hope for men condemned to life imprisonment.[8]

The penal condition is epitomized nicely by two quite trivial anecdotes, both reported by prisoners. Nathan Leopold relates that while he was an inmate in the Illinois State Penitentiary he was asked, by virtue of his having a college degree, to settle a fiery dispute that had arisen over the question, How long is a string?[9] Robert Size, imprisoned in Iowa, tells of a fellow inmate who spent endless hours training a cockroach to walk in a straight line. Asked why he had done so, he replied: "Well, you never know in here when you might need a cockroach who can walk in a straight line."[10]

In a more poignant view, Ignazio Silone, the Italian author, tells a story from his childhood, recalling an occasion when he saw a small, barefoot man being dragged through the streets of his village. "Look how funny he is," Silone said. Silone's father looked at him severely and then led him away. He had never been so angry with the boy.

"What have I done wrong?" Silone asked.

"Never make fun of a man who's been arrested! Never!"

"Why not?"

"Because he can't defend himself. And because he may be innocent. In any case, because he's unhappy."[11]

Among the more revealing studies of the bleakness of prison life is that of Willard Gaylin, a psychiatrist, who followed the fate of young men incarcerated as conscientious objectors for their refusal to register for selective service or to accept duty in the armed forces during the Vietnam War. Articulate, intense, and dedicated, sometimes highly self-righteous, and often very sensitive, these young men found their moral integrity undermined almost totally by the indifference of the prison system, other prisoners, the staff, and the remote personal and public audience toward whom their behavior inevitably was at least in some measure directed. One of the conscientious objectors said:

> I'm not sure how you write an article which can adequately describe this place. If you don't exaggerate, it makes it sound like a CCC camp, but it isn't. There's something different here, something horrible and destructive, something that forces a deterioration, and it is not rubber hoses and beatings. How can anyone describe it?[12]

Another prisoner put the same feelings in these words:

> It's not right that people should be locked up like animals. It's not the discomfort really, it's the whole thing. Everything that goes into making a prison. The food, getting up at a certain time in the morning, walking around the yard in a certain way—we always walk along the grass, counterclockwise. I don't know why. We always do it. Yesterday, I said we should walk around the other way. Everybody said why not, and we did. You know, it doesn't make any difference.[13]

But all this may be melodramatic, an expression of sentimental and mawkish feelings. Some maintain that many prison inmates prefer their condition and that this preference goes a long way toward explaining their otherwise seemingly inexplicable recourse to inept criminal acts so soon after they are released from prison. Prisons offer social amenities—sports, television, camaraderie—and most notably they offer surcease from the demands of initiative and choice. Gustave de Beaumont and Alexis de Tocqueville, the inquisitive Michelins of nineteenth-century American prisons, thought that the rule of silence that prevailed in our penitentiaries at the time was not at all burdensome for American inmates "whose character is taciturn and reflective," though they surely believed that such a regimen would be "more painful to Frenchmen."[14] Anthropologist Margaret Mead offers another cross-cultural insight on the varying meaning that imprisonment may have:

> It was not until fear of prison for the big men was substituted for the fear of punitive expedition that the Mundugumor came under government control. The leaders were willing to face death, but to face six months in prison wondering who had seduced or stolen their wives—this humiliating inactivity they were not willing to face.[15]

These homely observations caution us to add generalizations: prisoners differ and pains of incarceration vary according to the nature of the person suffering them. A middle-class college professor may agonize too much, in part out of reluctance, to suggest that persons in lower socioeconomic groups, used to less, may be satisfied more readily with less. Even if this is true (and it may not be), the idea seems cold and condescending; but all lives, after all, are lived under some constraint. The walls hemming in most of us may be as invisible as those that entrap Marcel Marceau in his awesome mime performance, but they are there nonetheless, quite substantial and impregnable.

Metaphors aside, imprisonment represents a particularly severe restriction of liberty and freedom of choice, and it seems to me that policymakers might usefully direct their energies toward keeping as many criminals as possible—if not all criminals—out of prison. There is, of course, a second, vital part to such an observation, one that suggests that penal policy must also provide satisfactory protection to innocent persons who might be victimized were offenders not locked up or otherwise punished or reformed (presuming that they would continue to commit offenses if there were not some effective intervention).

Philosophers have struggled mightly over issues of proper penal policy. It is clear that only under the most unusual circumstances will we imprison a person who, only suppositiously, is deemed likely to inflict injury on another. But the matter becomes less clear when we ask whether we ought to incarcerate a person longer than fairness dictates in terms of the law he violated, on the grounds that by doing so we possibly or probably can protect the innocent by incapacitating this offender or by deterring potential offenders.

Penal policy seesaws uncertainly, with the desire (among many of us) to keep punishment as benign as possible on one side and the interests in protecting potential crime victims teetering on the other. Additional items enter into the matter, too. Revenge is one of the most potent. It makes people feel better, more certain (in a paradoxical kind of way) that they live in a just world[16] if the depredator suffers, no matter what further purpose might be served by such an infliction of pain. Presumably, assuaging desires for revenge has its own social value, if only producing more contented citizens.

The dilemma persists. There may well be persons who, on reasonable and defensible grounds, will have to be incapacitated because we believe this will prevent their again taking possessions from or hurting others. That this may be necessary is shameful, though perhaps "shameful" is too weak and uninformative. It would be much better if we could all live in a state of harmony, particularly if the price for this harmony were not excessively exorbitant in terms of such things as self-determination and self-expression. Plato long ago pondered this matter in *The Republic* and concluded that the only way to establish such a condition was to perpetrate a "noble lie." The lie would proclaim that a divine being had created some persons of gold, others of silver, and still others of bronze and that each person was immutably tied to the prerequisites associated with whatever level at which he had been ordained to operate. Plato noted some gold parents might have silver children, and some bronze might produce offspring of a higher quality than themselves. And so it would be.[17] It is a simple-minded, tongue-in-cheek formulation, significant mostly for what it said about what cannot be done to reduce crime in a heterogeneous, fluid, cosmopolitan social system. Similarly in recent times, Albert K. Cohen in a brief monograph with a fine title, *The Elasticity of Evil*, ponders whether, in a country of paragons, minor idiosyncracies and deviations might not be elevated to the plane of censure that is today reserved for criminal offenses. Cohen suspects that the nature of the human animal is such that even if there were a centripetal movement toward conformity, "small improprieties and breaches of manners and good taste would become crimes." In short, he says, "there cannot be a society of saints because a process of social redefinition operates continuously to insure that all the positions on the scale from wickedness to virtue will always be filled and that some will be holier than others."[18]

Penal policy, then, is a function of seemingly inevitable criminal activity and the needs for protection from it (real or imagined) on the part of potential victims and revenge against it on the part of actual victims and their sympathizers. It is perhaps trite but also necessary to say that penal policy is closely interwoven with many other elements of the social structure, most notably with aspects that inhibit or elicit different forms of criminal activity. It is certainly tied to religious ideas, economic structure and well-being, and social attitudes, as well as fundamental views about the nature of human beings. The question is not whether a society, or at least this society, ought to have a penal policy excluding some persons from freer intercourse with their fellows but rather what form such a policy ought to take. It might be argued that the wrong persons are being imprisoned; indeed some wits maintain that honest folk ought to be locked up to protect them from the hordes of predators that roam at large.[19] Perhaps attention ought to be focused on the so-called white-collar offenders rather than on burglars and muggers, on the ground that retaliation against wrongdoing in high places will establish a social climate encouraging conformity to laws at all levels of society.[20] These are complex and somewhat theoretical questions, for it is obvious that penal policy responds very directly to public power and that the "haves," in part to protect the things that make them the "haves," are intent on seeing that obvious depredators are kept from robbing and hurting others and that similar protection is sought at all levels of the social system.

Crime, especially urban street crime, overpowers Americans. Part of their fear is instilled and aggravated by the prurient sensationalism of the mass media, but a good deal of it is very realistic. That the elderly must remain immured in their apartments at night is a testament to a rational instinct of self-preservation, not to hysterical paranoia.

What, then, can be done? The end-of-the-continuum options, aside from radical alteration of the external society, endorse making prisons more humane (and perhaps even abolishing them) or making them tougher. Obviously there can be diverse combinations of these items. For example, sentences can be lengthened, yet the manner in which they are served can be rendered more amiable. But that something is required is self-evident. A telling comment to this point is offered by a writer in the liberal *Village Voice*, who suggests that while it may be true that awful social conditions have turned some people into muggers, it serves no decent purpose to continue to allow these muggers to proceed unhindered in victimizing additional innocent persons.[21]

But many Americans recoil from tougher prison policies. To put the matter more precisely, liberals and criminal justice authorities, particularly judges, who have great power in such matters, resist intense pressures from the majority of the population to inaugurate harsher responses to criminal activity. The reasons for this are worth trying to understand, for they cut to the core of the irresolute manner in which the United States seems to be proceeding in matters of penal policy. There is an unwillingness to place offenders in prisons unless it appears absolutely necessary to do so, because of a widespread judicial conviction that incarceration represents the abdication of hope. It is believed that prisons only make prisoners worse; and since prisoners almost invariably emerge from their cells and return to the free society, this is a consequence to be avoided if possible. The criminal justice system is beset with irregularities that undermine any hidebound sense of an imperative response to a particular criminal act. So many persons manipulate the system in so many ways that it seems arbitrary, cruel, and pointless to move in a literal fashion against the remainder. Imagine, for instance, a juvenile thief whose parents plead for a chance to send him to military school rather than have him confined to a reformatory. Few judges would rule against offering the youngster such a chance; but just as few would not appreciate that this particular boy was buying his way out of incarceration, since it would be discriminatory to send youngsters whose parents could not afford military school tuition into penal confinement.

There is also, of course, an inevitable erosion of indignation in the face of massive case loads; and there is a keen appreciation that criminal activity of great enormity occurs in the well-to-do classes that remain far beyond the reach of the criminal justice system. Any day's reading of the *Wall Street Journal* indicates so many business frauds with official response of so mild a nature, if there is any response at all, that the singling out of street offenders for strong retribution reeks of hypocrisy.

The previous four chapters in this volume all deal with different aspects of the manner in which a social system should or should not approach the matter of dealing with law violators. We will begin our review of these contributions by considering the most concrete statement, that which discusses the penal program operating in Sweden.


### The Penal Program in Sweden

Cross-cultural emphases are often invigorating enterprises because they open up vistas far removed from those visible in more parochial inquiries. The history of criminal justice is replete with ideas that seemed impossible in a specified jurisdiction until it was demonstrated that other places had tried such curious things and apparently suffered not a whit for them. Experiences in England (to note a jurisdiction with which we share our common-law heritage) with narcotics, consensual sexual offenses, gambling, unarmed police, newspaper reporting of criminal trials, elimination of the grand jury, attorneys who serve as often as prosecutors as they do as defense attorneys, and a host of other matters all illuminate a range of criminal justice potentialities for the United States.

The utility of cross-cultural observation is even more pronounced with regard to Sweden. That small Scandinavian country's experiences have teased American commentators for several generations, most markedly since the appearance in 1936 of Marquis Child's panegyric, *Sweden: The Middle Way*. Two contradictory themes have pervaded American reviews of Swedish activities. The first is a glorification, marked by a strong tendency to see what Sweden has done as an admirable precursor of the things that America should be doing. Welfare, pensions, socialized medicine, abortion, and the use of heavy taxes to reduce alcohol consumption are among the Swedish programs that some Americans regard as admirable and worth emulation. The second is a strong sentiment that whatever Sweden has achieved that might appear attractive, it has done so by sacrificing something essential to the American scheme of things, something irreplaceable. A recent headline in *Time*, "Something Souring in Utopia," captures the nature of this belief.[22] The article enumerates Sweden's achievements ("a materialistic paradise" in which "neither ill-health, unemployment nor old age pose the terror of financial hardship"), but then notes a sharp increase in burglaries and robberies, as well as persistently high alcoholism and suicide rates.

Somewhere between the panegyrics and the muckraking lies the position that it matters not what Sweden is doing about this or that because Sweden is a unique place, quite different in significant ways from nations such as the United States.

Why does Swedish penal policy interest Americans, when it is obvious that the kinds of criminals that Sweden has and the cultural contours of the country present a picture so dramatically different from that found in the United States? Perhaps the best explanation is that, except for the Swedish prototype, American reformers have few other models toward which to turn. They are horrified at prison conditions in the United States. They are disenchanted with rehabilitation programs (which often involve strong elements of punitive vengeance lying beneath a semantic disguise). China and Cuba offer only cautionary tales: crime apparently can be reduced by massive social reorganization. Most Americans, for better or worse, clearly prefer to live with crime as it is rather than under more authoritarian regimes that appear to have reduced their crime rates with concomitant reductions in freedoms to do a wide range of other things besides commit crimes.

For these reasons, among others, the benign approach of the Swedes appears particularly attractive. The irony may be that the strength of the Swedish penal system may exist not in its enlightened policies (however advanced many of these may be) but rather in a considerable national ability to be self-righteous about what is done (rather than intensely critical).[23] Certainly this is hardly a full explanation, but it may contain an important germ of insight. So long as you think that what you are doing is good, both for you and for those to whom it is being done, you can take pride in virtually anything. Sweden does well in dealing with criminal offenders, Ward informs us, but perhaps not really all that well if criteria such as recidivism rates are examined closely.

The fundamental aim of penal practice in the United States has been to reduce the extent of crime, since crime is regarded as beyond the point of tolerance. In Sweden, on the contrary, crime is not seen yet—and in most regards reasonably so—as so significant a national problem; therefore it is not of paramount importance whether what is done to criminals has much impact on the amount of criminal activity. It might be argued that Sweden does not have much serious crime *because* it has a decent penal policy, but it seems much more likely that both the policy and the relatively low level of crime stem from the same cultural roots. It is quite possible that if Sweden had a tougher rather than a more indulgent penal policy, it might have even less crime than it now does.

As Ward notes, American attention was first focused firmly on correctional work in Sweden through a highly influential article written for *Federal Probation* in 1966 by Norval Morris, former dean of the University of Chicago Law

School. Morris' generally balanced overview was particularly handicapped at
the time by the absence of valid information regarding the consequences (at
least in recidivist terms) of the Swedish penal approach. But there was no
question that Morris was highly impressed by what he saw:

> [The average Swedish citizen insists that] the Swedish criminal or
> prisoner still remains a Swedish citizen meriting respect, continuing
> properly to enjoy a quite high standard of living and remaining a part
> of the community. . . .

> These sentiments were brought to his work by the prison officer who
> sees a Swedish quality of firm, decent, respective, and polite treatment
> between individuals as properly determining his attitude and behavior
> toward the inmate. It is a great asset, substantially diminishing the
> alienating prison subculture creating processes that are to be found so
> often in other countries.[24]

Morris's examination of the Swedish prison program has been updated
recently by Richard A. Salomon, a staff member of the Center for Studies in
Criminal Justice of the University of Chicago Law School, who spent two
months in Sweden. Salomon's portrait is an almost unrelieved paean of praise.[25]

Salomon credits the activities of KRUM, the Swedish prisoners' rights
union, with forcing the Swedish government to abandon plans for the construction of a network of large (420-inmate, very large by Swedish standards) prisons
and with obtaining concessions for prisoners in regard to visitations, mail censorship, and leaves of absence. Salomon notes that Sweden apparently (cross-
cultural comparisons, as he points out, must always be accepted guardedly)
imprisons about sixty-four persons per 100,000 population, while the United
States locks up about two hundred per 100,000 each year. In addition, since
1966 Sweden has reduced its prison population by 22 percent, while the nation's
population has risen 6.5 percent. Most Swedish prison inmates are sentenced for
drunken driving, and a vast majority of sentences (91 percent) are for less than
twelve months, while 76 percent of them run less than four months. The proprisoner stance of the mass media is said to encourage reform[26] (though certainly no group can have a stronger—and apparently uninfluential—champion than
American prisoners do in Tom Wicker of the *New York Times*).

Following his statistical review, Salomon moves into precisely the anecdotal
recitals that Ward regards as seductive snares for the unwary: mention of Tillberga, glamorization of the voluntary probation officer-prisoner relationship,
note of the center for education at Uppsala, and so on. We learn that isolation
cells have been converted into a photographic processing laboratory, and similar
oddments of admiration are forthcoming. As did Norval Morris, Salomon aban-
dons his unrestrained praise of the Swedish correctional regimen when it comes
to issues of probation and research. He finds the former disappointingly bogged
down in a morass of paludism, and the latter virtually nonexistent except for

a few stray, poorly designed inquiries. Finally, as so many other American commentators have done over the years, Salomon issues the penultimate call: "It would do well for us in the United States to seriously consider [Sweden's] reform efforts."

## On the Ward Critique

Ward's report on Swedish prisons fleshes out and, at times, contradicts the conventional popular wisdom on the subject in American circles. Ward has strong credentials to underscore his points. He did research in Sweden for a year and has returned for summers; so, compared with the visits of most American writers, his period of exposure was considerably longer. He brings to his task considerable penological experience. He worked for 18 months at a federal penitentiary in Terre Haute, Indiana, as part of the team that contributed to Daniel Glaser's study of the effectiveness of penal institutions[27] and conducted research for several years in the then highly regarded California prison system.

Ward attributes the public relations image of Swedish corrections prevalent outside the country in part to an understandable attempt by Swedish authorities to put their best foot forward. Implicit in this observation (though Ward does not suggest it himself) may be that the forty-four years of largely uninterrupted rule by the Social Democratic party had introduced into Sweden considerable unopposed control of the information fed by governmental agencies to outsiders. It is in such terms that American criminologist William Chambliss, in an as-yet-unpublished study based on an extended period of work in Sweden, insists that Sweden's official crime rates, when examined against the result of a victimization study he helped to conduct, are a good deal higher (and nearer to those of the United States, based on similar victimization inquiries) than official figures would lead a cursory observer to conclude.[28]

Several items in the Ward study might be singled out for further emphasis and annotation. I will focus briefly on day-fines, voting and volunteers, and research, recidivism, and relative deprivation.

### Day-Fines

The day-fine policy in Sweden represents a procedure that carries immediate appeal to an observer seeking "true" justice. Wrongdoers are assessed amounts calibrated not only in terms of what they have done in violation of the law but also with regard to their wherewithal. The poor man will have to pay $40 for a given offense while the wealthier violator is fined $400 for the same kind of behavior. It is easy to belittle the day-fine system by referring to Anatole France's oft-quoted remark that "the law, in its majestic equality, forbids both the poor man and the rich man to sleep under bridges, to beg in the streets, and to steal bread,"[29] and by suggesting that the patterning of criminal offenses is class-related and that penalties tied to wealth provide only a spurious facade of fairness and equality. But it is one thing to say that a system may not be perfect and another to charge it, on such grounds, with being unsatisfactory. The Swedish approach to fines is a good deal more equitable than any that I know. Its difficulty for America, it seems to me, is precisely where it draws its viability in Sweden. Swedes offer a good deal less resistance to matters which in the United States tend to be regarded as unwarranted invasions of privacy. All income tax reports in Sweden are open records, and any Swede can readily discover how much his neighbor earns—or at least reports. Each Swede has a six-digit *personnummer* which follows him or her from birth to death. The number covers every aspect of life—social security, military service, medical records, police reports, tax matters, and motor vehicle items—and these diverse records are easily collated.

Perhaps American resistance to such a registration procedure merely reflects an untamed antisocial impulse in the country's citizens, but a system of day-fines in the United States might create as much deception as it would induce equity. Nonetheless I would like to see it attempted, if only in one jurisdiction and for only one kind of offense, say, traffic violations.

*Voting and Volunteers*

Swedish prison inmates, as Ward notes, have the right to participate in local and national elections, a right that would be regarded, I suspect, as unconscionable by most Americans. In part, of course, Swedes vote by party not by persons, and I doubt that former inmates in Sweden find their way onto election ballots, as they obviously might and should in the United States in areas where the vote of a prison population, given the giant size of many American penal institutions, could control the outcome of an election.

Writing in a prison magazine almost a decade ago, I advocated that prison inmates be allowed to vote, primarily because it seemed to me to represent an essential element of fairness in a democratic society.[30] In a facility at which I was doing research, I had been impressed by the references former narcotic addicts often made to the precise date when they would have their civil rights restored. It seemed to me that this matter of readmittance to citizenship was of great importance to them. Also, a prison constituency would render a legislator much more sensitive to the implications of penal policy.

The entire subject of restoring or maintaining the rights of convicts is just beginning to receive the attention it demands in the United States. Prison inmates are extraordinarily diligent as injustice collectors, seeking assiduously to locate examples of ways in which they are being "done in". Their incarceration itself can be justified to them in terms of what they did to another human being. As commentators have noted, most inmates are probably quite supportive of penal codes barring acts like those they have engaged in. But when extra and extraneous punishments accrue, they rightfully become angry. I recall once trying to discuss with a group of inmates at the Terminal Island federal penitentiary the rationale of the law requiring them to register as ex-felons when they were released. It mattered not that the registration ordinance was largely pro forma; they wanted to know why it existed at all.

Bills have been introduced into the United States Congress to allow ex-offenders to vote for candidates in federal elections, and most states now have eliminated rules forbidding civil service employment for former felons. The reasoning behind such moves (and in support of the Swedish approach) is that gratuitous humiliation engenders only unnecessary hostility and alienation. This point comes through nicely in a vignette from a book by Hannah Green in which a mental patient explains why one attendant at the hospital is successful with the patients, while the other has so much difficulty:

> Deborah knew why it was Hobbs and not McPherson. . . . Hobbs *was* a little brutal sometimes, but it was much more than that. He was frightened by the craziness he saw around him because it was an extension of something inside himself. He wanted people to be crazier and more bizarre than they really were so that he could see the line that separated him, his inclinations and random thoughts, and his half-wishes, from the full-bloomed, exploding madness of the patients. McPherson, on the other hand, was a strong man, even a happy one. He wanted the patients to be like him, and the closer they got to being like him the better he felt. He kept calling to the similarity between them, never demanding, but subtly, secretly calling, and when a scrap of it came forth, he welcomed it. The patients merely continued to give each man what he really wanted. There was no injustice done.[31]

The extensive use of volunteers in the Swedish probation service is a matter that ought to receive a good deal more research attention than it apparently has. The scheme has a quick, initial appeal. I worked on the evaluation of a similar kind of endeavor in Santa Clara County, California, in which young attorneys were assigned to help supervise parolees. Our conclusion, based on intensive interviews (but no recidivism data), was highly flattering to the effort:

> This program is hardly a panacea, but no parolee was coerced into the program nor forced to remain with it, and the program's record shows that good things, decent and helpful things, were done for persons who throughout their lives had been neglected and overlooked by society. From that perspective, dramatics aside, it might reasonably be argued that the program represents a worthwhile endeavor, one that reflects a considerable credit on its participants. This, on the evidence we have gathered, is our judgment.[32]

We did discover that the attorneys tended to be highly unreliable in keeping appointments, and this appeared to further embitter some parolees who had relatively little trust in authority figures to begin with. There also were a number of status and role strains that developed between the regular parole officers and the volunteers, particularly when the volunteers unreasonably played the "good guys" and forced the agents into the roles of "heavies." In addition, with time the volunteers showed a considerable diminution in enthusiasm for the program. It was hoped that the attorneys (just as Ward notes in regard to the Swedish volunteers) might, over the years, acquire some insights into the criminal justice system that would serve to introduce improvements.

The entire area of supervising convicted criminals on the streets requires closer scrutiny. It always has been assumed, for instance, that parole agents and probation officers are interchangeably effective with all clients, so that very little attempt is made to match for maximum utility.[33] The assignment of paid civilians to supervise felons on a one-to-one basis, with the pay based on the degree of success in keeping the individual crime-free and abiding by stipulated rules to produce this result is a tactic that might be worth exploration.

### Research, Recidivism, and Relative Deprivation

What has the unique Swedish approach to criminal correction accomplished? It takes no research inquiry to conclude that if nothing else, Sweden offers a blueprint to other nations showing what can be done to provide humane conditions and certain amenities to persons who have been convicted of criminal offenses. Inevitably, though, the question must be asked: At what price?

Swedish penal policy has been notorious regarding the neglect of research information on which to base sophisticated assessments of what is being done. Only recently have a number of studies been published that move toward empirical examination of the Swedish plan for dealing with criminal offenders.

The results of the research work detailed by Ward are both intriguing and puzzling. Not having the original publications, I cannot say whether they meet the criteria of experimental sophistication. But unless prisoners were released randomly from institutions at diverse times, for example, it seems to me difficult to maintain, as Bondeson apparently does, that continued incarceration is related to the formation of more intensive ties to the criminal world (as measured by indexes such as the adoption of criminal argot). And if the offenders were released randomly, it is not beyond belief that those who missed out on the boon of release might have become considerably more antagonistic than they otherwise would have been.

That criminal argot absorption itself correlates with criminal behavior carries Bondeson's argument an important step further and suggests an approach that American researchers might well consider in their designs. But with the absence of longitudinal data, the logic of her argument seems treacherous. Presumably some offenders were released earlier than others because the former were regarded as lesser offenders by whatever criteria and those retained longer were believed to deserve such additional punishment. Those qualities on which such judgments were made rather than the length of incarceration per se might well relate to the adoption of things such as criminal argot and to participation in subsequent criminal behavior.

On the other hand, there is a certain commonsense aspect to the Bondeson conclusion that goes in the other direction. The longer you remain in the army, the more likely you are to behave like a veteran military person. But how does this translate into other behaviors, particularly when measured against alternative adaptions?

The argument for less incarceration that emerges from a study designed along the lines of Bondeson's inquiry does not seem compelling to me. The absence of those deleterious traits acquired in prison, for instance, was not notably effective in preventing the earlier offense, and there is a need to demonstrate (at least if fewer crimes is the criterion of success) that the extra time in the community, with the chance then to commit additional offenses, is outweighed by the criminogenic influences of the institutional experience.

The experience of "prisonization" (to use the term long favored by American writers to describe the taking on of procriminal attitudes within a penal institution) that is reported by Bondeson to increase unilaterally with increased prison time has been found to operate otherwise by a number of American studies. Donald Clemmer, the American warden who coined the term "prisonization," thought that it developed much as the Swedish workers say it does: "It can be stated that imprisonment, even in progressive institutions with their carefully developed training programs, frequently increases the criminality of the individuals it holds."[34] In a recent volume, however, Gordon Hawkins insists that Clemmer's view has "suffered a death by a thousand qualifications, [and is] so attenuated that even now there are those who are unaware of its demise."[35] Stanton Wheeler's study showed that as the time for release approached, prisoners abandoned prisonization views and moved back toward whatever conformist attitudes they originally had held.[36] Investigations by Peter Garabedian[37] and Daniel Glaser[38] confirmed this finding. Similarly, David Ward, in a study coauthored with Gene Kassebaum and Daniel Wilner, notes: "Aggregate data from our study . . . turned up no evidence of a curvilinear relationship in the endorsement of inmate norms and the time served in prison."[39] Thomas Mathiesen, a Norwegian who has been deeply involved in the Swedish prison reform movement as an advocate for the inmates, has reported that for the group he studied, "the population of inmates was characterized by a profound lack of solidarity" and the "inmates seemed to a considerable extent 'unprisonized'."[40] Reviewing the evidence, Hawkins notes:

> There is . . . evidence that some offenders benefit from some of the
> programs provided in prisons. . . . At the same time it should be some
> consolation that the belief that all who enter prison are ineluctably
> doomed to deterioration proves, on examination, to rest on no more
> rational basis than the antithetical idea that, if only we knew how,
> panacean programs could be devised which would transform all of-
> fenders into model citizens.[41]

The complex nature of judgment rendition in matters involving penal
policy will occupy the final segment of this chapter. Here I noted only that
the prisonization materials from Sweden provide but a single testament to the
fact that a decision on proper penal policy requires the most carefully designed
studies stipulating with some precision what the work seeks to measure. At the
same time, no policy can be recommended comfortably, unless some attempt
is made to assess other possibilities. It must be appreciated that all social interventions represent unique, almost idiosyncratic endeavors, which at best test a
general proposition only erratically.[42] The time, the personnel, the setting, the
internal dynamics, and a myriad of other contingencies inevitably undermine
the accuracy of the outcome of the experiment as it bears on the truth of the
general proposition that was being tested. The mixture of personalities in an
intervention will always be unique, and singular events—an escape, a fight, a
national election—can have profound consequences for the outcome. Then
when the results are in, there still remains the consummately involved task of
intruding on the research conclusion the value judgments about what is important to achieve, what the interpreter is willing to pay for such an achievement, and what other, largely unknowable, eddying consequences are likely to
flow from a particular approach.

The Bondeson findings indicate that recidivism remains about the same
whether offenders are incarcerated or are allowed to remain in the community
under supervision. This finding is taken to support a recommendation for less
use of prisons and greater use of community release, since "the benign Swedish
correctional institutions produce as few positive effects and almost as many
negative effects as the more repressive American institutions."

Several suppositions are implicit in such a conclusion. First, of course, there
must be a belief that the recidivism rate is satisfactory and that the society
should tolerate this later crime committed by convicted offenders. Otherwise
it would be logical, to conclude, as many Americans probably would, that since
community release and imprisonment fail to reduce recidivism, there is something drastically wrong with both of them and that things ought to be done
to redress the matter.

That the Swedes apparently do not regard such an option seriously says
much for the character of the society and probably much more for the nature of
the crime threat that for the moment is being posed to articulate, policy-influen-
tial citizens. Particularly little national anguish or anger is apt to be aroused

when so many offenders are "but for the grace of God" types, most notably drunken drivers and tax evaders. There is something quite compelling to be said for kind treatment when there is some likelihood that you are going to be the recipient of it.

On the other hand, the recidivism figures noted by Ward are a bit startling. That 85 percent of the persons incarcerated in youth facilities are said to recidivate, and that almost half those sentenced as drunken drivers get into trouble serious enough to be registered in the central criminal roster indicates that the Swedish approach (because it is too benign, too tough or, perhaps, quite meaningless?) does not have much of an effect on the ability of its clientele to remain free of later trouble. A warning though: recidivism figures must be regarded with great caution, particularly when cross-national comparisons are drawn. Robert Martinson, writing with Judith Wilks, reports that recidivism in the United States is actually 23 percent and probably declining, rather than 50 percent to 75 percent, as previously believed. Martinson and Wilks also found that persons sentenced to reduced-custody residential establishments, such as halfway houses and group homes, have a much higher recidivism rate (42 percent) than those sentenced to prison. Particularly eye-catching was the claim that the current recidivism rate of 23 percent was well below that of the 1960s, which was said to be 33 percent.[43] Whether, with congruent definitions and comparable populations, the Martinson-Wilks figures, the other American results, or the Swedish data will have to be readjusted remains a puzzling—and important—issue for persons seeking research conclusions on which to base policy decisions.

Bondeson's emphasis on *relative deprivation* as a concept to aid understanding of the "failure" of the Swedish prisons merits a moment's pause. The term originally was used by Samuel Stouffer and his associates in *The American Soldier* to refer to promotional prospects among noncommissioned military and air force personnel.[44] Later it took on the nuance of a discontent created (as Plato appreciated when he wrote of the need for the noble lie) by "the perception of discrepancies between the goals of human action and the prospects of attaining these goals."[45] Jackson Toby has noted that in the United States, where the ideal may be social ascent, the poor climber can be more bitter than the poor eater in other societies.[46] The term *perception of* represents the essential element in the definition. John Fowles captures the core theme of relative deprivation in the following observation:

> a much more interesting ratio is between the desire and the ability to fulfill it. Here again we may believe we come off much better than our great-grandparents. But the desire is conditioned by the frequency it has evoked; our world spends a vast amount of its time inviting us to copulate, while our reality is as busy frustrating us. We are not so frustrated as the Victorians? Perhaps. But if you can only enjoy one apple a day, there's a good deal to be said against living in an orchard

of the wretched things; you might even find apples sweeter if you were allowed only one a week.[47]

Swedish prisoners, Bondeson suggests a bit jingoistically, have had it so good in their nonprison lives that the mild deprivations of the benevolent prison experience may be regarded as intolerably harsh. The explanation may be correct, though I rather expect that it underestimates the true misery of imprisonment, no matter how normal a facade surrounds the experience. Lars Gorling, writing of a Norwegian penal institution, offers several pointed paragraphs demonstrating that the kinds of indecency that accompany captivity can produce a common bitter response:

> And they came up with new tests all the time. No one wanted to tell us what they were for—either because they didn't want to influence the results, or because they didn't want us to know; I'm not sure. They answered our questions with wisecracks, but were very anxious that we replied properly to *their* questions. Wisecracks or stony silence.
>
> They wanted to know everything; intelligence, likes and dislikes, interests, what it had been like when we were kids. About our parents, brothers, and sisters. Did we lay girls, and since when. And then we had to interpret various words.
>
> It was like eating yourself up, in daily portions. Afterward, you felt gnawed to pieces and hollowed out, squeezed dry and quite empty. It almost hurt you all over.[48]

Finally, Ward asks, as others also have done when they concluded their much more superficial reviews of the Swedish penal program: How relevant is this to the United States? His answer, with which I agree, is that at the moment the transferability is not great. The case would be a good deal stronger if there were more impressive research works demonstrating or buttressing the claims advanced for the Swedish performance in governmental public relations documents. But such documentation would go only so far. Sweden does not have the kind of crime that marks conditions in the United States. The attitudes of the Swedish people, perhaps because of this, are not antipathetic to freedoms for prisoners. Sexual opportunities, one of the hallmarks of the Swedish program, stem partly from the relaxed attitudes that Swedes traditionally have manifested in regard to sexual matters.

It will be particularly interesting to monitor carefully changes in Swedish correctional policy now that we have Ward's baseline materials. Allegiance in Sweden to the welfare emphasis remains very high. Swedes complain endlessly about the *skatt*—the tax—but their complaints rarely have the nasty edge that marks American attacks on welfare recipients; rather the Swedes complain that the tax rates are awful though they are necessary. Note, in this regard, three comments appearing in a recent book containing interviews with workers in the city of Vasteras: "We pay taxes until we're blue in the face and they get money from social services so that they can go on drinking." The use of the separative pronoun "they" is perhaps the most meaningful part of the sentence. And: "The tax is ten kronor . . . and the insurance went up to 49 kronor . . . because so many motorbikes are stolen and there are so many insurance swindles." And finally, with regard to foreigners beginning to settle in the city: "I don't get on with Italians and Spaniards and that sort. . . . They're so greasy."[49]

Whatever happens, Swedish penal policy is well worth serious and close American attention. It may not represent the middle way, but it is *a* way; and for a country such as ours, lost in a labyrinth, any way that promises surcease merits attention.

## Murton's Model

The approach to prison management advocated by Tom Murton seems to fit institutions  in the South and Midwest of the United States better than the tension-ridden, heavy-security prisons located in states such as Illinois, New York, and California. Murton himself had his major prison experience in institutions in Arkansas and Alaska, and he now teaches in Minnesota—three jurisdictions whose prisons have not been marked by the major crime problems associated with heterogeneous and angry urban populations. On the other hand, many of the cases he cites are from northeastern and far western sites, and the conditions in Arkansas during Murton's tenure were clearly worse than in most other sections of the country.

As he notes, Murton follows a long and honorable tradition of attempts in the United States and abroad to initiate prison reforms characterized by larger degrees of inmate participation in prison management. Such an approach operates on the principle that human beings, left to themselves except for the imposition of a democratic control structure, will behave in a decent, law-abiding manner. The evidence for the proposition, it hardly needs saying, is not all one way.

The first half of Murton's essay traces the admirable impulses that gave rise to the building of prisons; this is followed by a sharp critique of the contemporary conditions to which prisons have come. The text includes some tough or soaring metaphors and some fine lines that may be sly or inadvertent. Thus, he notes that Americans are too busy with other things to pay attention to prisons. Among the "other things" listed are "getting bread on their table and locks on their doors." Sometimes the argument seems controvertible, as with the insistence that because some persons steal even after the draconian punishment of having their hands chopped off, this proves that chopping hands off does not serve to inhibit thievery. But Murton also arrays a heavy line of documentation for the theme that inmate participatory government, allowed to operate, promotes astonishing alterations in prison atmosphere and inmate behavior.

The essential point of Murton's argument appears in this theorem: If inmates are allowed to participate in decision making, then they will tend to act more responsibly toward themselves, others, and the prison society. The corollary of this point is: If inmates develop a sense of responsibility while in prison, they may tend to act responsibly after release by committing fewer or no crimes. Murton makes no absolute claim for his position. He simply outlines what he would do if he were running a prison and asks the reader to judge, on the basis of good sense and history, whether the program seems worthwhile. As with the Swedish blueprint, Murton's model may be judged on several different levels. First, it may be deemed desirable because it is decent. Or it may be required to reduce crime to a stipulated level. Depending on the arena of judgment, different verdicts can be rendered on the approach Murton advocated.

## A Mexican Prison

Is participatory government necessary, or can any kind of prison management system that deals fairly and decently with the inmate population achieve similar results? The famous Hawthorne experiment in which factory workers registered increased productivity when their working conditions were improved, but then continued to turn out larger amounts when the boons were removed, offers a cautionary tale regarding the tendency to abstract from the total atmosphere of an intervention any particular content ingredient. The conclusion was that the Hawthorne workers did better, not because of improved lighting and similar things, but because they were made to feel special and important.[50]

Murton's blueprint can be compared to the ethos of an institution that the writers in this volume visited about two years ago. The Centro Penitenciario del Estado de Mexico is located forty-five miles west of Mexico City and three miles outside the city of Toluca. This prison, unlike the stereotype of Mexican prisons (that stereotype, like many others, has some solid foundation) was extremely well run and well tended. The grounds were carefully kept with a profusion of lovely flowers (though the inmates were said to be wary of these, insisting that they made them feel like "sort of queers"), and the institution was saturated with a continuous flood of classical music. The warden insisted that the uplifting nature of the music was in considerable measure responsible for the special atmosphere of the prison and for the low rate of violence. Mexican prisons, he said, averaged about one violent death each month; there had not been a killing in this institution in the past five years. Thoroughly skeptical, we observed that the warden himself reflexively turns off the speaker in his office when he enters. It is not that the music is so loud (though it is), but that it is unremittingly there.

The warden is intensely involved in the operation of the prison, fiercely loyal to the inmates, totally a benevolent dictator, and obviously very intelligent. He is quite meticulous and will drift toward a picture on the wall as he talks, adjusting it carefully so that it hangs straight. He is like a plantation owner, a pater familias, a type once very familiar in the operation of American prisons, but now no longer found here. There is an interchange that is revealing. An elderly inmate approaches the warden tentatively, takes his hat off and holds it awkwardly in his hands. The warden recognizes him, and they talk briefly. Apparently satisfied, the old man makes a sign of appreciation and shuffles backward out of the warden's presence, moving about ten feet before he puts his hat back on and turns away. "No prison in the world is good," the warden tells us. "This one isn't as bad as others." With some prodding he grants that, yes, he would say that this is the best penal institution in Mexico.

The prison holds 597 persons on the day that we visit, though it has a capacity of 900. The intake is controlled by the warden in his further capacity as director of the network of prisons of which this one is part. Food is raised on a prison farm, and some of it is distributed at no cost among the prisoners' visitors.

The prison yard is filled with swings and playground slides to be used by the children of families visiting the institution. There are rooms for overnight stays for wives, husbands, and male and female friends of the inmates. The rooms are neat, and many of them contain cribs for infants; but they are sterile and institutional in appearance. There is something of a brothel image to this section of the prison, and both the warden and his assistant include sexual innuendoes when they discuss the conjugal visiting program. We mention that California has begun such a program, but that the waiting list dictates about one visit each eighteen months. Surprisingly, the warden immediately interprets this as imposing an undue hardship on the prisoners' wives.

Prisoners dress in a wide variety of clothing styles. They earn moderate wages, below outside rates, but well above comparable American rates. About half their earnings go for food, and the remainder is split among savings, the institutional welfare fund, and personal expenses.

An American in the prison (he is one of three there) tells us that he had been incarcerated now for 6½ years and tries to convince me (and half succeeds) that this lengthy sentence is for nothing more serious than the possession of a few drugs at the time of the Olympic Games in Mexico City. The warden later details a much more serious criminal record, including multiple charges of burglary. The prisoners all report that marijuana is readily available within the prison to anyone who can afford it. A second American—held there while awaiting the determination of his final sentence—tells us angrily that he had been placed in isolation for several days merely because he had broken some property on the prison grounds. Later we learn from the third American that the second had shattered a window during an attempted escape. The long-timer says the prison is peaceful, the consequence, he suggests, of the fact that Mexican inmates have been "beat down" outside and have no heart for rebellion and resistance. He thinks the reportedly low recidivism rate is primarily a function of the fact that drug pushers, who he is certain would return to business, do not operate in the catchment area of this prison because they know how tough sentences are. If they do happen to be caught in the jurisdiction, they are apt to leave Mexico on release from prison, he says, and operate in South America. Therefore they do not show up in statistics on repeated crime by former prisoners.

By American standards, the classification hearing we attend is a bit astonishing. There are, besides us, about fifty students from a law class in a Mexico City university. The most personal affairs of the inmates being reviewed are paraded before the entire group. We mention to the warden later that this would be regarded in the United States as an intrusion into the inmate's right to privacy, and he seems taken aback by the idea, as if it were a bit strange.

One case we listen to involves a nineteen-year-old man, single, from Mexico City. He had been sentenced for the rape of his two sisters, ages ten and twelve. The sisters have been frequent visitors to the prison while he was there. Each staff person at the table—there are more than a dozen—offers some information and an opinion. The man's IQ is 90, says one. We learn, too, that he has worked hard in the institution, and now he is employed in a job outside but returns to the dormitory at night. He has learned to read a bit while in prison, but it is said he will never be much of a student. Someone adds that, yes, this is true, but he is a fine soccer player. On the outside, the man had not been entered into school until he was fifteen years old. Because of his age, the other pupils harassed him, and he did not remain in school very long. The neurologist says that the man is slightly neurotic but basically healthy. The prisoner still does not believe that what he did was a crime, but the staff feels that he has been impressed with the fact that if he does it again it will get him into trouble. There is no parole provision; the man would report to the police weekly. The warden listens carefully to all the information, then renders his decision: The man is to be released.

Later, in his office, the warden talks with us unselfconsciously about "love, comprehension, and good feelings" as the way to help prisoners. He believes that 80 percent of the men should not be in prison in the first place, though he thinks that the other 20 percent should be there because they are dangerous. He cites two studies on recidivism regarding his population. The first shows that 5.5 percent of the released inmates return to crime in a five-year follow-up period; the second sets the figure even lower, at 1.8 percent. The studies cover only persons sentenced to state institutions, but this embraces a large part of the prison population of the country. The usual recidivism rate for Mexico, the warden observes, is about 25 percent.

Are the patterns of crime for which offenders are incarcerated in the Centro

Penitenciario del Estado de Mexico important in conditioning the recidivism rate? The warden divided the population by offenses in the following manner: homicide, 47 percent; rape, 6 percent; drug trafficking, 12 percent; assault, 12 percent; and property offenses, 14 percent. Obviously, there is a disproportionate number of offenders who would be regarded as low-risk on recidivism scales by American researchers.

We ask him what he has learned as warden. "The only thing I have learned is that the inmates are better than I am." You could believe that he really means this, but we are cynical and tell him that it sounds too "saintly." He pauses, smiles good-naturedly, and chooses not to pursue this subject. "Prisons are useless," he says. We are told that he lives inside the prison, much as the inmates do, a most unusual arrangement for Mexican (or any) prison wardens.

What does this portrait of the Centro Penitenciario illustrate? The lesson might be that prisons can be run with compassion as Murton wants them to be, and that this kind of management can produce a reasonably satisfactory prison atmosphere and, perhaps, a very low rate of recidivism. The unusual nature of the inmate population at the Centro Penitenciario, in terms of the offenses that brought them to the institution, makes such a conclusion suspect, though. The program itself, which the warden was very proud of, probably was not very influential in producing the kind of spirit that prevailed. The specific treatment approach duplicated regimens that are now seriously questioned in the United States—mostly varieties of group and individual counseling. Perhaps the major point is that it does not matter much what is done in prison, at least within limits; but how things are done is extremely important.

### Participatory Management

The case studies offered by Murton of four wardens, including himself, who set out to introduce participatory management schemes into prisons are notable for the fact that each experimenter ended his work ingloriously.

A major key to their difficulties appears to lie in their failure to be sympathetic and responsive to the concerns of the staff personnel at prisons, a matter that arises as well in the Swedish system, as Ward has noted. Guards often believe that reforms make their jobs more difficult and more dangerous, and sometimes they do. Murton's presentation, with its accurate and sensitive understanding of the risks of pioneering, seems at moments to fall into the same trap that ensnared the triumvirate with whom he identifies. Thus he unlooses a broadside attack on the civil service—"the end product is a system which fosters mediocrity and punishes innovation." It probably will not do to identify with the inmates at the expense of other persons who have a working interest in the prison system. Perhaps there are no policies able to reconcile the interests of the public and its representatives and the prisoners, though

Murton's blueprint offers several specific recommendations aimed at easing staff problems.

Perhaps the most thoroughgoing assessment of the kinds of reform advocated by Murton is that attempted by Peter Scharf, my colleague at the University of California, Irvine. In a forthcoming book Scharf traces in some detail the work of the men on whom Murton relies in large part for his reform agenda. Scharf notes that prison democracy, like all democracies but more so, is limited by strict boundary lines. The inmates, for instance, cannot vote to free themselves, nor can they decide to jail their captors.

The trenchancy of this observation was brought home when I was doing research on a halfway house for narcotic addicts. The aim of the staff was to develop a therapeutic community, based on the model developed by Maxwell Jones.[51] Its work in this direction was epitomized in an endeavor to maintain an open kitchen. Residents absent at work who returned to meals later than the regular serving time often found no food remaining; others had eaten more than their share or had stolen food. The staff response was to refer the matter to the group for its collective judgment and action. The rationale for this policy appears in the following staff observation:

> I think there is a sound treatment premise behind having an open kitchen. We thought we should have some sign of creating an atmosphere. . . . We wanted at least to that extent to create a feeling of freedom in the house. . . . Even with an open kitchen, open doors, unlocked, without custody officers running round . . . the place is still perceived as a place of confinement . . . but anything that we can do to reduce the feeling is important.[52]

The open kitchen, like many such gestures toward realization of a therapeutic condition, was ill-fated and short-lived. For one thing, thefts of food created budgetary problems that made the staff susceptible to harsh criticism in its fiscal relationship with the central accounting office.

Also the posture of staff indifference to the shortages of food, buttressed by suggestions that if the men were concerned they themselves would do something about it, failed to impress the deprived individuals. These men had neither the interest nor, as they viewed the matter, the means to do anything constructive, and they complained bitterly about having to return from a day's work to the news that there was no supper for them.

The men were not persuaded by the staff's posture that matters such as these were none of the staff's business. The staff clearly exercised enormous authority throughout the program and obviously was quite willing to arrogate at given times any powers that it felt were requisite. Thus the seeming nonchalance about the food was generally taken for what in fact it undoubtedly was: a perplexing bit of play-acting.[53]

The work of Thomas Mott Osborne offers some insights into the problems that might be encountered by a prison reform movement such as that contemplated by Murton. Osborne himself was imprisoned for one week in Auburn when he first took the job as warden, in order, he said to gain a better, more personal understanding of the meaning of imprisonment. Osborne became best-known for his establishment of the Mutual Welfare League, which involved a mechanism for inmate determination of rule infractions and the punishments that should follow them. The prisoners also set up things such as a fire department and a prison bank. But Osborne's tenure was short-lived. He was accused of bypassing the regular authorities when his prisoners' court adjudicated a case of homosexuality that had taken place within the organization.[54] Within four years of Osborne's departure from the institution, his successor reported on the degeneration of the Mutual Welfare League into an inmate oligarchy:

> I found the League divided into two party camps. The energies of
> both parties were concentrated towards corraling votes. . . . As a result,
> the better element among the prisoners held itself aloof from the
> League and it became the Plaything of the less desirable class of men.
> . . . The League officials had full charge of all visiting parties. There
> were gratuities, of course. . . . Little supervision was given. The Judges
> were not always of the highest calibre. They would not examine the
> facts with impartial personality.[55]

We cannot know, from this experience, whether the approach itself was faulty or whether it had been foredoomed because of its threat to entrenched interests.

Scharf notes that reformers such as Murton tend to see the death of their aims as the result of external conspiracies, largely led and fed by hostile politicians. For Scharf, this view seems "perhaps overly charitable toward the noble, but often naive, democratic reformers." He attributes several common failures to the reformers themselves:

> The reformers, by and large, have been rather naive regarding the
> moral understanding of the inmates involved in their project. To read
> their writings one might perceive an image of the inmate as a hybrid
> of a Rousseauian noble savage (possessed of rationality and benignness
> towards his fellow man), and a well-meaning village Rotarian. Osborne
> refers to one Auburn road camp gang as "the most wonderful fellows
> I have every met." The reformers also tend to romanticize inmates as
> victims of circumstances and social casualties. Such a view ignores
> the reality stated by a contemporary of Osborne, who visited the Sing
> Sing League and reported that "the vast majority of inmates do not
> care to even attempt self-government."[56]

## Martinson's Arguments

Comments on Robert Martinson's chapter need not keep us overlong. In most respects the contribution speaks for itself, and in other regards it deals with matters that have been taken up during discussions of the other chapters in this volume. As I see it, Martinson's most fundamental point is his insistence that there is no evidence to demonstrate the accuracy of the most basic of the assumptions made about prisons—that they ought to exist, and that they serve a meaningful or necessary function. Martinson offers no evidence to prove that prisons are not essential for social protection; but I take it that he does not regard this as part of his task, which is only to set out some hypothetical lines of reasoning that, if true, could demonstrate the irrelevance of the prison. This is a long stride forward (or backward) from both the Swedish position as outlined by Ward and prison management as detailed by Murton. Current trends in the United States are toward harsher and more categoric responses to crime built around imprisonment. Martinson neither objects to nor approves of such ideas; he merely suggests that the prison is a supernumerary institution, perhaps serving no useful function at all.

The most avid reformers have paused uniformly before such an idea. Typically they call for a massive reduction in prison populations, but then at some infraction they say, yes, these men and women must be kept locked up. Sometimes they will also add that a very small percentage of inmates must be kept locked up even longer than their offenses warrant for those persons are, as best as can be determined, continuingly dangerous.

I suspect very strongly that Martinson is incorrect in his assumption that imagination, ingenuity, and good econometrical research can find a method more acceptable and more worthwhile than prisons or their prototype for the reduction of crime to an "acceptable" level. It seems to me very likely that the policy of isolating some persons from the mainstream of society in a congregate situation with some security probably will prove to be about the best we can do. It is possible, though, that technology might provide alternate methods that will prove more acceptable and more efficient. This is really Martinson's theme. If you forget about prisons, he says, if you make believe that they do not exist and had not been imagined, what other ways might be found to handle persons who violate the law? And how do these ways stack up against the prison?

Martinson offers but one example of an alternate arrangement, and it seems to be an unfortunate choice. He suggests that it might well be possible for the society to station one individual with one offender in open existence for the period during which it is deemed that the offender represents a threat to the society. Martinson insists, more pointedly, that we must remember that offenders do not offend all or even most of the time; therefore an efficient system would seek to guard against them only at those times when they are in jeopardy of doing things from which society desires to be protected. It would not, in theory at least, be necessary to maintain supervision over the offender on a one-to-one basis too often or for too long. This presupposes a magnificent insight into when the periods of danger and nondanger will occur. If we possessed such insight, we could just as well defend adequately against all crime, not just the recidivistic variety.

A point in Martinson's favor is that nobody has ever seriously considered doing without prisons. Many people agree that they are at best necessary evils, and that in our earlier history we managed without prisons, largely through more effective use of group pressure and control mechanisms, capital punishment, and banishment. Martinson does not exploit the polemical point that many revolutionary ideas such as his arouse initial skepticism and scorn, only to prove in the final analysis to be perfectly reasonable. Some revolutionary ideas, though, turn out to be more feckless than feasible; one need only note, as a passing illustration, the wondrous idea of the lower house of the Indiana legislature, which in 1899 decreed that the value of pi should be fixed at 4.0[57] To which category of ideas Martinson's belong is arguable at this moment. He merely asks that we argue them and investigate them. I find that attractive.

**Blumstein and Nagin's Contributions**

The chapter by Blumstein and Nagin presents a number of equations and models of diverse consequences of alterations in penal policy. The thinking at times is subtle and highly sophisticated; the ideas and the charts are well worth the attention of any scholar or administrator interested in better understanding possible consequences of his decisions. On occasion, however, the analyses seem to represent a drive for orderliness and mathematical precision more than a grappling with issues in a manner that can guide public policy decisions intelligently. There are clues, hints, and unexpected insights into what might happen as a result of different actions. But there is a lot of looseness too, camouflaged or deflected with definitional deftness that restricts the arena. Further, basic issues are by no means settled, so that the structure of the argument may be jerry-built upon shifting sands. For instance, the authors assume an increasing crime rate, as measured by *Uniform Crime Report* index crimes; but in fact it seems likely that there will be a decrease in crimes known to the police in the United States, presumably because of changes in the country's demographic pyramid. At another point, the authors observe that "there are now no reliable estimates of the magnitude of the deterrent effects of prison sanctions on index crimes." If such information is an essential ingredient in policy equations (as I believe it should be), then overall graphings and chartings may be a feckless enterprise despite the presence or even the likelihood of securing the necessary supporting data.

Basic to the Blumstein and Nagin chapter is the argument that societies imprison about the same percentage of their populations. This conclusion is based on examinations of the records in Canada, the United States, and Norway. With reasoning that contains a whiff of medieval teleology, the authors conclude that some force or other dictates this homeostasis, and that social systems will readjust what they label as crime and how they process such behavior in order to keep their imprisonment proportions constant.

The argument fails to persuade me, and I suspect that further cross-cultural evidence or time itself will render it obsolete. The very fact that the three countries investigated have different rates of incarceration indicates that variation is a function of a culture, and there is no gainsaying that societies change, sometimes dramatically. I suspect that an artifact has been elevated to a higher status and that the generalization has been allowed to influence policy considerations. Thus, unlike Martinson, Blumstein and Nagin assume that there will be a certain amount of a population imprisoned, and their greatest interest is in making more rational the manner in which the individuals chosen for this punishment are selected and treated in order to produce the maximum advantage. This idea dictates their recommendations for a sentencing commission that could juggle variables in a more rational fashion than the happenstance approach operating today.

There are some other hazards with this chapter, though the merits of its attempt to deal systematically with what has been rather chaotic conditions should not be undervalued. My statistics professor during my graduate days at the University of Wisconsin once told a story that strongly impressed at least one neophyte in the class. A farmer, he said, had used a new fertilizer on fifty acres of potatoes and doubled his crop. He thereafter increased the amount of fertilizer and reaped an even richer harvest. The third time that he raised the amount of fertilizer he was using, however, he found that his entire crop had been ruined by excess niter. The professor paused dramatically to allow this folksy tale to sink into the minds of his largely urban students. Then he spelled out for us the wisdom of the story: "Don't extrapolate beyond the data."

I think this is the peril of the Blumstein-Nagin model. It often implicitly accepts the idea that when some things are changed in a certain direction other elements will move as they have before. Another problem is that the results of more spontaneous evolutions often will not be reproduced when similar changes are introduced by dictate, because other, highly important variables associated with the more spontaneous emergence will no longer be operative.

An early illustration in the authors' presentation also merits critical attention. Allowing their imaginations to run about a bit, they suggest that a policy increasing the proportion of persons incarcerated in the United States might well have to be accomplished by means of a relaxation or elimination of a number of protections now guaranteed to a defendant in a criminal trial, rights such as the hearsay rule, and judgment based on the "reasonable doubt" standard. This conclusion, stated as a possibility, is puzzling, since the authors had pointed out earlier that only a very small fraction of the persons arrested and convicted under present protective standards are ever imprisoned. Presumably, the rate of imprisonment could readily be increased by a change in sentencing practice without any necessity to ease civil liberty protections.

Let us use the authors' example in terms of their larger theses. Suppose that what they say might happen, actually did. It would seem that under such circumstances all the equations and graphs could be rendered supernumerary in the face of a variable that was unmeasurable but highly significant.

In summary, as with many efforts to weigh and present in graphic and systematic form items that are both measurable and nonmeasurable, there is a tendency to underplay the latter and to focus on the former. Otherwise, the enterprise becomes feckless, replete with a hopeless array of "ifs," "maybes," and "buts" that render the neater formulations unacceptably fuzzy, even contradictory. Blumstein and Nagin are to be credited for the skill and ingenuity with which they attend to issues that often have floated about impressionistically; at the same time the inherent looseness and value-complexity of many fundamental matters involved with penal policy must be emphasized.

## Conclusion

It is obvious by now that the dimensions of a proper penal policy depend on an intricate blend of value judgments and empirical information. One is reminded of the children's puzzle in which the different digits have to be arranged in order, but when one is set in place at last, it often throws another number out of alignment.

Penal policy involves attempts to keep crime at an acceptable level through the use of intervention stratagems. These interventions are to bear on at least three distinct groups: the offenders, the would-be offenders, and the public. The last group includes persons with a direct interest in penal policy, such as politicians and crime victims, and those with only amorphous feelings about the matters. Various approaches can attain a single goal, but they usually do so at the expense of others. Massive use of capital punishment against all felons, for instance, would serve to keep the recidivism rate of one group of offenders under control. It might also deter potential violators because of its fearsome aspects. But it is not likely that the punishment would be tolerated by the society at large, particularly if it began to be applied to drunken drivers and embezzlers. At another extreme, it seems likely that failure to do anything about crime would encourage persons interested in easier acquisition of things that they desire to violate criminal laws. Most persons, of course, probably would not commit heinous crimes such as murder regardless of what penal policy exists. General deterrence issues, then, have to concentrate on the group wavering between conformity and illegality rather than on the population at large.[58] Judgments become even more difficult when other important considerations are inserted into policy equations, matters such as financial cost and the relationship between penal policy and other kinds of social programs (for instance, some persons want to know whether bad behavior is rewarded at the expense of good behavior). The level of crime and its form, matters most fundamentally beyond the ken of penal policy, also bear strongly on the nature of such policy.

The penal policy adopted by a society is perhaps a telling indication of the integrity of the society itself. Sir John Barry, for instance, noted that "it should be the objective of civilized and progressive society . . . to devise methods of punishment which do not deny the human qualities of the offender, because a denial of his humanity draws with it a denial of society itself."[59] In such terms it seems clear that American society must be guilty as charged of the offense of barbarism in its penal policy. What de Beaumont and de Tocqueville wrote more than a hundred years ago remains largely true today: "the penitentiary system in America is severe . . . the prisons of the country offer the spectacle of the most complete despotism."[60]

The five writers in this volume implicitly or explicitly reject the movement toward harsher correctional policy that marks conditions in the United States today. They see the need for more rational as well as more humane penal policies to involve both crime control and national rehabilitation, and each, in his own way, offers some ideas about how this goal might be achieved.

### Notes

1. Gary Wills, *New York Review of Books* 22 (April 3, 1976), p. 6.

2. Ibid., p. 8.

3. Kenneth Lamott, *Chronicles of San Quentin* (New York: David McKay, 1961), p. 265.

4. Curtis Bok, *Star Wormwood* (New York: Knopf, 1959), p. 50.

5. Robert W. Wilson, letter to the editor, *New York Times,* July 8, 1975. Copyright © 1975 by the New York Times Company. Reprinted by permission.

6. The extraordinary appeal of prisons to some of the world's more preeminent novelists is worth note. While studying law, Anton Chekov made an observation that remains largely true today: "All our attention is centered on the criminal up to the moment when sentence is pronounced, but as soon as he is sent to prison we forget him entirely. But what happens in prison? I can imagine." Later in his life, Chekhov studied the prison colony at Sakhalin Island. See Anton Chekhov, *The Island: a Journey to Sakhalin,* trans. Luba and Michael Terpak (New York: Washington Square Press, 1967). Of another famous author it has been said, "all his life . . . Dickens was obsessed with prisons, prisoners, and imprisonment." The first public building Dickens visited when he came to New York was the Tombs Prison. See Christopher Hibbert, *The Making of Charles Dickens* (New York: Harper and Row, 1967), p. 60.

7. Gresham M. Sykes, *The Society of Captives* (Princeton: Princeton University Press, 1958).

8. Quoted in Morley Callaghan, *That Summer in Paris* (New York: Dell, 1964), p. 72.

9. Nathan F. Leopold, Jr., *Life Plus 99 Years* (Graden City, N.Y.: Doubleday, 1958).

10. Robert Neese, *Prison Exposures* (Philadelphia: Chilton, 1959).

11. Ignazio Silone, "Visit to a Prisoner," trans. Harvey Fergusson II, in *Emergency Exit* (New York: Harper and Row, 1968), p. 1.

12. Willard Gaylin, *In the Service of Their Country: War Resisters in Prison* (New York: Viking, 1970), p. 212.

13. Ibid., p. 104.

14. Gustave de Beaumont and Alexis de Tocqueville, *On the Penitentiary System in the United States and Its Application to France,* trans. Francis Lieber (Carbondale, Ill.: Southern Illinois University Press, 1964), p. 121.

15. Margaret Mead, *Sex and Temperament in Three Primitive Societies* (New York: Mentor Books, 1950), p. 163.

16. Melvin J. Lerner and Carolyn H. Simmons, "Observer's Reaction to the 'Innocent Victim': Compassion or Rejection?" *Journal of Personality and Social Psychology* 4 (August 1966):203-210.

17. Plato, *The Republic,* § §414B-415D.

18. Albert K. Cohen, *The Elasticity of Evil* (Oxford: Basil Blackwell, 1974), p. 5.

19. A favorite story of Abraham Lincoln's was about a governor who visited a state prison. The convicts, one by one, told the same story of their innocence and the wrong done to them. At last the governor came to one who said frankly he had committed the crime and the sentence given him was just. "I must pardon you," said the governor. "I can't have you here corrupting all these good men." See Carl Sandburg, *Abraham Lincoln: the Prairie Years and the War Years* (New York: Harcourt, Brace, 1954), p. 375.

20. Gilbert Geis, "Deterring Corporate Crime," in *Corporate Power in America,* Ralph Nader and Mark J. Green, eds., (New York: Grossman, 1973), pp. 182-197.

21. "We Can't All be Victims of Society," *Village Voice,* October 10, 1974, p. 42.

22. "Something Souring in Utopia," *Time,* July 19, 1976, p. 32.

23. An observer of the Swedish scene, Bernard Weinraub, "Swedes Discuss the Impact of Welfare System on Freedom," *New York Times,* November 12, 1972 (Copyright © 1972 by the New York Times Company. Reprinted by permission.), has noted:

Publicly, of course, the Swedes are free to criticize, and freedom of the press and political rights are virtually limitless. On a personal level, however, many Swedes remain fearful of the bureaucracy—a

remote, powerful, and, by tradition, somewhat mandarin establishment—and suspicious of their newspapers and television, and clearly
inhibited by social pressures.

Henry Kissinger has offered a contribution to the lore of what he labelled
Swedish "self-righteousness." Reacting to an antiAmerican demonstration in
Stockholm, the former secretary of state noted venomously, "I know I'm per-
forming a very important sociological function here by demonstrating to the
Swedish public the depths human depravity can reach." See Craig Whitney,
"Reporter's Notebook: a Relaxed Kissinger on a Partly Sentimental Journey,"
*New York Times,* May 27, 1976.

24. Norval Morris, "Lessons from the Adult Correctional System of
Sweden," *Federal Probation* 30 (December 1966):3-13.

25. Richard A. Salomon, "Lessons from the Swedish Correctional System:
a Reappraisal," *Federal Probation* 40 (September 1976):40-48.

26. The proprisoner stance is not universal among the Swedish media,
however. Goran Albinsson of the influential *Svenska Dagbladet,* for instance,
suggests that "while the Swedish penal system is often held up as a model of
enlightenment, Swedes themselves doubt whether it is really functioning as
well as foreign believers seem to believe." Albinsson finds a "schizophrenic"
approach to justice in Sweden, epitomized by tough sentences for tax evaders
and relatively light penalties for street offenders "on the theory that they can
be rehabilitated." He believes that the police are "discouraged" and "often
make very little effort to find and arrest offenders." "With all this," Albinsson
concludes, "even Swedish reformers are beginning to express the opinion that
the progressive approach to crime and punishment here has not been successful." See Goran Albinsson, "Sweden's Prison System Soft in Wrong Places,"
*Los Angeles Times,* November 22, 1976.

27. Daniel Glaser, *The Effectiveness of a Prison and Parole System* (In-
dianapolis, Ind.: Bobbs-Merrill, 1964).

28. William Chambliss, "Crime Rates, Crime Myths, and Official Smoke-
screens," unpublished manuscript.

29. Anatole France, *The Red Lily* [*Le Lys Rouge*], trans. Winifred
Stephens (New York: Dodd, Mead, 1927), p. 91.

30. Gilbert Geis, "The Right to Vote," *Presidio* 35 (July-August 1968),
p. 5.

31. Hannah Green, *I Never Promised You a Rose Garden* (New York:
Signet, 1964), p. 66.

32. Gilbert Geis, Steven J. Simmons, John Monahan, Duff Zwald, and
Howard Bidna, "Attorneys as Friends Out of Court: an Examination of the
Santa Clara County Volunteers in Parole Program," *Santa Clara Lawyer* 15
(Summer 1975):817-854.

33. Gilbert Geis and Fred W. Woodson, "Matching Probation Office with Delinquent," *NPPA Journal* 2 (January 1956):58-62.

34. Donald Clemmer, "Observations on Imprisonment as a Source of Criminality," *Journal of Criminal Law and Criminology* 41 (1950):319.

35. Gordon Hawkins, *The Prison: Policy and Practice* (Chicago: University of Chicago Press, 1976), p. 63.

36. Stanton Wheeler, "Role Conflict in Correctional Communities," in *The Prison: Studies in Institutional Organization and Change,* Donald R. Cressey, ed., (New York: Holt, Rinehart and Winston, 1961), pp. 229-259.

37. Peter G. Garabedian, "Social Roles and Processes of Socialization in the Prison Community," *Social Problems* 11 (Fall 1963):139-152.

38. Glaser, *Effectiveness of a Prison.*

39. Gene Kassebaum, David Ward, and Daniel Wilner, *Prison Treatment and Parole Survival* (New York: Wiley, 1971).

40. Thomas Mathiesen, *The Defences of the Weak* (London: Tavistock, 1965).

41. Hawkins, *Prison: Policy and Practice,* p. 80.

42. Gilbert Geis, "Program Description in Criminal Justice Research," in *Criminal Justice Research,* Emilio Viano, ed., (Lexington: D.C. Heath, 1975), pp. 87-95.

43. Robert Martinson and Judith Wilks, *Criminal Justice Planning: a Preliminary Report* (New York: Center for Knowledge in Criminal Justice Planning, 1976), summarized in *Criminal Justice Newsletter* 7 (October 25, 1976):1-2.

44. Samuel Stouffer, Edward Suchman, Leland DeVinney, Shirley Star, and Robin Williams, *The American Soldier,* vol. 1; and Samuel Stouffer, A.A. Lunsdaine, Marion Lunsdaine, Robin Williams, Brewster Smith, Irving Janis, Shirley Star, and Leonard Cottrell, *The American Soldier,* vol. 2 (Princeton: Princeton University Press, 1949).

45. Ted R. Gurr, "Sources of Rebellion in Western Societies: Some Quantitative Evidence," in *Collective Violence,* James F. Short, Jr., and Marvin E. Wolfgang, eds. (Chicago: Aldine, 1972), pp. 132-148.

46. Jackson Toby, "Social Disorganization and Stake in Conformity: Complementary Factors in the Predatory Behavior of Hoodlums," in Daniel Glaser, ed., *Crime in the City* (New York: Harper and Row, 1970), p. 132.

47. John Fowles, *The French Lieutenant's Wife* (Boston: Little, Brown, 1969), p. 279.

48. Lars Gorling, *491* (New York: Grove, 1966), pp. 142, 145.

49. Sture Källberg, *Off the Middle Way* (New York: Pantheon, 1973), pp. 108, 302, 309.

50. F.J. Roethlisberger and W.M. Dickson, *Management and the Worker* (Cambridge, Mass.: Harvard University Press, 1939).

51. Maxwell Jones, *The Therapeutic Community* (New York: Basic Books, 1953).

52. Gilbert Geis, *The East Los Angeles Halfway House for Narcotic Addicts* (Sacramento, Calif.: Institute for the Study of Crime and Delinquency, 1966), p. 231.

53. Gilbert Geis, "A Halfway House is Not a Home: Notes of the Failure of a Narcotic Rehabilitation Project," *Drug Forum* 4 (1974):7-13.

54. Frank Tannenbaum, *Osborne of Sing Sing* (Chapel Hill, N.C.: University of North Carolina Press, 1933).

55. Lewis E. Lawes, *Twenty Thousand Years in Sing Sing* (New York: Long and Smith, 1932), pp. 113-114.

56. Joseph Hickey and Peter Scharf, *Toward a Just Community Approach to Corrections* (San Francisco: Jossey-Bass, forthcoming).

57. Ray Ginger, *Six Days or Forever? Tennessee v. John Thomas Scopes* (Boston: Beacon, 1958), p. 8.

58. Robert F. Meier and Welton T. Johnson, "Deterrence as Social Control: Legal and Extralegal Factors in the Production of Conformity," *American Sociological Review* 42 (1977):292-304.

59. John V. Barry, *Alexander Maconochie of Norfolk Island* (New York: Oxford University Press, 1958).

60. de Beaumont and de Tocqueville, *On the Penitentiary System*, p. 79.

# Index

Alaska prison system: model prison of, 14; regionalization in, 13–14; rehabilitation in, 14–15

Albinsson, Goran, 232n

Amilon, Claes, 39

Arkansas prison system: abuses in, 15–16; participatory management in, 31–32

Arrest record, deterrent effects of, 179–180

Austin, Paul Britten, 93

Barry, Sir John, 230

Bishop, Norman, 127

Blumstein, Alfred, critique of, 227–229

Bok, Curtis, 202

Bolshevo Colony, Russia, 41, 47

Bondeson, Ulla, 133–135, 214–215, 216, 217, 218

Borden, William, 140

Bultena, Louis, 96–97, 102

Caging. *See* Incarceration

California, determinate-sentence laws in, 196–197

California prison system, 45; volunteer parole supervision in, 213–214

Categorical restraint, 61

Chekhov, Anton, 230n

Child, Marquis, 208

Clemmer, Donald, 215

Cohen, Albert K., 206

Community prison. *See* Village prison model

Community service work, sentences to, 47–48

Community treatment. *See* Field supervision; Halfway houses

Conjugal visiting, 18, 112, 221

Connecticut prison system, private service contracts in, 48

Conrad, John, 96

Correctional Care in Institutions Act (1974), Sweden, 136–139; critique of, 140–141

Correction system, alternative: contractual *vs.* governmental model for, 35–38, 48; field supervision in, 66–67; organization of, 34–35; residential community project in, 48–49, 149; village design of, 38–44. *See also* Prison reform

Correction system, Sweden: citizen and community input in, 141; legislation for, 136–141; organization of, 107–110; penal sanctions in, 101–107; policy directions in, 141–144, 157n; social welfare model for, 99, 149–156, 218–219

Correction workers: in civil service system, 36; and inmate relations, 19; under participatory management, 223–224; professionalization of, 10; selection criteria for, 34; women as, 95. *See also* Warden

Criminal behavior: effects of imprisonment on, 12, 69–70, 134–135, 214–216; effects of punishment probability and severity on, 79, 81–83, 85, 229; incentives to, 71–73, 74, 76–77, 78; restraints from, 56–57, 73–74; in Sweden, 144–146, 153, 209; U.S. rate, by state, 155; victim restitution and, 47. *See also* Juvenile offenders

Criminal record: deterrent effect of, 193; for juvenile offenders, 193–194; maintenance policy on, 192–193

Davao Penal Colony, Philippine Islands, 41, 47

Deterrent effect: of criminal records, 193; of imprisonment, 12, 141, 174; of incarceration, 81–82; of legal threat *vs.* restraint, 62–63, 83–86; of punishment probability and severity, 78, 81–83, 85, 229; of sanctions, 80–81, 179–180, 183–186

# About the Contributors

**Alfred Blumstein,** professor or urban systems and operations research and director of the Urban Systems Institute at Carnegie-Mellon University, has extensive experience with criminal justice systems. He served on the President's Commission on Law Enforcement and Administration of Justice, and directed its Task Force on Science and Technology. He also served as the chairman of the Panel on Research on Deterrent and Incapacitative Effects of the National Academy of Sciences. He is currently the past-president of the Operations Research Society of America. Dr. Blumstein received the bachelor degree in engineering physics and the Ph.D. in operations research from Cornell University. He has conducted research on air traffic control, urban mass transportation, military operations, and law enforcement and criminal justice.

**Gilbert Geis,** professor of social ecology at the University of California at Irvine, is a former president of the American Society of Criminology. He received the Ph.D. from the University of Wisconsin. Among his recent publications are *Forcible Rape, White-Collar Crime, Not the Law's Business,* and *Public Compensation to Victims of Crime.*

**Robert Martinson** is currently professor of sociology at the City College of the City University of New York. He received the Ph.D. from the University of California at Berkeley. He is coauthor of *The Effectiveness of Correctional Treatment, Rehabilitation, Recidivism, and Research,* and is in the process of completing a study of recidivism and correctional treatment funded by the National Institute of Law Enforcement and Criminal Justice. He was a member of the Committee on Corrections, Law Enforcement Assistance Administration, and has been a consultant for the state of New York and the National Council for Crime Prevention, Department of Justice, Sweden.

**Thomas O. Murton** has been the warden of various institutions including the Arkansas Penitentiary. He has a Ph.D. in criminology from the University of California at Berkeley and is currently professor of criminal justice studies at the University of Minnesota. He is the author of *The Dilemma of Prison Reform* and *Accomplices to the Crime: the Arkansas Prison Scandal.* His present activities include a historical study of the territorial prisons in the United States.

**Daniel Nagin** received the Ph.D. from the School of Urban and Public Affairs at Carnegie-Mellon University. He is currently affiliated with Cambridge Systematics, Inc., on leave from Duke University. Dr. Nagin is a coeditor of the

National Academy of Science report, *Deterrence and Incapacitation: Estimating the Effects of Criminal Sanctions on Crimes*. Recent publications have appeared in the *Stanford Law Review, Operations Research,* and the *Journal of Criminal Law and Criminology*.

**David A. Ward**, currently professor of sociology and chairman of the Department of Criminal Justice Studies at the University of Minnesota, received the Ph.D. in sociology from the University of Illinois. He was a Fulbright Scholar in Sweden and Denmark in 1971. He has coauthored *Women's Prison: Sex and Social Structure; Delinquency, Crime and Social Process;* and *Prison Treatment and Parole Survival*. In addition to serving as an editorial consultant for the *Journal of Criminal Law and Criminology,* he is presently involved in a study of 1500 inmates who served time at Alcatraz.

# About the Editor

**Marvin E. Wolfgang,** professor of sociology and law and director of the Center for Studies in Criminology and Criminal Law at the University of Pennsylvania, is also the president of the American Academy of Political and Social Science and a member of the American Philosophical Society and the American Academy of Arts and Sciences. He received the Ph.D. in sociology from the University of Pennsylvania. Dr. Wolfgang has served on numerous boards and commissions, including the Panel on Social Indicators, the National Commission on the Causes and Prevention of Violence, and the National Commission on Obscenity and Pornography. His publications include *Patterns in Criminal Homicide, The Measurement of Delinquency, The Subculture of Violence, Crime and Race, Delinquency in a Birth Cohort, Criminology Index*, and *Evaluating Criminology.* His current projects include a follow-up study of *Delinquency in a Birth Cohort*, a longitudinal study of biosocial factors related to delinquency and crime, and a national survey of crime severity.